Writing for Academic Journals

Writing for Academic Journals

Fourth edition

Rowena Murray

 Open University Press

Open University Press
McGraw-Hill Education
8th Floor, 338 Euston Road
London
England
NW1 3BH

and Two Penn Plaza, New York, NY 10121-2289, USA

First published 2020

Commissioning Editor: Vivien Antwi
Editorial Assistant: Karen Harris
Content Product Manager: Ali Davis

A catalogue record of this book is available from the British Library

ISBN-13: 9780335248407
ISBN-10: 0335248403
eISBN: 9780335248513

Library of Congress Cataloging-in-Publication Data
CIP data applied for

Typeset by Transforma Pvt. Ltd., Chennai, India

Fictitious names of companies, products, people, characters and/or data that
may be used herein (in case studies or in examples) are not intended to
represent any real individual, company, product or event.

Printed and bound in Great Britain by Bell & Bain Ltd.

Praise Page

"*Rowena Murray has approached publishing in a journal with scientific rigour. Following this book's recommendations will make it impossible to find a convincing excuse for failure to publish. She herself writes with a high level of artisanal skill; this book is fast paced, stylish and highly readable. Her own extensive experience in supporting journal article writers tempers this book with the credibility of a seasoned veteran. Best of all, there is a wealth of wisdom here—in advising on how to publish, Murray is also advising on how to live a satisfying life as a writer.*"

Associate Professor Susan Carter,
University of Auckland, New Zealand

"*In* Writing for Academic Journals *(4th edition), Rowena Murray's voice is direct, down-to-earth and wise. Drawing on a depth of practical experience as both published author and writing teacher, she conveys the message that, yes, publishing in academic journals is demanding, but it's also very possible. And that once you are successful, there is still much to be learned from reading books like this one and hanging out with others in writing groups and workshops. To that end, the book is a trove of tips and techniques helpful to all who pursue the challenging craft of (good) academic writing.*"

Barbara Grant, Associate Professor in the School of Critical Studies in
Education at the University of Auckland, New Zealand, and
author of Academic writing retreats: A facilitator's guide

"*This book was already a classic, but the update makes it even more useful. From finding time to write, doing a short literature review and identifying scam journals, Rowena Murray provides an excellent, concise and accessible companion for writing academic journal papers, which is appropriate for both students and working academics.*"

Associate Professor Inger Mewburn, Director of Research Training,
The Australian National University, Australia

Dedication

For all writers – solitary and social

Contents

Preface

This book is based on the assumption that writing skills we learned in school – when most people learn most about writing – do not equip us for our entire career. We can develop writing skills throughout our careers, and writing development – or whatever you want to call it – is not remedial; far from it. On the subject of writing for academic journals, there are other potentially problematic misconceptions:

You cannot write for academic journals until you have immersed yourself in the literature.
You cannot write for academic journals if you have not done any research.

These and other conceptions about writing for academic journals have, of course, an element of truth in them; you do have to know the literature, and you do have to contextualize your contribution in relation to other work and others' writing.

However, 'immersing yourself' in the literature is itself a long-term process. If you wait until you feel you have achieved that, you may never write. If you wait until you have found your place in the literature, you may lose the creative spark, the germ of your own idea and your commitment to write. In reality, it is the process of publishing a paper that helps you to establish your place in the literature, and writing is one way of developing your understanding of previous work.

Moreover, there are many reasons for writing – sharing knowledge, developing knowledge, making a difference – and many different types of writing – professional, academic, pedagogical – and you might want to develop different types of writing so you can speak to different audiences.

If this is true, then you need strategies to write and develop your ideas while you are still learning about academic writing and research in your field. You may also have to overcome the misconception that you cannot publish anything because you have not done any 'real' or empirical research. In some fields that may be true most of the time, but there are many varieties of paper published in different disciplines. So, thinking about which discipline you want to write in is part of the process.

Many see writing as a discipline-specific activity and will wonder how this book can possibly address new writers in every field, but a generic approach to writing can help. While each discipline is different, there are similarities in writing published in journals across disciplines.

Yet each field does have its own rhetoric; in fact, each journal has, in a sense, its own genre, its own prevailing conventions and values at a specific time. Analysing journal articles from different fields in specific periods demonstrates the process of working out what editors and reviewers are looking for.

In addition, other forms of writing can be involved in writing for academic journals: blogs, podcasts, websites and social media – these can be ways of developing ideas and writing.

Finally, while writing is an individual act, there are ways of talking about writing that can help you to work out what you want to say, realize that someone else may be interested in that and work through or around potential barriers to your writing, such as finding time to write, in writing groups. Even when we have writing skills and something to write about, there can be tensions around the act of writing and conflicting motivations – are you writing because it matters to others or to you? Writers' groups are spaces where we can navigate this tricky terrain.

What's new about this edition? People tell me the previous edition was useful, but I have responded to reviewers' and many users' feedback in making improvements:

- Because creating writing time is still a major problem, I explain writing plans, tasks and programmes, clarifying distinctions between them and explaining how to use them.
- To make this book easier to read and use, there are now clearer distinctions between different types of text – such as explanation and example.
- There are brief suggestions on using online resources and electronic bibliographic tools, although these things change all the time.
- There is a new section on scam journals.
- Every single page has been revised and updated. Many are now more concise, though I decided to keep many of the explanations, because it helps to have rationales for writing in particular ways.

This new edition is relevant for people in various professions and disciplines:

- academics across the disciplines writing about research
- academics writing about the Scholarship of Teaching and Learning in Higher Education
- researchers
- Early Career Researchers
- Mid-career Researchers
- PhD students and students on other doctoral programmes
- practitioners
- clinicians
- Masters students aiming to publish from their projects
- writing teachers
- practitioners as researchers
- those who advise academic writers: PhD supervisors, line managers, research directors.

Acknowledgements

Once again, I want to thank everyone at Open University Press/McGraw-Hill for the high standard of their support and advice.

I also want to thank the reviewers who critiqued the third edition of this book and provided detailed, thoughtful and useful suggestions for this new edition.

Dr Morag Thow MBE of Glasgow Caledonian University continues to provide unstoppable support.

Many others, at many other institutions, in writing groups, courses, retreats, one-to-one interviews and informal discussions have helped me understand what goes on when we write. Thank you all.

Introduction

Writing cannot be reduced to a set of professional imperatives. Given the lack of immediate, or even long-term, reward for publishing, there must also be personal motives. The satisfaction that writing a paper brings only comes later, sometimes much later, long after the writing is finished.

The dominant characteristic of those who do academic writing may be persistence:

> A writer needs obstinate perseverance to succeed. Writing is a fairly thankless undertaking. I think people get tired of it pretty quickly, so sticking with it is the greatest part of the battle.
>
> (Messud, quoted in Roberts *et al.* 2002: 50)

This makes the process of developing effective, meaningful, motivational and behavioural strategies complex.

Theoretically, what might be seen as the primary purpose of writing for publication – achieving 'hits' in significant research audits – must, therefore, be broadened to encompass what might be seen as less rational motives: self-expression, creativity, personal meaning, pleasure and enjoyment. In reality, however, these two types of motivation – what we might call the political, or social, and the personal – may work in opposition. There are those who would argue that academics and professionals are eternally plagued by a tension between 'idealism and practicality' (Rossen 1993: 5). Perhaps the competitiveness endemic in academic writing can be read as an externalization of this internal conflict?

This book

This book is aimed at all writers. This includes academics, students, professionals, clinicians, practitioners and the many others who write – or want to write – for academic journals and published writers, those who have not written as much as they want and non-published writers. Writing and publishing, and finding a purpose in doing so, can be a challenge. There can be tension between 'scholarship as a means to an end or as an end in itself' (Rossen 1993: 3). The same could be said of writing for academic journals.

What distinguishes this book from others on the subject – apart from its exclusive focus on the writing of journal articles – is that it deals not only with increasing or improving output, but also with changing writing practices. Productive strategies are provided to help writers change their practices.

Change takes time. Stages in the process of becoming a regular, productive writer are outlined. By adopting and/or adapting these strategies writers will become more productive, will write more readily and will find more enjoyment in the process. There is also evidence that they will be successful. By working through this book, writers can discover their own reasons for writing.

Not everyone wants to write more. 'Productivity' is not always the goal. Making writing less stressful, more manageable, is one of the goals of this book.

Every chapter has writing activities that progress a writing project in stages, from start to finish, from finding topics to responding to reviewers and, finally, marketing your article to a wider audience. All the activities were tried and tested in writers' groups at many universities, old and new, in many countries and in other types of institution. Chapters are linked by questions or comments repeatedly raised by writers because, unless these issues are addressed, a writing project can falter or fail.

In practice, some writers immediately take to some of the writing strategies described here; others find them counter-intuitive or not immediately productive. The trick is to adopt or adapt them, as appropriate, and, more importantly, to stick with them for long enough to see the benefit. Clearly, reading about a writing strategy in this book, or even trying it once or twice, could have little or no impact on your writing practice or output.

This book argues that you may have to change your writing habits; for example, in order to become a regular writer, you may have to use *both* 'snack' and 'binge' strategies. Writing is not treated as a skill that you learn once and for all time, but as a professional task that continues to present challenges to new and experienced writers alike. (To be honest, this is what makes it interesting.)

Writing for academic journals is often perceived as one of the most discipline-specific activities. Many academics, researchers and professionals assume that it is not possible to discuss writing in a generic way, and that only someone in their area can provide useful feedback or instruction. Yet, this is to ignore the deep structures of research arguments across a wide range of subjects, as illustrated in this book. This material is, therefore, relevant to all disciplines.

The emphasis is on what writers do. Although the role of the reviewers is also discussed in this book, the focus is on how writers can respond to feedback in order to move their writing towards publication.

> That nature of the academy (and of academic work) is to foster rivalry through discrimination between various theories and ideas, which are largely – as critics of the academy delight in pointing out – subjective, which heightens the tension between scholars all the more.
>
> (Rossen 1993: 3)

Instead of fixating on this 'rivalry' or being distracted by your critics' 'subjectivity', you can focus on getting on with your writing.

Further reading

McGrail, R.M., Rickard, C.M. and Jones, R. (2006) Publish or perish: a systematic review of interventions to increase academic publication rates, *Higher Education Research and Development*, 25(1): 19–35.

Mayrath, M.C. (2008) Attributions of productive authors in educational psychology journals, *Educational Psychology Review*, 20: 41–56.

Murray, R. (2008) Incremental writing: a model for thesis writers and supervisors, *South African Journal of Higher Education*, 21(8): 1067–77.

Chapter 1

Why write for academic journals?

> Reasons for writing • Reasons for publishing • Internal and external drivers • Career implications • Research profile • What is academic writing? • What can research on academic writing tell us? • Can it be learned? • Is it innate? • What is 'research'? • Reasons for not writing • 'I haven't done any research' • Intellectual capacity • Turgid writing • Narrow range • Pre-peer review • Guilt, fear and anxiety • Procrastination • The writing self • Team and collaborative writing • Barriers to writing • An integrative strategy • Checklist • Further reading

This chapter explores the potential purposes of scholarly writing – why do we do it? What's in it for us? The aim is to prompt readers, particularly if you have not published much or at all in academic journals, to address your motivations. These can be quite mixed. New writers are often ambivalent about academic journals, even, sometimes particularly, journals in their field, and this can be a barrier to writing. It is crucial to address the issues that come up most frequently in discussions at this stage; if the issues are not addressed, it is unlikely that there will be any writing.

You may not like the kinds of writing you see in journals in your field. Many new writers express a strong antipathy to what they see there:

'I don't want to write that turgid stuff.'
'I want to write something that I would want to read.'
'No one will read it if it's published in that journal.'

On the positive side, many new writers have something 'in the locker', something they have been meaning to write about for some time. Many feel guilty. A starting point is putting the sense of failure – of not having written – behind them. In order to do this, re-tuning of motivation might be needed.

The reason why addressing this question – why write for academic journals? – is so important is because there are competing tasks in academic and professional lives, and they all seem to impinge on writing (Carnell *et al.* 2008; MacLeod *et al.* 2012). There is competition not only to get published in journals but also to find time to write, and this can lead to huge pressures on the individual (Hey 2001; Ball 2003; Gill 2010). The trick is not just to work harder or longer (Acker and Armenti 2004), but to find personal reasons for writing.

Reasons for writing

Since it can have so many effects, there are potentially many personal and/or professional reasons for writing:

- working out what you think, clarifying your thinking or starting to think;
- having a 'rant', letting off steam, 'uncluttering' your brain;
- telling others what you think;
- persuading others to take it on board.

This list is no more than a starting point for thinking about where you are in what could be seen as a continuum between writing for yourself and writing for others: which is more important to you now? Which do you feel more ready to do? Which do you want to do in the short term? Starting today? If you have always had a feeling – as many seem to – that you would like to write, if only you knew how to go about it, then now is the time to start.

Some writers argue that they like writing and do not lack confidence, but see no reason to get into print. They have other ways, they argue, of gaining professional recognition and other outlets for their communications. Of course, this is always an option, as long as you are clear about and comfortable with any consequences there may be for your career. And what about consequences for your learning? If you do not submit your writing to journals, where else will you get the type of hard critique provided by reviewers?

Reasons for publishing

Your reasons for publishing may be much more closely linked to external drivers – and to other people's criteria – or, perhaps, to your awareness that you are expected to establish such a link.

Reasons for publishing in academic journals

- career progression – moving up to the next rung on the ladder
- gaining recognition for work you have done
- stopping someone else taking credit for your work or using your materials
- personal satisfaction of completing a new goal
- setting yourself a new challenge
- helping your students to gain recognition for their work
- learning how to write to a high standard
- contributing to knowledge
- building your institution's status
- developing a profile

Some of these reasons are more altruistic than others. Co-authoring with students, for example, can help them in their search for a job after graduation, in some professions. They will certainly have learned from publishing, provided you help them to participate in the process, and you will have modelled a form of continuing professional development. In addition, if you have not published before, this is an excellent way of developing a small-scale piece of work for an article.

Internal and external drivers

For writing, as for other professional tasks, there is a complex mixture of internal and external motivations. What is interesting is that when it comes to writing for academic journals, these motivations may seem to be in opposition, and they can work against each other. Even in discussion among those who want to write for journals, there can be resistance to actually doing it.

Both external and internal drivers may combine if your aim is to get on in your career, yet this might be complicated by your ambivalence towards the writing you see published in the journal articles in your field. You may be ambivalent about joining what you see as one big 'game'. You may even develop feelings of antipathy towards those who regularly publish. This may be compounded by your or others' scepticism about the publishing process.

When I say in writers' workshops – in an attempt at humour rather than cynicism – that the quickest, surest way to get published is to change your first name to 'Professor', there is often rueful laughter, followed by an important discussion of the differences between articles published by those who already have a body of work and an established profile in the discipline, and articles published by 'unknowns'. Of course, reviewing should be blind, but even when it is, it can be easy to identify authors from their references or from gaps in their references (i.e. if they have anonymized references to their own work).

The important lesson is that once you have a body of work and experience, you may write different types of articles, and these may be very different from your first publication.

Internal drivers include your intention to develop your writing skills, yet you may feel ambivalent about feedback you receive from peers and reviewers. You may invest time in researching a journal, yet feel that they have 'missed the point' of your article, or been too harsh in their critique, or that they seem to be confusing it with another article entirely. You may flat out disagree with the feedback. The criticisms may indeed be unfair and unhelpful, but your reaction may be as much about the emotional side of receiving criticism as about research debates. You have, after all, invested so much of yourself in your writing. Until you have been through the process several times, you may find yourself taking criticism personally, and even then it may still sting.

It will come as no comfort to know that as your knowledge of writing for academic journals deepens, you may uncover new layers of ambivalence: once you are regularly publishing, you may feel that you know what you are doing and resent reviewers who seem to think that you don't. This might be the best indication yet that it is an on-going struggle to bridge the gap between your internal and external drivers. You may continue to feel that what started out as your distinctive voice has morphed into journal-speak.

This is why it is important, particularly when you are getting started, to have a way periodically to refocus on what's in it for you to publish in academic journals.

There are those who will find all of this a bit pathetic. Of course we all have to publish as part of our jobs – why all this ambivalence? Surely it is your responsibility to add to the store of knowledge and to keep yourself up to date for the sake of your students, your colleagues and your field? If this is your view, you will, in theory, find it easier to make time and space for your writing, although when you start to, for the first time, there will be consequences for other people:

> You have to be very clear, if you want to write, what place it occupies in your life. I'm afraid that if you're ambitious, it often has to have first place – it sometimes has to take precedence over human relationships and anything else.
>
> (Mantel, quoted in Roberts *et al.* 2002: 75)

No matter how much time and energy you plough into other roles, supporting students when no one else will, representing your department on more than your share of committees, and being course leader on more courses than your colleagues, there will be people who refuse to see all your efforts. 'How did you find time to write', they wonder, 'if you really are so busy?' Come the day you actually defer a task in order to finish an article, there may be a reaction. You may be branded as someone who is prone to 'dropping the ball' or not being a 'team player' in that workplace, and perhaps beyond.

The point of this one-sided narrative is to characterize another type of external driver: the increasingly negative reactions – real or imagined – that your writing may provoke in other people. These can work against your writing, convincing you to make less time for it, not more. You have to make writing more important than anything else at some point, in order to get it done. If you never make it the priority you will never do it. You have to ask yourself, what exactly are you waiting for?

> Write as if you are dying. It works. Imagine if you've only got a year to live or something. I think that's the best motivator to get you to do it.
> (Gemmell, quoted in Roberts *et al.* 2002: 57)

While this view will seem extreme to some, it does raise the question of how long you have to get started and to become a regular writer for academic journals. How long are you going to wait to get started? Another few months? Another year? Or two?

Career implications

Progressing in your career is a compelling reason to write for journals. You may not enjoy the career appraisal or review process, and you may not find it useful; yet it does give you an opportunity to make connections between what you want to do in your writing and what is valued in your place of work.

These connections are not always apparent to heads and managers, who may not read what you write. The same goes for your applications for promotion: do not expect senior officers to read your work, or even to have a grasp of its significance in your field, or in any sense. They are just as likely to read your publications as you are to read theirs – i.e. perhaps unlikely? As long as they don't stop you doing what you want to do – in your writing – you can consider yourself to be in a privileged position.

You may think that your work is so directly linked to the priorities in your workplace that it hardly needs to be said. Think again. Take every opportunity to make that link explicit. As you develop your publication plans and intentions, think about how you can, if not 'align', then simply explain them in terms that are relevant to workplace strategies and priorities. In some disciplines, this will be superfluous; in fact, you may think the whole process of formal career review is superfluous. But in some areas, and perhaps at some times, it is much more important to make these links explicit. No one will do this for you; in fact, it may be that no one else can do it as well as you can.

As you are contemplating the publishing component of your career, therefore, you may have to update your answers to four questions:

1 What are the precise or general targets for publishing in your area/department/faculty/institution?
2 What are the current themes/priorities for research and scholarship in your discipline/department/faculty/funding bodies?

3 Have you discussed with your head of department/manager – as part of your appraisal or review – how you will meet those targets, including resources you will need?

4 Do you have general or specific, formal or informal, agreement to your publishing plans from your head of department, line manager and/or research mentor/advisor?

Find out, if you can, others' answers to these questions, noting the array of answers and areas of convergence. Note any dislocations, however minor, between the stated agenda and what is going on in practice, without, if you can avoid it, becoming too involved in what others are doing or not doing. You have no control over that, and is it really any of your business, unless there are opportunities to work together? The purpose of this dialogue is to gauge your colleagues' views, not to compare your outputs to theirs.

This is not to say that your output should be fixed for your entire career. You may want to do different types of writing for publication at different stages in your career, from 'initial career', when you might still be developing publications from your thesis; to 'middle career', perhaps a time to write a single-authored book, proposals for external research funding or other appropriate output; to 'later career', when you might be asked to contribute to an edited volume or a special issue of a journal, etc. (Blaxter *et al.* 1998a: 140). Again, it depends on your discipline and, above all, on your understanding of how people construct a programme of publications at different stages in their careers.

Take a look at some websites: what and where are junior and senior researchers publishing in your discipline or sub-discipline? Study the trajectory of their publications over their careers.

The broader context for your writing in research assessment – in whatever form it takes in your workplace – will probably provide increasing pressure to publish in high-ranking journals. The history of research assessment in various countries shows a trend from 'benign' to having 'bite' (Gilroy and McNamara 2009: 321), not only affecting universities' research incomes but also leading to the closure of university departments. There is intense pressure on academics and professionals in increasingly performative settings (Hey 2001; Acker and Armenti 2004).

Research profile

Developing a research profile is a compelling reason for writing journal articles. Are you thinking ahead? Do you want to be published in certain journals, not in others, and think you have no chance of getting into the high-ranking journals? It may seem premature to be thinking of developing a research profile, but your first publication may present you to the research community in a particular way. It is important to think about that as you select target journals.

If you want to develop a profile, will you have to focus your publications in a certain area, not publishing too widely?

Or will you use diversity in your writing to make a broader impact, thereby reaching a range of audiences? Will this be valued?

Would it be useful to co-author with someone who has an established research profile? Who will be first author? Could this be a long-term writing partnership, where you take turns as first author?

What is academic writing?

> The craft or art of writing is the clumsy attempt to find symbols for the wordlessness. In utter loneliness a writer tries to explain the inexplicable.
>
> (Steinbeck 1970: 14)

Academic writing is a set of conventions. We see it in a thesis or published article in our discipline, a definition that becomes more precise when you analyse published writing in your target journals.

Some argue that academic writing is a narrowly defined set of specialisms and knowledges, so narrow that it leaves 'huge gaps in our understanding':

> It is the desire to think and write more, to fill some of these gaps that informs my desire to leave the academy – to think and write on subjects of my choice, in the manner that I wish to write, in whatever voice I choose.
>
> There is so much emphasis on asserting a one-dimensional 'voice' in academic life. I enjoy writing about many subjects in different ways.
>
> (hooks [sic] 1999: 141)

hooks – who refused to use capital letters in her name as part of her resistance to systems of oppression, including language – argues that our subjectivity is 'colonized' in academic writing, and it is certainly true that across the disciplines subjectivity has traditionally had little or no value. This has begun to change recently, in some disciplines, but in others such change is inappropriate to the enterprise of research.

Words associated with writing about research

- objective
- hierarchical
- focused
- conservative
- neutral

If hooks's argument applies, then there are gaps not simply in the literature, but created *by* the literature. An academic approach to research – and academic styles available for writing about it – is limited. Those who find it limiting are not necessarily limited; it is important to acknowledge that much of what we think, say and do in the course of our work can become invisible when we publish.

That accounts for academic writing, the product, but what about the process? A published article creates an illusion of linear progression, when, as we all know, writing is a dynamic, cyclical process. While the merits of published articles are often discussed, there is relatively little discussion of how writing actually gets done: what are the stages, and how do we manage them in relation to other tasks? How do productive writers manage it? – a question to be asked not so much in awe or envy as in anticipation of a practical answer.

What can research on academic writing tell us?

There is a body of knowledge on writing – about how it is learned and how it is done, about what constitutes good writing and how it is achieved. There is a substantial amount of scholarship on how undergraduate writing skills can be developed and on the writing academics and professionals do. While Blaxter *et al.* (1998b) argued that research on academic writing was 'patchy' then, now there is a knowledge base to draw on. (And to which we can contribute.)

For example, there is research on strategies used by productive academic writers (Hartley 2008). Hartley and Branthwaite (1989) studied British psychologists and found that their results matched closely those of Boice (1987). This research offers pointers that later researchers endorsed:

1 Make a rough plan (which you needn't necessarily stick to).
2 Complete sections one at a time. It may help to do them in order.
3 Use a word processor if possible.
4 Revise and redraft at least twice.
5 Plan to spend about two to five hours writing per week in term time.
6 Find quiet conditions in which to write and, if possible, always write in the same place (or places).
7 Set goals and targets for yourself.
8 Invite colleagues and friends to comment on early drafts.
9 Collaborate with longstanding colleagues and trusted friends.

(Hartley and Branthwaite 1989: 449)

What is interesting, and still useful, about this list is that it shows the way to a productive writing process. There is advice on how many hours to aim to spend on writing per week, which does not sound like much, but it is probably more manageable than the higher figure many new writers would set themselves. Point 6 sounds like study skills advice we tell students. In this context it sounds a bit rigid, but this is what worked for the productive writers in the study. Perhaps, as psychologists, they were better at identifying productive behaviours. They would, for example, understand the power of goals and targets in both theory and in practice.

A 2008 study shows that productive writers (in a social science discipline) have particular attributions, are adept at disengaging from other professional tasks in order to write and are no less busy with these other tasks than their colleagues are (Mayrath 2008).

Some of the best books on academic writing focus on strategies for productivity (Boice 1990a; Bolker 1998; Silvia 2007). Many of these draw on psychology, which helpfully brings in the behavioural dimension of writing (Murray *et al.* 2008) – academic writing is not just technical (grammar, punctuation and paragraph structure) or cognitive (strategies for thinking about writing); it is about what we actually do when we write, and how we manage our motivation. Boice's research showed that many writing problems are related to writing behaviours.

Boice (1987, 1990a) developed writing strategies for academic writing, backed up by empirical evidence. His approach is still relevant, though contentious: he advocates regular writing in short bursts, 'regular' meaning daily and 'short' meaning as little as thirty minutes. This 'snack writing' approach goes against the seemingly prevalent 'binge writing' mode.

Elbow's (1998) freewriting – both public and private, i.e. to be read by someone else, or not – is a valuable technique for all writers, though some need to be persuaded of its value. The value of what he calls 'low stakes writing' cannot be overstated; although all writing is targeted at a specific audience, it is important to have a space to write without judgement, because anticipating judgement can inhibit or delay thinking and writing. Overdoing this anticipation can make an emerging article lose its focus.

Boice and Elbow were influential in the development of the approach proposed in this book: their idea that good, productive academic writing occurs through regular writing – and might not be achieved without regular writing – was novel at the time and surprises academics and professionals to this day.

In addition to these apparently individual writing strategies, this book draws on my research showing the impact of writers' groups (Murray and Moore 2006; Murray and Newton 2008). While solitary writing may be the most familiar model of academic writing, there are benefits to writing in different types of group.

What is new in this book is the development of an integrative writing strategy. When thinking or talking about academic writing, again and again I come back to the question of whether it is possible or sensible to talk about any one of the dimensions of writing separately from the others (Murray 2008). Can we talk about rhetorical skills without, for example, talking about the need to – and the skill to, the confidence to – negotiate time to write on a daily basis?

People tell me all the time that there is no time to write. They feel they constantly have to switch tasks and roles around, stretching deadlines for other things in order to write – and sometimes, they say, it is simply impossible to write. Surely making time for writing is also a skill? Although, do we not already do that in other areas of our professional lives? Negotiating processes are involved in writing and in time management, and my work has opened up some of these individual and group negotiations, which have generally remained tacit or hidden from view both in the literature on academic writing and in routine discussions in institutions (Murray and Newton 2009; MacLeod *et al.* 2012; Murray *et al.* 2012).

A systematic review of academic writing development in 2006 found very few studies (McGrail *et al.* 2006), but since then there have been more studies of different aspects of academic writing. For example, Sword has written about academic style (2012) and about what expert writers do (2017). To sum up, research on academic writing involves several disciplines:

1 Psychology, including motivation and meaning making;
2 Social – usually seen as solitary, but can benefit from groups and communities;
3 Rhetoric, including not only the mechanics of writing, but also persuasive strategies;
4 Cognition – ways of thinking about writing, including attribution and self-efficacy.

Links between the first and last of these convey the complexity of academic writing and make the case for strategies that integrate approaches.

There are also many online resources, such as #AcWrit, the Thesis Whisperer blog (https://thesiswhisperer.com/), Pat Thomson's blog, Patter (https://patthomson.net/), the Research Whisperer blog (https://researchwhisperer.org/) and so on, and podcasts like Changing Academic Life, with advice for academic writers.

Debate about writing research and development continues. There are those who blame schools; others blame new technologies for what they see as the degradation of students' grammar. In reality, some academics and researchers will be as unsure of how to use the semicolon as students. Perhaps we can admit that what we learned at school about writing – whether that included grammar or not – was never likely to be sufficient for writing a journal article.

There is also a misconception that writing can be separated from learning and research: I have heard it said, by a very senior keynote speaker, opening a conference that I had been invited to address on the subject of academic writing, that 'We all know that it is the quality of the research that matters, not the writing.' Was he singling out my session for censure, since this was the subject of my presentation listed in the conference programme he had in front of him? This remark potentially discouraged others at his institution from seeking, or perhaps providing, writing development. Moments like that explain why people do not generally talk about the challenge of writing.

Can it be learned?

How much of this literature on academic writing is familiar to academics and professionals? To what extent are these tried and tested strategies taken up in academic and other research settings? It has been argued that academics, researchers and other professionals who write journal articles learn about writing in the course of their careers:

> Successful university lecturers are likely to have spent many years developing acceptable ways of constructing their own knowledge through their own writing practices in a variety of disciplinary contexts.
>
> (Lea and Street 1998: 163)

Yet many, even those who completed research degrees, say this is not how it works; it is simply not possible to learn everything you need to know about writing as you go: 'It was unspoken but it just seemed obvious: that's what one does. And then it turned out that I was terribly bad at it' (Ellmann, quoted in Hanks 2003). While it would be interesting to research why this might be, the purpose of this book is to address the need for guidance in writing for academic journals, particularly for new writers: there is no need to pretend that you know all you need to know about writing.

When they experience writing development, many are surprised at how little they know about writing and some are relieved finally to be able to admit it:

> The writing process was something I hadn't given much thought to before starting the [writing] course. . . One of the first topics explored was how is academic writing learned? The answer . . . seems to be by trial and error. On reflection I cannot recall being given formal instruction on the specifics of academic writing during my undergraduate career. This trial and error process is not just confined to academic writing; it extends to all forms of writing.
>
> (Participant in Academic Writing module,
> Advanced Academic Studies)

Is there an assumption that writing development or instruction is only for those who struggle with writing – non-native speakers, or those with poor writing skills? In some disciplines, support is provided during the doctorate, but in others there is nothing at all. What exactly we need to learn about writing at the doctoral level and beyond is itself a matter of debate.

Meanwhile, the pressure on academics and professionals to publish in journals increases year by year. In addition, as more institutions are granted university status, and new disciplines join higher education, the case for support is even more urgent. These writers, some highly experienced, face even more intense pressure to participate in audit exercises that make publication targets very specific. Many of these lecturers will not have published in the past, but will be expected to do so immediately. They have to run to catch up with other, established disciplines with whom they will be compared. This pressure to publish is international, as is the demand for development and support. The stigma previously attached to what I call 'writing development' is thankfully being eroded, as academics, postgraduates and undergraduates recognize that it is in their interest – and not just their universities' interest – to raise the standard of their writing by learning more about it.

Writing for publication requires a complex transformation for those who recently completed – or are still working on – a thesis or dissertation. This can involve several dimensions of change. Many new writers do not have rhetorical knowledge – knowledge of the techniques of persuasive writing that are the building blocks of scholarly writing. Consequently, they may make errors in their first articles, some of which, in my development work across the UK and elsewhere, I find recur across disciplines:

New writers' errors

- Writing too much about the research 'problem'
- Overstating the problem and claiming too much for their solutions
- Overstating the critique of others' work
- Not saying what they mean, losing focus through indirect writing
- Putting too many ideas in one article

Defining the problem is clearly a crucial step in an argument. Yet many new writers spend too long on this, in their early drafts, and produce an over-long first draft that then has to be radically cut. Alternatively, perhaps they have an article that asserts there is 'a problem', but new writers do not always perceive the gradations of argument that are available and end up overstating the critique, demolishing the opposition and drawing fire from reviewers. They are often able to say, immediately, when asked, what it is they are trying to write, which is why it helps to have dialogue with colleagues who can say 'write that down'. Balanced, usable sentences often appear in discussions that are focused on a journal article and, if that is an obvious point to make, then it should be noted that such discussions – focused on the writing of a specific article for a specific journal – are not routine in the working lives of academics, researchers, clinicians or practitioners. Nor do new writers know how to initiate this discussion. This is why such practices are described in this book.

Of course, any writer can make any of the above errors at any time, but these seem to feature particularly in new writers' texts. What these early errors have in common is the writers' lack of rhetorical development of their argument. They assert points, without the necessary definitions and justifications. Once these flaws are pointed out to writers – as flaws – they can quickly modulate their tone, trim their critique and prune their article. It is possible, therefore, to learn about writing; in fact, it can happen very quickly, once the principles are pointed out. For that reason, this book defines and illustrates many of the key principles of academic writing, with examples from different disciplines.

For instance, whenever I introduce the subject of paragraph structure – and its role in argument – to academics, professionals or researchers, I inevitably use such terms as 'topic sentence' and ask them if they know what it means. Almost always, a silence falls. 'Is that the silence of "we know this already, move on" . . . or the silence of "we don't know, tell us"', I ask. Usually, a few immediately respond that they do not know. The point here is not that these writers should study grammar or linguistics, but that they have gaps in their knowledge about how sentences and paragraphs work. This can affect how they talk about writing with students or colleagues and how they manage their own writing.

If academic writing can be learned, then can it be un-learned? People who do not write regularly, who have stopped writing for a while, or feel that it is difficult, say, 'I've forgotten how to write.' The cure is, as always, to start writing again – 'It's not till I write that I realize that I can', as one put it – but perhaps write in new ways. It is possible to have a sense of incompetence at the very thought of writing, and this, if it goes on for long enough, can be aversive: it will stop you writing. This is something you have to find ways to avoid, if you are to write for academic journals.

Is it innate?

On the few occasions when writing ability is discussed in universities there are popular assumptions about what makes some people productive writers, and it is not all about technical skill:

- These people are just good writers.
- Some are better at making time for writing.
- Those who publish are more selfish; they don't care about students/patients/colleagues.

For new writers and emerging researchers there is a potential double bind here: you should be able to write already on the basis on your education and experience, yet if you were really good enough you would already have written more than you have.

The ability to write for academic journals is not, of course, innate, although, interestingly, some still think that it is. This is not an excuse for avoiding writing development or, importantly, writing discussions. There are strategies for productive writing and ways of making time for writing in overloaded academic and professional working lives. Perhaps you do need to think about being more 'selfish', if that means putting your goal – writing – first. Perhaps you do need to overcome the sense that writers are a breed apart. Perhaps you need to learn new tricks.

What is 'research'?

I discovered long ago in collecting and classifying marine animals that what I found was closely intermeshed with how I felt at the moment.

(Steinbeck 1962: 181)

This suggests that what constitutes 'research' will be closely related to your interests and perspectives. All sorts of studies 'count' as research, in some disciplines, with growing rigour and credibility.

Research is as much about the work you are currently doing, including teaching, as anything else. If you have expertise, experience and a profile in an area, then it makes sense to find your research in that area, unless you hate it with a passion. If you can find the right journal, and can construct a sufficient contribution, then you have a potential publication.

For example, a brief survey of the sub-field of social work dealing with residential childcare produced the following types of work in published journal articles:

1 **This is both** a review **of . . . as well as** an attempt to place the issue in a practical and reasonable context (Anglin 1999).
2 **A theoretical model** is offered . . . (Pazaratz 2001).
3 The author draws upon **30 years of experience** in . . . (Gavin and Lister 2001).
4 This article **looks at how** . . . There is a **discussion** of practical **skills** and training **directions** (Ziegler 2001).

The first example shows how what the author considers an 'issue' can be the subject of review and research, while still being relevant to practice, a feature many new writers say is important to them.

The second example demonstrates that a new model, developed by the author, can make an important contribution.

The third explicitly draws on extensive experience, making the case that this is itself an important body of knowledge.

In the fourth, relatively non-academic terms such as 'looks at' were sufficient. Such options will not be available in all fields, but they are available in more fields than many new writers realize.

In other fields, personal experience, the personal voice and the first person, 'I', are off-limits, both stylistically and philosophically. In some disciplines, they simply cannot constitute the ingredients of new knowledge. This will be obvious to writers in those disciplines, but it is important that writers are not put off by criteria that drift across from other disciplines. In your discipline, you know what does and does not count as new knowledge from your reading and other academic and professional activities. This is no time to be distracted by writing in other disciplines.

Brew (2001) argued that academic research is itself narrow, requiring closer links to living with uncertainty, ambiguity and the actual processes of researching. Calling for more 'reflexivity' and 'critical questioning', Brew opened up new possibilities, for some disciplines, for a rigorous critique of research itself and the development of new ways of thinking: 'We cannot escape seeing an outdated epistemology infusing practice' (p. 177). There is also a prompt here for analysing practice. In other words, while experienced colleagues may attribute your views on the narrowness of academic writing in your discipline to your inexperience and naïvity, you have grounds for critiquing existing work and established principles. There is bound to be some such critique in your own discipline; you will not be the first to have these feelings or ideas about academic writing in your discipline.

Even failure – with, of course, a careful definition of what constitutes 'failure' – can be a fruitful topic for academic writing:

> Research must acknowledge its disasters as well as its achievements; its rigidities as well as its creativity; its power and its powerlessness; its openness and its dogmatic blinkers.
>
> (Brew 2001: 186)

Research can be quite narrowly defined, but acknowledging that narrowness, carefully identifying its nature and form, can strengthen your arguments. (Identifying the 'causes' of such narrowness would be a more complex argument, since cause-and-effect arguments are much more complex than arguments about the 'way things are'.)

Brew (2004) analysed the conceptions of research held by established senior researchers and identified four categories of research experience: 'The domino (series of tasks), trading (a social phenomenon emphasizing products), layer (excavating reality) and journey (research transforms the researcher)' (p. 214). Whether or not you feel you already have, or aspire to, one of these, it is as well to consider your own orientation as something real, part of your identity and, therefore, worth defining. Otherwise your concept of 'research' might remain amorphous or even internally contested. Work out where you are coming from, which definition of 'research' is meaningful to you, and then you can start to give the tasks, trades, layers or stops on your journey some definition in real time and space, among real people. Brew's perspective, it should be noted, was underpinned by research.

Of the orientations Brew proposes, the 'trading' variation is interesting for its social nature:

> Whether the research outcomes are conceived in terms of publications, research grants, the achievement of objectives or social benefits, more often than not in this variation, research is described in terms of relationships, activities or ideas of other people (e.g. research assistants, collaborators or other researchers in the field).
>
> (Brew 2004: 221)

This implies that networks, collaborations and beneficiaries, in a variety of senses, are positioned in the research process at a more than conceptual level.

A related aspect of this variation, one that might link directly to writing – interesting that Brew uses the word 'variation', perhaps to emphasize plurality – is the idea that research is for an audience. Clearly, this suggests that it is important to develop not just an internal sense of audience, but also real external audiences, for our research and writing.

The strongest link to writing is, in fact, with this trading orientation, as Brew illustrates with a quotation from one of the participants in her study:

I'm with the school that believes you should always be writing while you are researching and I always tell my . . . students too, that it's fatal just to go away and read for a year. You should always be writing, . . . even if what you have written is discarded you should always be writing . . . Half the time is reading, half the time is writing.

(Brew 2004: 222)

This suggests that if you want to publish research regularly you should get yourself into the habit of writing during the research process, but that you should not try to do all this on your own; your social situation, including the social context of your professional life, can enable or inhibit your writing. This last point may come as no surprise; many of those who say they want to write say lack of support is a barrier. But you can change this: build peer relationships that provide a forum, both critical and supportive, for your research. Develop some of this 'trading' mentality and find others who have it too. The motivation for doing this is that the trading variation is more likely to lead to publication (Brew 2004).

You will, of course, come across others with whom you want to work, but whose orientation towards research clashes with yours. This may mean that they can, for a while, perhaps not forever, be research colleagues for you and you for them. Getting your different definitions of 'research' out in the open at an early stage can help you bridge the gap. This discussion can also sharpen your understanding of research, in a variety of senses.

To complicate matters further, you may change your orientation to research as you do more of it, or as you write more about it or as you learn from reviewers' feedback. This too could be a topic for peer discussion, as long as the focus is on external products (the 'trading variation').

Much of this, including what some will see as the potential narrowness of Brew's or others' conceptions of research, can itself be a topic for your writing. In fact, in some disciplines, the question of what does and does not constitute research is a recurring subject of debate, and not just in the academics-versus-practitioners contest. Looking across a range of disciplines, you can see that making the case for your research as sufficient to be given the name is often among the first steps in the argument. This is another reason to write about it, and it may, in fact, be part of the text you write. This is a subject that you can write about now.

Alternatively, you can use this as an 'excuse' to get started: writing about potential orientations towards research, writing your response to Brew's 'variations', writing about your work in relation to what others have called research and constructing links between the two could be an important part of your reorientation as a researcher.

You can take this a step further and consider writing in different forms – as a conscious development process, but with the possibility of publication in mind – such as narrative: outline your history as a researcher; describe your journey towards research; describe your attitudes, feelings and approaches at different stages in the process. What might start out as exploratory writing might become redefining, recovering and developing an identity as a researcher: how are you positioned as a researcher or writer in your scholarly community? Is there integration, alienation or both?

This is not just a matter of writing a 'how I see myself now' snapshot diary entry or essay, but writing yourself into research. Many people who are new to research have written themselves out of research and, as their careers take shape, found it difficult to write themselves back in.

Although academic writing in your discipline may not allow such subjectivity, there are potential benefits in developing a subjective response to research; it may be important for your long-term motivation. If academic writing – and a great deal of research – has its origins in positivistic assumptions, then it may be productive to explore the limits of these assumptions. In some disciplines, their dominance is being challenged in any case. In others, they are ripe for debate: 'Historically, subjectivity has been the privilege of those with the power to control institutional discourses' (Bensimon 1995: 599).

Academic discourses were constructed over time, they have been tried and tested and are now widely trusted; but this does not mean that the 'rules' of academic writing never change. It is not only cynics, the excluded and the disenchanted who take issue with what constitutes research. Some creative thinkers never tire of challenging established and/or privileged concepts.

In some disciplines, this will seem like wasting time; there is no need to develop an orientation, since researching – and writing about it – is obviously what academics and researchers do. Yet Brew's research into this included a wide range of disciplines, and so we can learn from her work what established senior researchers see as research, and there are even hints about how they do it. Surely this is a more sensible way of learning about research than 'simply getting on with it'?

Reasons for not writing

Reasons for deciding not to write provide insights into the nature of professional workplaces and the terms and conditions of those who are expected to write for publication:

- I don't have any time for writing.
- I can't write in my office.
- I'm not ambitious.
- My teaching comes first.
- I review journal articles, but I don't write for journals.
- I don't want to play the publications game.

- I'm too tired when I get home to do any writing.
- I resent giving up so much of my personal time to writing.
- I do a lot of writing, just not for publication.
- No one will read it anyway.
- I'm probably just afraid of rejection.
- I don't write well.

The problem is that there is little or no progressive discussion about how advanced writing is learned, about who needs to learn about it, or which modes of learning might work best for them or, most importantly, who might teach it.

You may feel that you already know that your work 'makes a difference' and feel no need to 'publish for publishing's sake'; you may feel that there is no point. Secure in your knowledge of your work's significance, you decide not to write.

There are, therefore, reasons behind the reasons: like many, many others, you may find that you lack the education, support or environment for writing. The sooner you find the support you need the better. You can start by looking for a course, group, mentor, programme or website, and the writing activities in this book will help you to start, progress and complete a journal article.

'I haven't done any research'

This barrier to writing is popular among academics in universities that have relatively recently included research and publication in academic workloads and professions in which writing journal articles is new. Many think they simply have nothing to write about.

One option is to join the Scholarship of Teaching and Learning debate: writing about your teaching and students' learning. This is a massive body of work, with national and international conferences, communities and conversations. It includes research on doctoral supervision.

Until you reconfigure your work and ideas – in writing – they may seem too modest for academic journals. Yet, most journal articles make modest contributions. Define what yours is, as this is an essential element of most articles anyway. Until you do, the voice telling you that you did not do that work as 'research', and therefore should not be representing it as such, will keep droning on and may stop you writing.

Intellectual capacity

Some years ago, in the midst of my discussion of ways to become an effective and efficient writer, one response was, 'Well, yes, that's all very well. But you're assuming that everyone has the intellectual capacity to write for publication.' Well, yes, I had been assuming that everyone in the group of writers and potential writers in front of me was capable of finding something to publish somewhere. I did not think it was my remit to judge writers' capacity; nor was I qualified to do so across the range of disciplines represented in the group.

It is a legitimate question, but what was he really asking? The intellectual capacity to do what? To analyse the literature, to work out what still needs to be done and to plan a piece of writing about that? And how would that intellectual capacity have been measured? Do we all need to have first-class undergraduate degrees? PhDs with distinction? Royal Society Fellowships? What would be sufficient demonstration of 'intellectual capacity'?

And how would that intellectual capacity have developed in the first place; could it be that writing for academic journals is one way of developing it, teaching us how to raise the standard of our work, our thinking and our writing? You have to handle the question of your intellectual ability carefully; it can be transformed into a reason not to write. Surely some of what experienced writers know about writing for publication was learned *through* writing for publication?

Many people will challenge your ability to write for academic journals. This challenge is, of course, legitimate, although critique can be wearing. Academics and professionals who are deemed 'non-research-active' – i.e. not publishing in journals, or whatever definition and term apply in your context – may have to justify time devoted to research and writing. However, few of them are likely to have dedicated writing time in any case.

Whatever your starting point, writing for journals provides an opportunity to develop. The purpose of your academic writing is to persuade readers to think about your ideas, at least, but it is also to develop those ideas to the point where they are publishable.

In the end, I do still assume that everyone has something to write about. The question is, can everyone find the right journals for their work?

Turgid writing

They make it so tedious – footnotes and bibliographies! They're just ridiculous. Who cares what you read? Just get on with it.

(Ellmann, quoted in Hanks 2003: 20)

New writers are often dismayed at what they find in academic journals. They reject the inherent value of articles published in a style they do not like. They resist the implicit injunction to 'write that way'. They reject the opportunity to transform their ideas into a new genre. Ironically, they often use the dominant styles and structures to construct arguments for not writing for academic journals.

This argument then provides a rationale for not writing at all; after all, the argument goes, who would want to join such degraded, self-serving, navel-gazing debates? In some discussions, in many different institutions, this has been given as a reason not to write for academic journals at all. Again, that is, of course, an option, but not one endorsed in this book.

Critiquing the dominant norms and forms of academic journals is an important activity. Negotiating the extent to which we choose to reproduce what we find there is an essential part of the writing process. Seeing publication as some kind of 'game' can stimulate new writers to find out what the 'rules' are and how the 'referees' apply them, so that they can then go off to 'train' and 'play' to 'win'. Discussing the pros and cons of targeting journals we do not enjoy reading – though they might 'count' heavily in research league tables – is an important stage in developing and sustaining the motivation to write.

However, writing for academic journals is not about performance; it is about persuasion. People in our fields will not read our writing, no matter how fresh we think our style is, if we do not make some allowance for their perspectives. This may mean adjusting our writing style to suit our audience.

We already do this. You already know this. You have to at least consider adopting some features of the styles you see used in published writing. This might require a change of your perspective: for example, if you think some points in the articles are too laboured, sentences too long and ideas too obvious, this might indicate areas that have to be carefully, perhaps more extensively, argued in that journal, ideas that are more contested than you think they should be.

Deciding not to write for a journal because you do not like its style is paradoxical. It may even indicate a lack of understanding of why the journal is written in a certain way. Accepting that you may have something to learn from analysing – and producing – different styles is more likely to develop your writing skills and your understanding of what it is that gets published in your field.

This is a contentious point; feelings run high in discussions of what constitutes 'acceptable' writing and 'new knowledge'. Personal preference is powerful; people have strong views about what makes good writing. Once we have our preferences in perspective, we can begin to see that a range – not an infinite range, but a range, all the same – of options is open to us, one of them being to redefine what you think constitutes 'turgid' writing.

Narrow range

While some see the range of writing options available in academic journals as just too narrow, others see it as a plus, as it helps them decide what to write and how, in the sense that they see it as a framework for their writing.

Finding options in the narrow range		
Only certain topics are accepted	◊	I can relate my work to those topics
They do not publish my method	◊	I can focus on other aspects of my work
We're never allowed to write 'I'	◊	I can discuss subjectivity in the methods

Those who have not yet published are sometimes uncomfortable with this approach, seeing it as exactly the kind of game playing they despise. But it is about being rhetorical (Murray 2010). It involves looking for a way to join a conversation that has been going on, in the literature, in a specific journal, in specific terms for ten or twenty years or more.

Pre-peer review

Most people who spend any time thinking about or doing research know how important peer review is, but it is even more important to get feedback on your writing before you submit it to a journal – pre-peer review. You may think your writing is not ready to show to anyone else, but it is probably a good idea not to expect that feeling to go away, even when it is published.

What stops writers showing their writing to others? Lack of confidence? Lack of understanding of how it might help them? Lack of trust in colleagues? Lack of definition of the sort of feedback they are looking for? A bad experience: they gave writing to someone once and were severely critiqued? Not leaving enough time – just wanting to submit it?

If you had bad feedback on your academic writing, why was that? Did you ask for the feedback you needed? Did you say you wanted constructive feedback? Or did you take it for granted that that was what you would get? Did you react emotionally or analytically to the feedback? Did you ask the wrong person? All of these happen some of the time, but the trick is to keep going.

In 'pre-peer review' you might be looking for feedback on the continuity of your argument. Does it seem convincing? Does it make a contribution? Does it seem appropriate for the journal you are targeting? That might be sufficient feedback. Write these questions on a separate page, staple it to your article, highlight them in colour, put it all in a plastic envelope so that the front sheet cannot become detached, and negotiate a deadline with your readers for their feedback.

I once asked a senior colleague for feedback on a draft article that the journal had returned with major revisions required. Eight months later he put it in my mail tray with one comment written at the top of the first page: 'I presume this has already been submitted.' Why did that happen? In hindsight, I can see that I asked the wrong person. The experience taught me not to ask him for feedback – but I only found that out by asking him in the first place.

Another way of getting feedback in the early stages of developing an article is to email the journal editor to check that both your proposed subject and what you intend to say about it are of sufficient interest – as they see it – to readers of their journal (see 'Contacting the editor' section in Chapter 2). Without this early check, you might write an article that they are interested in, but not in the form that you wrote it, because, for example, it takes a direction that they think moves away from the journal's focus at a specific time.

Who can you ask for pre-peer review?

Reviewer	Type of feedback
Mentor	Advice about journals and editors
Senior colleague	Guidance on writing about your subject
Someone who has published in your target journal recently	Specific information about journal's editorial preferences
Colleague in any discipline	Feedback on your article's 'contribution'
Colleague in department/ discipline	Constructive critique of your idea
Constant ally	Encouragement to write at all

These are just suggestions. This is not to say that every writer has to have every type of feedback; it can be difficult enough to find one person who is prepared to supply feedback of any kind. The purpose of this list is to prompt writers, particularly new writers, to think about finding feedback.

Don't forget to tell your reader which type of feedback you are looking for; it can save everyone time and effort. This is easier said than done: people are very busy. They do not have much time to read other people's writing.

Guilt, fear and anxiety

Many people report that they can be quite creative in finding ways to avoid writing: numerous cups of coffee . . . washing the cups right away . . . and drying them . . . checking references . . . writing emails . . . updating . . . various things . . . putting on the washing . . . cleaning the bathroom . . . taking out the washing . . . hanging it up . . . cutting the grass . . . watching it grow . . . making another cup of coffee . . . washing the cup . . .

There are potential distractions in almost endless lists of domestic and important professional tasks. Many new and experienced writers say these avoidance tactics are related to their uncertainties about their writing, but they may also be related to writing itself. How many of us were ever taught strategies to start writing quickly and easily, so as to avoid procrastinating?

On the other hand, some see displacement activities as essential steps in the writing process, even if they are not entirely happy with this process. This is often cited as a reason for not trying the generative strategies proposed later in this book: 'What can I possibly write in half an hour? It takes me half an hour to get started.' These writers say that they cannot simply 'start writing' on demand.

Whatever the purpose or value attributed to so-called displacement activity, if they work to stimulate your writing, then well and good. If they do not, guilt follows. Guilt at not having done 'enough' is a recurring theme in many writers' discussions.

Fear and anxiety recur so often that it seems important to invest time in confidence building (Moore 2003). If you want to become a successful academic writer, it might not be enough simply to learn more about the technical skills; it might be equally important to invest time in developing your confidence through new types of writing activity, dealt with later in this book.

I keep suggesting changes *you* can make because the institution where you work is not likely to change for you. It is unlikely to give you more time to write and more recognition for your writing, but you can develop an identity as a writer within that context. Over time, as you publish more, guilt, fear and anxiety do not disappear, but they will not stop you writing.

In case you find this discussion demoralizing or patronizing – neither is my intention – I recommend you consider the real risks of submitting your work to an academic journal. While 'risks' is perhaps the wrong word – some might say 'challenges' – it can nevertheless *feel* risky for a number of reasons:

- Your work is subjected to the hardest critique you have known.
- Experts scrutinize your research and your writing.
- You make mistakes.
- You 'put your head above the parapet'.
- You attract criticism.
- You unintentionally criticize an authority, causing conflict.
- You develop your argument beyond what you can logically claim and beyond the evidence you have.

These are not imaginary risks. Writing for academic journals means writing at the edge of your – and perhaps others' – certainty. Until your article has been peer reviewed, you may not be sure that you have made a contribution. In addition, I have seen other risks for new writers:

- What you have decided not to say is seen as a serious omission.
- Your critique of others' work is seen as too strong.
- Your statement of the problem is seen as too general, under-referenced.
- You haven't cited key people in the field, even those you disagree with.
- Linking your work with that of established figures is seen as presumptuous.

Even successful, published authors can encounter new risks:

- Unsuccessful colleagues passively or actively loathe or seek to undermine you.
- Your growing confidence is seen as arrogance.
- What you write about is devalued in your institution; its relevance to research strategy is questioned.

The trick is to get to grips with these potential risks, work out what could hold you back and discuss this with trusted colleagues who want you to succeed.

We have all had these thoughts. We all have our particular trigger, the one that makes us lose confidence from time to time. In practice, over time, these thoughts can be destructive prompts, that is, prompts that tell you not to write (see Chapter 4 for more on writing to prompts). They can also make you lose focus in your writing, as you try to strengthen your arguments with added detail, evidence or references. This may be why so many new writers put so much into their first drafts of their first articles. They often have two or three articles' worth of material, but feel that they need to bolster their article, when, in fact, making the case for the work they did or making the proposal that it needed to be done might be publishable articles in their own right, in some disciplines.

This section has explored fears and anxieties in some depth because new writers seem to find many reasons not to get started, or, once started, to give up when they are asked to revise, resubmit or re-resubmit articles. This is partly related to lack of understanding of the process, partly to doubts about their ability to meet this high-stakes challenge and partly to fears that go back to their early education:

> Throughout my twenty years of teaching at a number of universities I have witnessed the terror and anguish many students feel about writing. Many acknowledge that their hatred and fear of writing surfaced in grade school and gathered momentum through high school, reaching a paralyzing peak in the college years.
>
> (hooks 1999: 169)

Submitting an article to an academic journal can leave you feeling precarious, but that is not just because you are weak and inexperienced; it is the very nature of the writing act, some would argue, and may be embedded in previous experiences of writing.

Procrastination

Putting off writing until you have 'more time'? Until you feel 'ready to write'? Convinced that if you had more time you would write more?

Tasks that have deadlines get done before those that do not. You already know that a deadline forces you to prioritize. Anything with a deadline is automatically more important than something without. This is a professional approach to competing priorities, and learning to manage competing priorities is a key stage in becoming an academic writer (MacLeod *et al.* 2012).

For some academics, teaching is the priority. For other professionals, seeing patients or clients is the priority. Sometimes, the priority is non-negotiable, such as when marking exam scripts consumes large periods of time at certain points in the year. In many workplaces writing comes last in a long list of tasks. As long as it has no fixed deadline, it is the first to be dropped. Even when writers put writing time slots in their diaries, it often proves difficult to protect them. For some, it is impossible.

There are, therefore, very good reasons for putting writing off, as other priorities arise. It may even feel subversive to be thinking about ways to lever writing into your timetable. Do you need to ask permission to do this? Who else will you tell? Who will support you as you do this? Who will undermine you? Is it easier to procrastinate, rather than risking the hostility of colleagues?

Those who write for a living know what to do to keep writing – perhaps because they have fewer competing priorities? – and we can learn from them how to keep writing. We all have to find our own antidotes to pressure and uncertainty and persevere when those fail us:

> You need perseverance, courage, bloody-mindedness, a capacity for hard work, endurance . . .
>
> (Weldon, quoted in Roberts *et al.* 2002: 7)

The writing self

Academic writing is not neutral. It is gendered, raced, classed and, therefore, potentially discriminatory in these and many other ways. These factors affect the role and status of the writer in academia and will impact on the new writer's learning needs in relation to academic writing. The community of academic writers is diverse, though the community of editors and reviewers may be less so. Some will see these issues as irrelevant to the development of the writing self; others will see the writing self as positioned by the organization of other writers and the position of publishing in their disciplines. For them, the whole enterprise may seem so fixed as to give the illusion of transparency, particularly to those who are already publishing in journals. Where does the new writer fit into all this?

Do you really need to let yourself be pinned down? There are ways of finding room for yourself in academic journals. For example, an interesting strategy is noted by Blaxter *et al.* (1998a: 146): 'You can, of course, use a number of different styles and voices. You might also use different names, as some academics [and professionals] do, for different kinds of writing.' While some will find this a bit extreme – and limiting to their developing research profile – others will see that perhaps they have more options than the exclusivity of certain journals suggests.

However you choose to deal with the selectivity that operates in journals across the fields, it might help to think of yourself as a writer and to think through what it means for your sense of yourself:

1 I have a reason to write that is not just about meeting other people's standards.
2 I make writing meaningful for myself.
3 I reward myself for making sacrifices for writing.

4 I take care of myself, as a writer: physically, mentally and spiritually.
5 I have found someone to have open discussions about my writing, not just analysing barriers, but ranging over possibilities and experiences.

The sheer numbers of us trying to get published create experiences and perceptions of academic writing as fierce competition. But this need not be your motivation to write. Some people are simply not motivated by competition; they find it demotivating. If you expected universal collegiality in your workplace, you may be disappointed by this. But there is no need to feel that you are in an endurance competition until you retire. This is not to say that choosing not to publish is your best option – though it is certainly one option – but that you have to find some way of either ignoring other people's sense of the on-going competition or find other reasons to write, some of which you might keep to yourself, if you feel they would put you at risk in your context. However, others will argue that 'keeping it to yourself' is exactly the kind of self-silencing that power structures depend on, so perhaps this should also be a topic of discussion with others who write.

Team and collaborative writing

This is a good way of not 'going it alone', or, as one new writer put it, 'We can begin to run in packs', and you may also be creating an island of collaboration in this world of competition, with all the advantages – if you manage it well – of pooling strengths, skills and contacts.

It might help, if you are just starting to write, to have someone who can help you make writing decisions, help you with writing dilemmas or who will simply listen.

You may be able to work and write with, and learn from, more experienced colleagues. You may be able to step outside your territory or tribe. There may be issues of voice, ownership, career implications, politics and time that you should discuss at the start of the collaboration. These may relate to the requirements of the organization that funded the research.

However, there may also be disadvantages for new writers, and over the longer term this should not be your sole strategy, if it is the case in your discipline that 'those without sole publications are not rewarded for their team-playing skills' (Blaxter *et al.* 1998a: 144).

Barriers to writing

The greatest problem I can see for academics [and professionals] in post is not finding the motivation to write but the time amidst all the pressure and heavy workloads of teaching and administration.

(Anonymous reviewer)

This reviewer is right. Time is definitely, absolutely and across all the disciplines *the* inhibiting factor for people who want to write for academic journals. This is evidenced in evaluations, focus groups, questionnaires and informal discussions where academics, practitioners, clinicians, students and professionals cite lack of time as the barrier they could not overcome.

As the reviewer points out, even those who say that they have the 'motivation' to write cannot do so if the time does not exist in which to do it, or if they are so exhausted from other work that they have no energy left for writing. This suggests that even if you succeed in motivating yourself and are ready to write, you still have this problem to solve: how will you find time for writing and, even when you do, how will you protect it from all the other demands on your diary?

But are 'motivation' and our use of 'time' as separate as the reviewer makes out? Is your use of time not driven by your motivation? Do you not allocate your time to tasks that you decide to perform, knowing how much is needed for each task? Or is that too simplistic? Are you really free to decide how to spend your time, when there are so many external demands that simply must be met?

In theory, you know that you are the one who decides how much – or how little – time to spend on each of your professional tasks. In practice, however, there are so many interruptions that academics and professionals report that they rarely even get through their 'to do' lists. They do the work that must be done – and there are various definitions of 'must', as you know.

This is the reality of many academics' and professionals' lives (Hey 2001). Can any amount of talk about your 'motivation' really make a difference in this context? If your context does not provide time for your writing – see 'It's not a hobby' (Murray 2013) – is it, again, up to you to create it? – see 'Time is not enough' (MacLeod *et al.* 2012).

A key to understanding this barrier may be holding on to the idea that you have tried, really tried, to make time for writing, and everything you tried did not work the way it did for other tasks. I am not trying to make light of this barrier; there are many, many people who are at this point, which is one of the reasons I wrote this book, but there are those who managed to get beyond it.

I do not want to make light of what is a difficult journey – from not-writing to regular publication. In fact, I would argue that there are situations where barriers to writing are indeed insurmountable: anyone with a family and/or others to care for, anyone going through a break-up or bereavement, or anyone who is ill should not, in my view, try to solve this problem.

Having said that, some people find that a new challenge gives them just what they need to take them out of themselves, to look beyond their situations and move forward in their lives. This is a very personal matter. Some decide – rightly or wrongly for their own and others' wellbeing – that it is too risky for their careers to take time out.

Whatever your situation, the purpose of this chapter is not to analyse reasons for not writing – though that can be instructive – but to open up discussion of ways of solving the problem of finding time to write, even when it seems impossible.

The key point is that if you are in the position of having no time to write, it is time to face up to the need for change. This may involve casting off some of the writing strategies you currently use – they aren't working. Not talking about your writing with people who focus on barriers to writing – they aren't helping. Not trying to solve this problem with people who are not writing journal articles – they aren't writing. This book describes many writing strategies and ways of working with others to overcome barriers to writing. These strategies not only help to solve the problem of making time to write but also take up less time, use up less energy and – for new writers particularly – reduce the need for endless, potentially demotivating revisions.

Because it is such a huge challenge, a whole chapter is devoted to ways of making time for writing: Chapter 3.

An integrative strategy

Writing can be integrative in the sense that it is related to other academic and professional roles, and you can find many outlets for the types of writing that you can develop from your different roles: 'biographical, confessional or developmental' (Blaxter *et al.* 1998a: 139).

Writing can be integrative in another sense: it is one of the themes of this book that new writers can – and should – work on more than one dimension of writing. Rather than using just one of the strategies proposed in this book, or sticking with the one that you have, this book encourages you to move towards an integrative strategy, combining different strategies in your writing practice.

For example, you can get words down on paper and then work on them later, filling in the blanks, making improvements. Or you can structure your article in detail before you start writing. Either way, you can start a project – without procrastinating – and make progress.

The strategy you use may depend on the time you have available, the type of writing you have to do or your familiarity with the subject. You can choose the strategy that suits the stage of writing you are at, at any time. You can adapt as you go along. In other words, having a range of strategies – rather than just one – can help you to write through the various challenges that writing presents.

Having said all that, it would not do to give the impression that writing is forever integrated and 'flows' once you have mastered these strategies; there is no way round the 'interruptedness' of writing in academic and professional lives and settings, nor is this unique to writing, of course. Continuous flow in your writing, as in other academic or professional tasks, may not be an achievable goal; what you can do is adapt and adopt strategies that help you to connect the stages of writing that are dispersed among the activities of your work and your life.

Checklist

- Consider writing about your current work; don't wait until you have new 'research'.
- Write about a project you completed some time ago; you may think it is out of date, but you had a reason for doing it then, have acquired knowledge on the subject and can weed out what is irrelevant and update what is out of date.

- Own up to procrastination, if you like, but focus on why your writing about this subject may be needed or valued and why you might want to write about it now.
- Find personal reasons to write – what are the reasons that matter to you?
- Form your own views on journal articles, published writers and the imperative to write, but don't let all that stop you writing. Think about how you will join the conversation or debate going on in a specific journal.
- Combine different writing strategies. Which ones do you use now? What works? What needs to change?
- Try changing a writing habit – what do you want to stop doing? What do you want to start doing?
- This book is not a course textbook; instead, it provides a set of writing activities to produce text.
- Use these strategies together to make up your productive writing process.

Further reading

Boice, R. (1987) Is released time an effective component of faculty development programs?, *Research in Higher Education*, 26(3): 311–26.

Hartley, J. (2008) *Academic Writing and Publishing: A Practical Handbook*. London: Routledge.

Torrance, M., Thomas, M. and Robinson, E.J. (1993) Training in thesis writing: an evaluation of three conceptual orientations, *British Journal of Educational Psychology*, 63: 170–84.

Chapter 2

Targeting a journal

'That's interesting!' • Getting to know the journals • Judging journals • Scam journals • Journals that 'count' • Choosing a journal • Peer reviewed or professional? • Instructions for authors • Journal resources for authors • Websites for authors • Analysing a journal • Working out what is acceptable • Analysing abstracts • Defining genre • Joining the conversation • Cloning or creativity? • Mediating • Personal negotiations • Contacting the editor • Editors' responses • Wait time • Checklist • Further reading

The main point of this chapter is that, as with other forms of communication, you have to address the needs of your audience. Of course, you will know the journals in your field from reading them over the years. But now that your intention is to write for them, you shift your focus to your target journal's instructions for authors and its published papers in order to work out what type of paper that journal's editors and reviewers are looking for at a particular time.

What they find acceptable can be defined in terms of what editors and reviewers have already accepted, that is, what they publish in the journal. When you write for a journal find a way to bridge the gap between what you want to say and what they want to hear.

Research your target journal. Become a scholar of that journal at this time. Identify dominant issues and conventions. As with other aspects of research, keep your knowledge of journals up to date.

This is, of course, information that this book cannot supply: it would be impossible to provide advice on targeting every journal in every field. What this chapter does provide is advice on how you become an expert in your target journal and how to start writing your paper at the same time.

'That's interesting!'

'That's interesting!' may be the last thing you want to say about papers you read in academic journals. Once you have started to study them closely, you may be more tempted to say 'That's obvious', 'That's boring' or 'Who cares?' Yet someone found something 'interesting' – perhaps not new theory, but something sufficiently new – in every paper published in your target journal.

Many years ago, an article with exactly this title, 'That's interesting!', described research into what makes an article 'interesting' to readers (Davis 1971). The author concluded that it is not just articles that follow a journal's lead that get published; articles that go against the grain may be even more 'interesting' and equally publishable:

> QUESTION: How do theories which are generally considered interesting differ from theories which are generally considered non-interesting?
>
> ANSWER: Interesting theories are those which deny certain assumptions of their audience, while non-interesting theories are those which affirm certain assumptions of their audience.
>
> (Davis 1971: 309)

This does not, however, mean that the published articles Davis studied broke all the conventions, but that they offered a clear contribution that explicitly stood out from the rest of the work in an area. Of course, you can do this while still following the conventions of your target journal; you do not have to break all the conventions in order to inject your papers with a 'that's interesting!' factor.

Davis's study provides a useful question to help us work out what would constitute the 'interesting' factor at a certain point in a journal's history: if an interesting paper attracts the attention of readers, you have to work out, 'Where was the [readers'] attention before it was engaged by the interesting?' (p. 310). It might, in fact, be valuable, if you have not already developed this knowledge, to learn about the types of 'interest' represented in a selection of issues of your target journal over the past year. Such an analysis would give you a very real understanding of what is – and is not – likely to be published in that journal.

A further implication of Davis's argument is that you should develop not only your knowledge of your subject, but also 'an intense familiarity' (p. 337) with your audience's assumptions about your subject. While these may seem self-evident, you can use them to focus your article:

- What does your audience assume about your subject?
- Which aspect(s) of your subject do they assume is/are still open to question?
- Which aspect(s) of your subject do they assume is/are not open to question?
- Will you challenge any of these assumptions in your paper?

On the other hand, you have to be wary when certain areas are branded as important for research and writing, careful that these areas do not lock you out of other areas that are equally worthy of research, areas that you might have an interest in researching.

An early step in writing for academic journals, therefore, is understanding what 'that's interesting!' means in your target journal. Find out exactly how that quality is put into words in papers published there in the past year. If you do not find any of the papers interesting, you may have to revise your definition of 'interest' for this context. You may realize that you have a different set of criteria. You may have to review your understanding of what constitutes publishable work.

Getting to know the journals

Identify the types of journal in your field. For example, Blaxter *et al.* (1998a) define six types: popular, professional, applied, academic, multi-disciplinary and electronic (p. 150). Is there the same range in your field? Do you have all these options?

In any case, you know you have to make explicit the connections between your work and the work of other published authors, showing how your article takes the field forward, complementing others' work and/or taking the field in a different direction, or at least point in a new direction. Thinking this way will shape your article.

Or make a list of possible topics, perhaps sketching other articles you can write for other journals.

More specifically, browse the titles of articles published in your target journal. Think about how you might package your work by describing it using one of these types of titles. Examine a few types of title in detail. For example, you may find that some titles are definitive, while others are more tentative or propositional. Some signal what type of article it is – such as a review article or research article. Others foreground methodology. Then there is the title-plus-subtitle option, allowing two types of heading to be combined in one, thanks to the use of the colon. Perhaps there is a topical title before the colon and something more generic (within which genre?) or descriptive after the colon. Is this style of title used in your target journal? Some of these forms, you know already, will not fit in your potential target journals. However, the point is to overcome the potential barrier of making stylistic adjustments to this minor, but important, element of your article. Writing the title is another focusing device in the early stages of writing your journal article.

Writing activity

A key writing task at this stage is to write several different working titles for your article.

Write yourself a list of titles – appropriate to your target journal – that you are prepared to use for your article.

This is not just about making it up, pretending to write an article, but about beginning, with an appropriately modest goal, to write. Of course, your title will change, possibly many times, as you write, but, on the other hand, if you choose a title that will fit easily into your target journal's agenda, then you may find that you have a useful focus for the rest of your writing process.

Moreover, by writing a working title, you link journal article writing and your identity as a writer: 'the titles of published papers also help to frame an academic's public identity' (Blaxter *et al.* 1998a: 147).

Over the longer term, you could create a pattern of titles in your papers, if this works with the range of journals you target: 'it is worth giving some attention to the ways [the title] may contribute to creating a sense of cohesion across ... several research projects' (Blaxter *et al.* 1998a: 147). This helps you to develop a focus in your chosen area. You may find it helpful to read whichever of the many books on writing for journals in specific disciplines relates to your field. For example, for psychologists there is Sternberg's *Guide to Publishing in Psychology Journals* (2000).

Judging journals

Anyone thinking of writing for academic journals should have a knowledge of how journals are ranked and how to update their information regularly. At the time of writing, this information is easily accessible on the Web of Knowledge. You can search a full listing of journals in your field, rank them according to their impact factors, other factors and 'half-lives' and study citations. If you don't know how, consult a librarian. In fact, get regular updates from librarians – they always have the latest techniques for information search.

In case this is not absolutely clear, the impact factor and citations are represented as numbers. It is not enough to say a journal has a 'high impact factor', and if someone tells you this you should ask for the specific number. This type of information, particularly journal impact factors and citations of articles, is now routinely included in the *curriculum vitae*.

Other devices for measuring the quality of journals include bibliometrics, journal rankings, university rankings and many different systems of research assessment. The most recent cycle of the UK's research assessment is a good source of information on how specific publications were ranked in the recent past. Although it features the UK, this easily available source of information has international currency because it shows which publications, by which people, in which departments at which institutions are ranked highest. Using this source, list the top three researchers and/or top three institutions in your field and see what they published and where. Then update this information by tracking their more recent publications.

Because publication in high-ranking journals is often linked to research funding, which in turn generates further publications and increases impact, some will say you should always target journals with a high impact factor. Others will advise a 'stepping stone' approach, where you target lower ranked journals initially and then work up to the higher ranked journals, in the knowledge that you really need to be published in them in the next couple of years if your publications are to 'count'.

Scam journals

Warning!

So-called business model journals are out to make a profit, but aren't all journals? The 'scam' part only really makes sense if you are scammed, i.e. if you have to pay for something that turns out to have less value than you expected, or no value at all, if there was no peer review, for example.

You may already have received emails from scam journals. There are also 'predatory' journals and predatory open access. This is another research task for you: find out how to spot scam journals in your field. Find reliable sites you can use to check.

If a journal that I had never heard of emailed me directly, and put the proposed charge for publishing my article at the end of the email, or if it was not there at all, I would assume it was a scam journal. If I were to name journals that had done this – and there have been several in the past year or two – I would be drifting into legally troubled and troubling waters, even if I suspected it was a scam.

So, heed the warning. Find out how to check. Be suspicious if they want to charge you for publishing your article, though, to be fair, that too may change in the next few years.

Journals that 'count'

Who decides on the status of journals? In some countries there is a list of journals that researchers must publish in, if their publications are to 'count'. In some disciplines, there is a prescribed list, ranked in order, of journals that 'count'. However, that list may change from time to time.

Some journals count in research audits and league tables, some do not. Some count for more than others. Find the scale being used in your system, institution or country. If you want to have the option of working in different countries, check other countries' systems. If you see someone publishing in a different sector, national or institutional system from you, find out if their work 'counted' in their careers. Study a few cases. Look at their publishing choices. Check their career progression, research funding and whatever else interests you.

Check the citations index for your discipline to determine a journal's status:

Citations have three merits: they reflect the view of the international community rather than that of a small expert panel; they are objective and transparent; and they are immune to grade inflation. Drawbacks include bias towards established researchers and against excellent work in obscure fields. Poor work may sometimes be cited in order to correct it.

(Smith and Eysenck 2002: 15)

Not everyone agrees that citation counts are key indicators of a journal's status, but some will still see them as a 'gold standard'.

Choosing a journal

There are many reasons for choosing to write for a specific journal. It is not just about the appropriateness of the subject of your article, which you know is relevant to certain journals. It is not just about the journals that you like. It is not just about the journal's title, since the word 'international' in the title does not guarantee that it has a high impact factor. It is not just about targeting the journal that your senior colleague tells you to, since your choice has implications for your career. It may not even be about reaching the widest audience, since many new writers report that they can reach much larger and wider audiences in other forms of publication, some of which have no impact factor.

While choosing a target journal is straightforward in some fields, in others a more complex mix of factors comes into play: the power of the journal, the power wielded by colleagues and your own sense of empowerment to make a choice.

The open access debate may complicate your choices. It is clear that this mode of publication will change how research is accessed, but it may also influence how it is evaluated, and this is another factor in choosing target journals or other outlets.

These forces need not limit new writers' choices; instead, they offer opportunities for writing. For example, a new writer reported that having chosen a high-ranking target journal, he then researched the editor's work, noted that the editor took a certain theoretical approach in his own writing, read up on that approach, applied it in his analysis and submitted his paper to the journal, which was quickly accepted, and a second was accepted by the same journal a year later.

This will seem like extreme 'targeting' to some, but the result is that the writer learned more about that theoretical approach and its use in analysis. He was also published in a high-ranking journal, which was, after all, his goal.

Peer reviewed or professional?

New writers often spend a fair amount of time debating the pros and cons of publishing in 'academic' or 'professional' journals. The academic journals, they argue, will reach a minute readership, while professional journals will reach many more people, including those who can implement the writers' ideas. At this point I usually ask the question, 'How many papers have you published in this or that journal?', and the answer is 'none'. In other words, there is a quantity of informal knowledge about these two types of journal that is often not based on experience or even on hearsay.

This is not to say that new writers are lacking in ability, but that they often seem to form beliefs about journals and readers that are difficult to modify and may inhibit their motivation to write. Although this discussion is a crucial moment in a writer's development – without it they may never overcome their resistance to writing for academic journals – it can lead to a block.

One solution is to see the value in both types of journal and to consider, over the long term, whether you could or should publish in both. 'Academic or practitioner' is, therefore, less a dilemma than a set of rhetorical choices. In practice, there are journals in some fields that bring the two together:

Academic	Professional	Both
Research	Practice	Study of practice generates new knowledge
Small audience	Large audience	Mixed
Values theory	Values experience	Researches experience

You can probably identify the journals in your field that combine 'theory' and 'practice'. This may involve you in updating some of your assumptions about what constitutes an academic subject.

In practice, however, this discussion of choice has to be much more specific to your subject area, and this would be a good topic for you to write about now, even using the informality of style and writing in the first person singular in order to explore what you really think:

Writing activity

- What experience can I draw on?
- What do I want to analyse?
- What is the underlying theory?
- What theory can I relate my work to?
- What new perspective do I want to bring?
- How can I relate that to others' perspectives?

Practitioner journals may have less status, particularly if they do not use peer review. It is worth checking, however, whether this distinction still applies to the journals you are considering.

Frequently, new writers have enough material for both types of journal, but they do not realize it. Hence the need for focused discussion with experienced writers about your publication plans. You do not have to limit yourself to one type of journal, and you may argue that this is not a healthy, motivating strategy in any case: 'it is dangerous for us to allow academic institutions to remain the primary site where our ideas are developed and exchanged' (hooks 1999: 140).

Instructions for authors

Many editors report that, incredible though it seems, submissions ignore the journals' requirements. This section is here to spell out the point, however obvious, that you must follow your target journal's instructions for authors to the letter.

What not to do

- Invent a referencing style, use the wrong one or provide incomplete or inconsistent references.
- Exceed the journal's word limit.
- Omit abstract/summary, author biography or other requested elements.
- Submit your paper single-spaced.

Instead, always use the recommended style manual or the journal's house style. Of course, you know all this already, and cannot believe that an astonishing number of writers do not follow the journal's guidelines. If you need any further motivation, some editors claim that they will not even consider papers that do not follow their guidelines.

Another part of your 'instructions' as a writer is the journal's aims and scope. Unlike the guidelines for presentation, these are open to interpretation. If possible, talk to someone who was published in the journal recently to check and sharpen your understanding of how these aims are put into practice.

There may be other important requirements for submissions, such as ethical approval, statement of potential conflicts of interest, any financial support you had for the work described in your paper or specification of who did what in multiple-author papers.

Journal resources for authors

In addition to specifying how authors must submit their articles, some journals occasionally include articles about how to write for publication. Others provide resources for authors. For example, the website of the *British Medical Journal* (*BMJ*) https://www.bmj.com/about-bmj/resources-authors not only explains the whole process from submission through peer review to publication but also provides guidance on writing. In addition, there are *BMJ* publications that shed light on the requirements of journal article writing in this field (Hall 1998; Greenhalgh 2019). Search for this type of resource in your fields and in your target journal.

Websites for authors

There are also resources online at publishers' websites (e.g. Emerald, Taylor and Francis Journals Online), so check both your target journal's and its publisher's websites. There may also be video and audio interviews with editors and authors, which give more information on what journals are looking for. And there are always websites on how to get published (e.g. www.academicladder.com).

If you do not already know them, check out the websites of the relevant professional body for your research area. These provide a wealth of reliable, relevant information about research in your field and how to grow your knowledge of it, often in specific sub-categories.

Analysing a journal

Part of the process of targeting is analysing features of a journal in detail. Again, this is not to say that you are a complete novice; you already know the journal well. Instead, the point is to develop your knowledge of the journal further through systematic analysis of how articles published there recently are constructed.

How to analyse a journal

1 Read the full instructions for authors. Some journals only publish an extract in certain issues.
Check the website. Read titles and abstracts.

2 Skim and scan the last few issues for topics and treatments.
Which topics appear most often and how are they treated?
How can you adapt your material to suit the journal's agenda?

3 List the headings and sub-headings used in two or three papers.
How are articles divided up: number of words per section, proportion of each section?

4 Which methodologies or theoretical frameworks are used?
How long, how defined, is that section of each paper?

5 Discuss your analysis with experienced, published writers in your field, preferably those published in your target journal recently. Ask them: 'Are the editors/reviewers likely to go for an article about . . .?'

Look at how structure is signalled in each article. Even in short articles, there are versions of the generic structure of academic writing – rationale, aims, methods, results, meanings, though not always in these terms – but what form do they take in your target journal?

In some journals, it is less important to signal the structure of the article; it is more important to signal the research process.

How the research process is signalled

The identification of . . . remains **one of the most difficult challenges** . . .
Seeking and detection of . . . **could provide a [sic] valuable information to** . . .
. . . a first study was undertaken to **evaluate** . . .
Four collection means **were tested** . . .
A **statistical assessment** of the results indicates . . .
The evaluation . . . was then carried out using . . . Collection was made using . . .
The results show . . .
The results of this preliminary study **are in agreement with** other previous researches . . .

(Darrer *et al*. 2008: 171–8)

The research narrative – a research question leading to a research answer – may be made explicit in the matching of terms at the start and end of the abstract, as in the following example. Writing in this way, if it is appropriate for the target journal, makes the contribution clear and the argument consistent.

Recent research has been concerned with **whether speech accommodation is an automatic process or determined by social factors** (e.g. Trudgill 2008). This paper investigates phonetic accommodation in New Zealand English when speakers of NZE are responding to an Australian talker in a speech production task. NZ participants were randomly assigned to either a Positive or Negative group, where they were either flattered or insulted by the Australian. Overall, the NZE speakers accommodated to the speech of the AuE speaker. The flattery/insult manipulation did not influence degree of accommodation, but accommodation was predicted by participants' scores on an Implicit Association Task that measured Australia and New Zealand biases. Participants who scored with a pro-Australia bias were more likely to accommodate to the speech of the AuE speaker. Social biases about how a participant feels about a speaker predicted the extent of accommodation. These biases are, crucially, **simultaneously automatic and social**.

(Babel 2010: 437–56)

For structured abstracts, where the headings do all the work, it is not necessary to write in complete sentences, as in the following examples. The proportions of each element of an abstract – in terms of the number of words in each element – are very clear. An emphasis on methods (of both data collection and data analysis) is clear in the next example.

Background: Television viewing time, the predominant leisure-time sedentary behaviour, is associated with biomarkers of cardiometabolic risk, but its relationship with mortality has not been studied. We examined the associations of prolonged television viewing time with all-cause, cardiovascular disease (CVD), cancer, and non-CVD/noncancer mortality in Australian adults.

Methods and Results: Television viewing time in relation to subsequent all-cause CVD, and cancer mortality (median follow-up, 6.6 years) was examined among 8800 adults ≤25 years of age in the Australian Diabetes, Obesity and Lifestyle Study (AusDiab). During 58 087 person-years of follow-up, there were 284 deaths (87 CVD deaths, 125 cancer deaths). After adjustment for age, sex, waist circumference, and exercise, the hazard ratios for each 1-hour increment in television viewing time per day were 1.11 (95% confidence interval [CI], 1.03 to 1.20) for all-cause mortality, 1.18 (95% CI, 1.03 to 1.35) for CVD mortality, and 1.09 (95% CI, 0.96 to 1.23) for cancer mortality. Compared with a television viewing time of <2 h/d, the fully adjusted hazard ratios for all-cause mortality were 1.13 (95% CI, 0.87 to 1.36) for ≥2 to <4 h/d and 1.46 (95% CI, 1.04 to 2.05) for ≥4h/d. For CVD mortality, corresponding hazard ratios were 1.19 (95% CI, 0.72 to 1.99) and 1.80 (95% CI, 1.00 to 3.25). The associations with both cancer mortality and non-CVD/noncancer mortality were not significant.

Conclusions: Television viewing time was associated with increased risk of all-cause and CVD mortality. In addition to the promotion of exercise, chronic disease prevention strategies could focus on reducing sitting time, particularly prolonged television viewing.

(Dunstan *et al.* 2010: 384–91)

This last example is a wake-up call to those of us who sit for long periods every day, increasing our risk factors, not just during television viewing, but also, according to the conclusions of this article, 'possibly in other prolonged sedentary behaviours' (Dunstan *et al.* 2010: 389), such as writing.

By doing this kind of analysis you develop a profile for each journal, updating it routinely. You will probably already have internalized a lot of this information, but it can help to make your observations, and therefore your choices in your own writing, more explicit. You can then check your observations and your choices against others. Moreover, this analysis is likely to prompt you to develop the title and abstract for your article.

To extend this analysis, with/without colleagues or in a writers' group, analyse a journal in detail by looking at how the arguments are articulated across all the abstracts in one issue. For example:

Analysing abstracts in one issue of your target journal: example
British Journal of Educational Technology, **32(1), 2001**

1 Ford and Chen

Starts with 'This paper + verb': 'This paper presents results'.
Followed by specifics of the study.
Results take up the bulk of the abstract.
Key word at start of sentence: '*Significant* differences in'.
Implications in second-last sentence in propositional style: 'The findings provide support for the notion that . . .'.
Last sentence refers to future research, but is not specific.

2 Pedler

Starts with background/context statement in general terms.
'This paper + verb' comes second: 'This paper examines'.
This structure in also used in sentences 3 and 4: 'It first describes . . . It then presents . . . and finds that . . .'.
Sentence on findings included.
Implications stated as a proposal statement, minus the phrase, 'The findings suggest': 'Spellcheckers need to use'.

3 Morris

Starts with 'This paper describes'.
Method is described in general terms: 'A summative evaluation study'. 'However': good link word to signal balance of interpretation.
'The implication of this research outcome is considered', but not specified.

4 Holsbrink-Engels

General opening statement.
Almost half the abstract is background.
General statements in the continuous present tense.
Then 'The results are described': good sentence variation, but too cryptic?
Explicitly signals 'The main conclusion'.
Wordy (in my view): 'is considered as having the potential to assist'.

5 Sandberg, Christoph and Emans

Change of style: 'In this article *we*'.
Uses narrative structure, with time words: 'First we established . . . Then the requirements were . . . description . . . evaluations . . . Conclusions'.
Pros and cons of findings referred to, not specified.

6 Salmon

Starts with 'This paper describes and discusses critically'.
Claims study is 'unique' in first line.
'Useful lessons' learned from the study are semi-specified.

The next step is, of course, to analyse a whole article in your target journal.
Once you have decided what type of article you want to write, choose one of

that type and take it apart. Work out exactly how it is constructed and how that construction is signalled in words. What styles and forms of argument – in any terms – can you see in that article? Study topic sentences (first sentence of each paragraph):

Analyse an article: study the topic sentences

Hamilton *et al.* 'Too little exercise and too much sitting: inactivity physiology and the need for new recommendations on sedentary behaviour'

Introduction

There is now broad agreement among clinicians . . . that . . .

However, a question that arises from consideration of . . .

In this regard, the updated recommendations . . . have sought to clarify . . .

However, this 'background' may be equally important for . . .

Sitting is the most common sedentary behaviour of adults . . .

In this article, we consider 'too much sitting' a distinct health hazard and describe recent findings from . . .

Epidemiologic evidence supporting an increased emphasis on reducing sitting time

Epidemiological observations from the middle of the 20th century showed . . .

New data . . . strengthen the case for seriously addressing . . .

The Australian Diabetes, Obesity and Lifestyle Study (AusDiab) has provided a unique opportunity to examine . . .

Does meeting physical activity guidelines obviate concerns about sedentary behaviours?

A recent report from AusDiab examined the relationship of . . . Recognizing the subjective nature of self-report data . . .

Light-intensity activity had a strong inverse relationship with sedentary time.

More recently, breaks in sedentary time . . . were shown to have beneficial associations . . .

This set of findings from AusDiab shows important patterns of association with . . .

The emergence of the inactivity physiology paradigm

The term inactivity physiology was first put forward in 2004 to describe . . .

The effects of postural allocation . . .

Generic association studies have suggested . . .

The most definitive experimental evidence . . .

Studies have used . . .

If physical activity is thought simply to be . . .

In summary, studies using sophisticated . . . methodologies have found . . .

This perspective may have some radical implications for public health . . .

Research directions: understanding and influencing sedentary behaviour

While the evidence . . . is compelling . . . much remains to be understood . . .

Laboratory studies with humans could be carried out . . .

Real-world experimental studies might be conducted . . .

New directions for future guidelines and public policy

Given this new understanding . . .

Communicating this new perspective . . .

Conclusions

Coming to grips with the new evidence that we have described will pose challenges.

Because insidious health hazards are common and affect most of the population . . .

This analysis has three benefits: (1) it helps with targeting a specific journal by defining the type of writing required; (2) it provides a framework for structuring an article for that journal; and (3) it prompts writing, if, when doing your analysis, you write sentences for your article for your target journal.

Working out what is acceptable

You will know that some journals have only two or three types of article, while others have several types, such as 'conventional academic articles . . . research notes, viewpoints, work in progress, responses to previously published articles, review articles, autobiographical pieces and poems' (Blaxter *et al.* 1998a: 146).

Although it is contentious, the case can be made that you can define what is acceptable for publishing in your target journal in terms of what has been accepted, although there are, of course, exceptions in some fields: 'Many of the more recently established journals . . . allow for and even encourage less conventional kinds of writing' (Blaxter *et al.* 1998a: 146).

You may find that you resist or reject this approach to targeting. You may even be uncomfortable with the idea of targeting. Yet this is what constitutes effective writing – writing that persuades its audience – and it also, it has to be emphasized, defines the work you have to do to write your article.

Analysing abstracts

This section is about learning to look for the shapes of argument that a journal has accepted recently. It is also about seeing patterns that occur across disciplines, such as problematizing sentences, methods for approaching the research problem, contingent answers to your chosen question, and so on. Many abstracts begin with what is known, then move to what is not known and needs to be researched, then to the justification of the work done, followed by the argument that it needed to be done, and so on.

Three abstracts from one field are analysed in detail in this section. If you think the field of academic writing – as an area of research in itself – is likely to be narrow, wait until you see the range of current research on this subject and the different journals in which it is published. This means that in this area – as in many others – different types of writing are available to writers, but for any paper you are writing, you work to match your research and writing with the journal you are targeting at this time.

These examples also illustrate an important point for new writers: if you can adjust the pitch of your argument you can write about your topic in different ways for different journals. This is not re-hashing your material, but developing it in new ways, sometimes taking your thinking or research in new directions. These abstracts deal with different types of research. This is how you can develop a writing portfolio: not by writing about a new subject in each article, but writing about the same subject, even writing about the same data, in new ways, in new analyses, in different journals for different audiences.

Even if higher education studies is not your field, this section shows the kind of analysis I suggest you do on abstracts in your area. Doing this analysis outside your area, in the first instance, is one way to avoid being distracted by the articles' contents. Since you might not care too much about the content of the papers in my selection, you can focus on the analytical approach I am demonstrating, and that, I argue, you should use.

Perhaps more importantly, although this activity is meant to be analytical, it often draws out academics' and professionals' personal preferences. Some people just do not like certain styles of writing or certain research paradigms. There is nothing wrong with that, as long as you can put your stylistic preferences on hold, as required, in order to produce a style that is acceptable to your target journal.

The first abstract begins with a good example of that clever rhetorical device, the 'uncontentious opener', marked in bold. The opening sentence problematizes an issue without drawing fire. While it makes a sweeping statement, the terms are general enough to stay on the right side of overstatement and familiar enough not to require references at the end of the sentence. The case is made for the work conducted without critiquing the work of other researchers. This is skilfully done.

Abstract 1: the review paper

During the last two decades the higher education system in the UK has moved from an élite to a mass orientation, while academic careers have become less secure and more demanding, and a greater accountability has been imposed upon the system. In the light of these changes, it is appropriate to ask what is known about the nature of academic work. For the purposes of this article, academic work has been conceptualised as involving one or more of five overlapping roles: the commonplace triumvirate of teaching, research and managing, plus writing and networking. **The existing literature** on each of these roles, and on academic careers in general, **is reviewed**. At the time of writing, there was **no single comprehensive text available** on academic work in the UK.

While much has been written in recent years on the teaching role (and, to a lesser extent, managing) **relatively little** of a cross-disciplinary nature **appears** to have been written on academic researching, writing or networking. **The future development of** these, and other, areas of writing on academic careers, **is considered**.

177 words

Blaxter, L. *et al.* (1998b) Writing on academic careers, *Studies in Higher Education*, 23(3): 281–95

The second sentence creates a brilliant, economical shift of gear from the context to the work reported in the paper: 'In the light of these changes, it is appropriate to ask'. The authors do not say, 'We have to consider' – which would be more debatable – nor do they propose that this is a neglected area of study. Like their opening sentence, the way they put it is also relatively uncontentious, because, in many fields, it is *always* 'appropriate to ask what is known about' a subject. This is an excellent way of introducing a review paper. The authors build a solid foundation for the sentence, 'The existing literature . . . is reviewed', so that their review develops logically from the context.

One statement in this abstract often strikes researchers as overstated – 'no single comprehensive text available' – yet, on closer examination, we see that while it might be foolish to claim that 'no text was available', what the authors have said is that there is no 'single comprehensive' text, a claim that is not as extreme as it first seems. Likewise, 'relatively little' qualifies the statement 'little has been written on', as the authors suggest merely that there is less on this area than in other related areas. The word 'appears' prevents the authors from sounding categorical in their assertion – a standard device in academic writing, whereby the authors acknowledge that what they assert remains open to debate.

Finally, what the authors provide that is new is described only in general terms – 'the future development of . . . is considered'. We are not told the outcome of their review, analysis and 'consideration'. Some find this unsatisfactory; they want to know whether or not it is worthwhile reading this paper, and they make that judgement based on the abstract. However, this paper was published and therefore was judged adequate in its present form. This is not to say that papers published in this journal never specify the outcome of the research in the abstract, but it does mean that this is an option, whether or not every writer would choose to write that way. Moreover, it is an appropriate option: when writing about a subject that has not been extensively researched, such a tentative assertion of 'contribution' to the field is appropriate.

In the second example – still about research on academic writing, still in the field of higher education – the writer does more work to establish that there was a gap in the literature.

Abstract 2: defining the research gap

A review of literature on released-time programs shows a trend away from uncritical acceptance. Emerging skepticism about released time from teaching or service **stems from a lack of evidence supporting** its usefulness and from the mixed messages it gives about the value of teaching. **Four demonstrational experiments** confirm that skepticism by **showing that (1)** verified assessments of normal workloads contradict faculty claims of being too busy for additional scholarship; **(2)** faculty given released time usually persist in old habits; **(3) new faculty showed no obvious benefits of a typical released-time program; and (4)** faculty in released-time programs verbalized real doubts about how to use extra time for meaningful scholarship. **A fifth experiment suggests an alternative to** traditional released-time programs: faculty who claimed too little time for regular scholarship learned to produce significant amounts by finding time for brief, daily writing sessions.

142 words

Boice, R. (1987) Is released time an effective component of faculty development programs?, *Research in Higher Education*, 26(3): 311–26

The first sentence, 'A review of literature on . . . shows a trend away from [or towards]', is one we could all write regularly. This is not to say that we will plagiarize this paper, or any published writing. The point is that there is a limited range of rhetorical techniques that work in each discipline, and a limited number of ways of saying that your work needed to be done. What is interesting about this variation is that the author did not write, '**There is** a trend away from', but rooted his assertion in literature, or at least the review of it, which 'shows' such a trend.

'Emerging skepticism' develops the point that such programmes are no longer viewed uncritically, while the term 'released time' is given more definition. This sentence also identifies that ubiquitous trigger for research: 'lack of evidence'. It is logical to assume that if we had more evidence of effect, we might be more willing to consider a programme. This is a recognizable argument for research.

The essential link between the literature, and the question it leaves unanswered, on the one hand, and the author's research, on the other, is implied, rather than explicit: 'Four demonstrational experiments'. The link between the statement of the need for the work and the beginning of the description of it is made by repeating the word 'skepticism'. Like abstract 1 (Blaxter *et al.*), this abstract tells us nothing about methodology. It does not say how 'experiments' were conducted or how data were analysed. Yet, clearly, this was judged appropriate for publication in that journal at that time.

Some readers like the listing and numbering – 1, 2, 3, 4 – of research outcomes. It makes for a very long sentence (66 words), but each element of the list follows the same pattern, making reading easier. Yet many feel relief when the last sentence breaks the pattern with 'A fifth experiment'. Some find it more difficult to read than the first, perhaps, they say, because they are less familiar with its more scientific style; others say the opposite. Whether or not you like this style, it has recognizable, generic rhetorical manoeuvres that you will see in your field. Again, it is important to conclude this part of the discussion with a reminder that the paper was judged acceptable by the reviewers and editors.

Finally, a third example – same discipline and research area, different method and journal – shows a different approach. No contextualizing opening sentence; it goes straight to a description of the study.

Abstract 3: straight to the study

Three different two-day thesis writing courses were designed and evaluated. Forty-one graduate research students completed a product-centred course which taught grammatical and stylistic rules for good research writing. **Thirty** students completed a cognitive strategies course which introduced heuristics for generating and organising thesis content. **Thirty-three** students completed a generative writing and shared revision course which entailed the production of an unplanned draft followed by extensive revision on the basis of reviewing by peers. **All three courses** were well received by the students, **but** those who attended the product-centred and generative writing courses **showed significantly greater improvements** in productivity than did the students who attended the cognitive strategies course. **These findings suggest that** short writing courses **can be of benefit** in teaching research writing to graduate students **but** that such courses should focus directly on the production of text rather than on strategies for generating and organising information and ideas prior to composing.

152 words

Torrance, M. *et al.* (1993) Training in thesis writing: an evaluation of three conceptual orientations, *British Journal of Educational Psychology*, 63: 170–84

In this example, the first word of the first sentence tells us that this article is about three studies. We then follow a pattern: reporting on each, as each subsequent sentence starts with a number, again setting up a pattern. Unlike abstract 2 (Boice), with all its results presented in one long sentence, here each result has a separate sentence. Then there is a synthesizing sentence, beginning 'All three courses', which neatly pulls them together and makes a positive statement about them, quickly qualified in 'but'.

'These findings suggest that' is another generic phrase that we will probably all write at some time. Certainly, there is no avoiding the word 'suggest' in academic writing, particularly at the conclusion of academic argument, implying as it does the process of interpretation – rather than proof – in research.

We would all probably be happy to say that our work led to 'significantly greater improvements' in our field (whether or not that means statistically 'significant' will, of course, have to be clarified, but not, apparently, for abstracts in this journal at that time). Stating your paper's 'contribution' is required by some journals: does your work contribute something 'new', 'fresh' or something that 'can be of benefit'? How are contributions described in your field – exactly which words are used in the closing sentences of abstracts and conclusions in journals in your field? Significantly, in this third abstract, the claim that it makes a contribution is qualified, again with the word 'but', as the authors not only clarify their claim but also do not appear to claim too much. Is this current practice in your target journal?

These three examples show the range of rhetorical choices made by writers in one discipline. Although the three are, in some ways, quite different, there is not an infinite variety across any one field; if you study your journals in this way, you can develop your understanding of how successful, accepted papers are put together. With this understanding, you can make appropriate choices in structure and style – appropriate to your target journal.

If you become a scholar of abstracts in your discipline, conducting this level of analysis, then you are more likely genuinely to have learned about how writing is produced in your discipline's journals.

What you can learn from studying abstracts

- How to write 'uncontentious opener'/problematizing/rationale sentences
- How to make the case for your work
- How to link what is known/not known and your work
- How much to write about your methodology
- How much detail to give on your results
- How to define your contribution – options and specific terms to use

---

Defining genre

Every academic discipline has distinctive ways of thinking, stating ideas, and constructing and pacing arguments. Within each discipline there are sub-genres, represented by or within different journals. Some features of the genres of academic writing appear across disciplinary boundaries – generic features of academic writing.

I thought this was a relatively uncontentious position until I was vigorously challenged by a scientist who strongly disagreed: 'How can you say that there are such generic features? How do you know? What is your evidence?' The fact that we were, in that moment, analysing examples from his and other disciplines that had similar features did not make him see it that way. This was an important reminder, for me, of how differently we perceive writing in our different disciplines – but the strength of his reaction was interesting. Is it wrong to think of academic writing as a genre? Is it true that comparisons cannot be drawn across disciplinary boundaries?

While it is crucial to study the genre of writing in your discipline, it is equally important to learn about the generic forms available to all disciplines. Later in this book examples from different disciplines are used to illustrate classic, generic features of academic arguments. Will you only read those from your own discipline? Taking the 'anti-genre' view? Knowing that various readers have various reactions to the idea of generic features in academic writing, I have kept examples short.

Even as you learn about genre, there may be others in your discipline who think like our colleague mentioned above. They may think that you are naïve, that you still do not really know what is going on in journals in your field, that you are just too new to the game. Some may even think that you are proving too slow at picking it up, particularly if you seem to want to debate their views, rather than just acting on their suggestions. Clearly, you will have to gauge for yourself which, or perhaps whose, advice to follow and how to express your responses to it, but as you learn more about writing you may find that you have opened a new debate in your department.

Perhaps, even as we differ on this issue, we can agree that academic writing is not infinitely various; there are recurring patterns and dominant norms and forms within and across disciplines. Consequently, the range of structures and styles at your disposal is not infinite. Your writing choices are limited by the conventions in your target journal at this time. Each journal has its own genre. Certain types of arguments are privileged over others, as illustrated by those who study genres:

> Gould's synoptic history of evolution **unfolds as a kind of narrative.** **Life begins** (prokaryotic cells), **develops** (eukaryotic cells), **diversifies** (Ediacara and Tommotian creatures), **explodes** into the modern fauna of the Burgess Shale and **then subsequently subsides** through large-scale attrition **until we arrive at** the ever diminishing number of extant species co-habiting the planet **today**. To make his point Gould rewrites Darwin's model of evolution as a puzzling story, whose climax (the Burgess Shale) is clear, but whose interpretation is a matter of considerable debate.
>
> (Halliday and Martin 1993: 36, emphasis added)

This example uses a narrative genre: linking points using words that suggest the passage of time: 'then', 'subsequently', 'until'. This definition of continuity and stages may itself be open to question in the field of research – does everyone agree that these are the key stages? – and perhaps avoids the more complicated cause-and-effect mode. Simply saying that one thing followed another is still open to question, but it may require a different type of evidence than causal analysis. Some might question the link made by the words 'we arrive at', since it implies a connection that either has already been well argued or is about to be.

The point is to identify the genres that are used not just in your discipline, but in your target journal at this time. If not narrative, then what?

Joining the conversation

By writing an article for a journal you are joining a conversation, which may have been going on for many years, and you can analyse this conversation:

Analyse the conversation

- Who is already participating in this scholarly conversation?
- Who decides who can join in?
- Do you know anyone who is already taking part?
- Who has been excluded?
- What are they all talking about?
- What is already being discussed?
- What have they not talked about for a while?
- What do you want to tell them?
- Can this be modulated to relate to their conversation?
- What do you need to do and know in order to join the group?
- How are they likely to react to what you say?

Your answers to these questions could, in some fields, be topics not only for exploratory freewriting (see Chapter 4) but also for your academic writing.

You have to establish your place in the conversation: on what terms can you join the debates in your field at this time? Even when you have thoroughly analysed the conversation, make a clear case for your contribution, as persuasion counts more than performance in this type of conversation.

Use writing at this stage to develop your ideas. If you do no writing at this stage, as you study the writings of others, will you be distracted by others' ideas – a real risk for new writers. In fact, writing regularly can help you to develop your ideas, perhaps exploring several potential lines of argument.

Besides, it should be clear to you now that even those whose papers you find dull or unoriginal have put a fair amount of work into getting published. They may be well aware of the flaws and deficiencies in their writing. Yet, experienced people at the journal judged them to be adequate.

Taking this thought a step further: can you see yourself as part of a community of writers, all facing the same challenges? If so, you can position yourself, as a writer, not on the outside looking in, but on the inside looking around at how other people are getting on with their writing.

Cloning or creativity?

It is precisely because common structures of evaluation and advancement in various academic jobs require homogeneous thought and action

. . . that academia is often less a site for open-minded creative study and engagement with ideas and more a space of repression that dissenting voices are so easily censored and/or silenced.

(hooks 1999: 140)

Some feel that targeting a journal by becoming a scholar of it is like 'cloning', losing your identity as a writer, losing your own voice. Some new writers say this feels like compromising, blending in, losing your originality.

Yet, it can be the opposite: targeting is about working out where, within the on-going discussion in your discipline, what you want to say can be rendered relevant and, at the same time, original. This is not about losing creativity; it is about applying your creativity to finding ways to have your say.

This is not a way to lose your voice; it is a way to choose how to give voice to your message, rather than just expressing it in the way that suits you. This is a process of giving external voice to your thoughts and ideas. Finally, if you do not test your writing, by submitting it to peer review, then you will have no voice, only thoughts and ideas.

In any case, as has already been acknowledged in this chapter, you may be very far from 'cloning' if your paper is going to fill a gap in the journal's publications: 'Matching your subject to a company's [or journal's] strength may be the single best placement strategy, but matching it to a company's [or journal's] obvious weakness can make sense too' (Appelbaum 1998: 81).

You can see an area in which your target journal has not published as a 'gap' in a different sense: 'pick a topic from within a journal's remit on which it has published little' (Blaxter *et al.* 1998a: 152).

The best strategy is to know what is dominant in the sub-field of your discipline represented by those who are published in your target journal, and to let that influence your writing, while, if it is feasible, still being able to move away from that when you choose, and still get published, which is still the goal. It may be that to write with too much of an eye on the business of what 'counts' may change 'the nature and spirit of the words that come together on the page' (hooks 1999: 163).

Mediating

Rather than take yourself out of the running, there are ways in which you can build the apparent interrogation of your ideas into your writing. Anticipate refutation of your work. Build it into your paper. Show the debate in your writing. Establish a mediated position for your paper.

You can redefine some of the terms that you think might be thrown at your writing: 'practice' orientation, for example, can be defined in many different ways, not all of them pejorative. If you check the literature, you will probably find many of these definitions, allowing you to recover the term for the purposes of your argument. If you cannot find a sufficient range of definitions of this particular term in your own field, check out other fields. If this is not a relevant critique of the type of writing you do, anticipate other critiques and redefine their terms.

In the case of the 'practice' example, your work could be based on a body of practice, draw on practice-based research, use research conducted at one institution to prompt research at another or establish connections between practice and research orientations, arguing that this is, in some cases, a false distinction.

In other words, potential tensions between what you want to write and what they want to hear can be included in your writing rather than excluded from it: you can make it the subject of part of your paper. In some fields, this might be the subject of an entire paper.

Personal negotiations

Do I contradict myself?

Very well then. . . . I contradict myself;

I am large. . . . I contain multitudes.

(Whitman 1855, 'Song of Myself': 84)

It is not certain that you will hold to the same position, in the scholarly debates you enter, for your entire research or writing life; you may change your mind.

As your ideas develop, you may take a different slant, or you may disagree entirely with something you wrote earlier. You may have new findings that contradict the previous ones. Or you may find that you finally do accept to modify your argument in light of recurring responses.

Whatever the reason, there is nothing wrong in making this shift, as long as you signal it, define and justify it, and make it as explicit as is appropriate for your discipline and target journal.

Contacting the editor

This can be an important step in article writing. It can provide you with information that is not available anywhere else.

Many new writers are surprised by the suggestion that they email the editor of the target journal as a first step in the journal article-writing process. Yet only by doing this can you check that the journal you have decided to target is interested in (a) your subject and (b) what you want to say about that subject. Because this is *only* an initial enquiry, you can legitimately email several editors at once, to see if one is more likely than the others to be interested in your article.

While the purpose of this email is to check that the journal has not moved on, that your proposed paper still has relevance, this strategy has also helped many new authors to adjust the slant or emphasis of their papers so as to achieve a better 'fit' with the journal and thereby to increase their chances of being published in it.

For example, I wanted to write a paper about writing development for academic staff and emailed the editor of the journal I was targeting to that effect. He replied that his journal was a 'research' journal and thus not receptive to papers on staff development. I adjusted the pitch of my paper to focus more on the evidence of impact in my work: focus groups, questionnaires and actual published output showed that my programme worked. I could still write about the same subject but could demonstrate research outcomes: there was evidence of an effect. I emailed this back to the editor. He was much more receptive to this approach. I wrote my paper that way, careful to make it clear, in my article, that it was not about staff development, but about research, and it was published.

The point of this narrative is that I would have wasted months of time had I not sounded out the editor initially. The editor's one-sentence response was enough to guide me in shaping my paper to fit in with his agenda, while still – important point – writing about the subject I had chosen. This is not to say that we should all ask editors how we should write our papers – that is not the purpose of this initial enquiry email – but should be sounding them out at the earliest stage to see if they are interested at all in what we are writing.

As writing and publishing in journals has become increasingly competitive, I think this is even more important. See it as helping editors to screen papers. They receive masses of articles all the time. See this initial enquiry step as saving them time.

As always, there will be disciplinary differences in this: according to one senior scientist, emailing the editor with an initial enquiry about your paper is not done. What you do, she said, is write the paper and send it in; everyone knows what they have to do, she argued, and discussing it with the editor is wasting everyone's time. This point was put so strongly that either you have to believe it is true all across the board in that discipline or it is, in some ways, challenging to this senior scientist's practice. However you interpret her response, get a response from more than one published author in your field, particularly if you are new to the game. It might also be fruitful if you are not new to the process but aiming to raise your game.

It has to be said that there is no great risk in trying out this strategy – if editors think it is wrong to approach them in this way, they will surely tell you so. Some journals – including some scientific journals – explicitly ask you, in their 'instructions for authors', to contact the editor before submitting a paper or abstract. Some want to see a summary first. Some make no such request, but this may not mean that they are not amenable to the practice. Check whether your target journal explicitly invites or forbids such early stages dialogue at this time.

A further reason for and potential benefit of this initial enquiry is that it can bring a confidence boost when the editor responds to say that he or she is interested in your topic. Such a positive response, from a senior figure in the field, is the first that many new authors have had. Even new authors understand that this brings no guarantees of publication; but they appreciate being given the 'green light' to write the paper. There is, at last, a real audience for the paper-in-progress.

Here is the suggested text for your email. In the subject line, put 'initial enquiry' or 'pre-submission enquiry'. Write four sentences in your email:

Emailing the editor

1 State the subject of your paper.
2 Say what you are saying about that subject.
3 Say why you think this paper would be of interest to readers of the journal at this time – not the obvious connection, make an explicit connection.
4 End with a question – to prompt a response.

With this version you are not giving the editor any work either in trying to work out what you want to know or in making the connection between the journal and your proposed paper.

Example of email to editor

Subject line *Journal of X Studies*: Initial enquiry

I am writing a paper on/about [insert the subject of your paper]. This paper . . . [insert what you say about the subject]. . . . This could/will be of interest to readers of the journal because it contributes [insert specific/timely/related to paper published in that journal link between journal and your article]. . . . Would this be appropriate for the journal at this time?

It may be important not to say that your paper is already written, meaning that you can still act on the editor's response. Keep your message short and you are more likely to get a quick – sometimes immediate – response. These four sentences are plenty. Keep the sentences short enough that your reader does not have to scroll down at all. If the editor wants more information than this, he or she will surely ask for it. End with a question mark to catch the eye and focus on what you are asking.

Editors' responses

If an editor has not responded to your initial enquiry within 24 hours, email him or her to check that your message was received, repeating the message.

If you still hear nothing back, try emailing another editor, if the journal has more than one.

If you still hear nothing, submit your paper when it's ready.

Wait time

After you have submitted your paper put a date in your diary, six or eight weeks on, or whenever the editor has said feedback will be sent to you. When that day comes, if you have not had a decision from the editor, and if there is no information about the progress of your article through the review process on the journal's website, send an email asking for an update on progress with your paper through the reviewing process. If you are going to be out of the office for any length of time, this is the moment – or find another excuse – to contact the editor.

Checklist

- Although you know the journals in your field very well, become a scholar of articles published there: study structure, style and rhetorical features.
- Find at least one article published there recently that you can cite in your article.
- Do some writing for your article: draft the title and abstract.
- Develop an idea for your paper that fits or challenges the norms and forms of your target journal.
- Email the editor before completing your article to check that it is the kind of thing they want to publish. Sometimes, when a journal has published a lot on one subject, editors decide to 'move on' to other subjects.

Further reading

Carnell, E., MacDonald, J., McCallum, B. and Scott, M. (2008) *Passion and Politics: Academics Reflect on Writing for Publication*. London: Institute of Education, University of London.

MacArthur, C.A., Graham, S. and Fitzgerald, J. (eds) (2016) *The Handbook of Writing Research*, 2nd edn. London: Guilford Press.

Finding time to write

Incremental writing • 'Binge' or 'snack'? • A writing plan • Goal
setting • 30-minute slots • Monitoring progress • Creating a place for
writing in your life • Becoming a regular writer • From process to
programme • Time-saving digital tools • Writer's block • Checklist
• Further reading

> If you set a short term deadline (even of five minutes) you *will* write
> something/produce something and more often than not, it's as good as
> what you would have done with double the time!
>
> (Writers' group participant)

There is a popular misconception that we need to wait for mood, ideas or inspiration before we can write, and that once we start we must keep going. This is what people often refer to as 'flow'. In accounts of how people actually write, this word does not appear often, but many new writers aspire to doing writing that 'flows' or experiencing 'flow' in their writing.

Along with this conception, there is the popular belief that even once you have decided to write, you have to 'work yourself into writing again each time' (Blaxter *et al.* 1998a: 141). Since both assumptions can make writers delay in getting started, particularly if they do not have much time, they are worth challenging.

How often do you have any time to write, let alone a time slot that coincides with your mood or inspiration? If your answer is 'not very often', or 'not often enough', then waiting for a writing 'mood' is a mistake.

Disappointingly, to some, Boice (1987) argued, based on his empirical research, that if you had more time, you would not necessarily write more. This finding makes some heads of department very happy, as they take it to mean that they can immediately cancel sabbaticals. This is not what it means. Boice showed that if you had more writing time, you would probably persist with the writing habits you have now, and this would not necessarily lead to writing more.

Explanations of the persistent time problem are many and varied. For example, at the end of a six-month writing programme (of monthly, half-day workshops involving many of the strategies covered in this book), one group of participants explained the persistent 'time' problem that came up again and again in discussions throughout the six months. It would not go away.

Making time for writing – what is the problem?

- 'Research is not a residual . . . But it can become that.'
- 'Maybe other things should become residual?'
- 'Put a notice on your office door.'
- 'Being selfish is not a bad thing.'
- 'Don't feel guilty about doing research.'
- 'Even when I have a half-day for research, I don't use it; something else comes up, like marking.'
- 'Any time we have for research is just by chance.'
- 'Technology makes it easier for people to find us.'
- 'Students always find you.'
- 'At certain times, students must take priority, for example at times of course work submissions.'
- 'You can't protect the half-day for research.'
- 'There is no space for research/writing at work.'

One person in this group suggested a more devious approach: putting a notice on her office door that said 'Please use other door', when there was no other door. Whether or not she did this, I do not know, but what is clear from the other comments about finding time to write is that there are blocks. It is difficult. Many find that people and tasks stand between them and their writing.

Even where there is a research imperative, there may be no facilities or 'permission' for writing. Making writing time is almost bound to feel as though you are going against the grain. It can even feel wrong, but this does not mean that you will never solve the problem. Many already have.

We need to consider changing our writing habits. The nature of that change should be regular writing in short bursts. Rather than waiting for inspiration or mood, you can get into the writing habit through regular writing. This may seem crashingly obvious, but writing for academic journals does not seem routinely to be done in this way or discussed in these terms.

There may be a good reason for this: academic writing requires the highest standards of content and writing; this cannot be achieved in small increments of time alone. The really intricate and difficult thinking work that goes into writing cannot be done in 15-minute bursts. This is true. And if you do have large amounts of time to write – and if you find you write plenty in the time you have – perhaps there is no need for you to change how you write. However, if you find that you are not achieving much – or anything, in terms of publications – in the time that you have, you may have to change your writing habits.

This chapter presents the argument that combining 'binge' writing – writing in large chunks of time – and 'snack' writing – writing a little often, for example in 30-, 60- or 90-minute slots – is an effective strategy for making time for writing in academic or professional schedules, and still having a life. This approach is similar to Zerubavel's (1999: 4) in the sense that there is a focus on developing 'temporal routines' to stimulate and sustain regular writing. However, while Zerubavel provides a framework for thinking about writing, this book provides many different writing activities for developing productive practices. Of course, these activities also involve thinking about writing.

This chapter is not, therefore, about finding your 'ideal' writing routine, but about developing a range of ways of writing (Murray 2015). Finding time to write may therefore involve changing writing concepts and behaviours.

Then there is the question of what is sometimes called 'selfishness', meaning putting yourself, and your desire to write more, first, more often. This is regularly cited by new writers as one of the explanations for how those who publish a lot manage to do so – they are more selfish. By contrast, according to these accounts, new writers are more likely to invest value in teaching, sometimes in over-teaching. This is a contentious issue: I am not suggesting that you spend less time on your teaching in order to make time for your writing. But, it is worth looking at how you spend your time. You are probably too busy already. Where will writing time come from? Something has to change.

What this range of issues indicates is that we have to find ways to fit writing into our lives; this may mean making changes in other areas of our lives and getting the support of others as we do so. Or, as others have put it – although they were referring to thesis writing rather than writing for journals – you can see finding time for writing as a 'lifestyle change' (Burton and Steane 2004: 98). This may lead you to think of writing in new ways:

> First, it helps you recognize the level of effort and the intensity of effort needed, and second it helps you to reflect realistically on how you spend your time now, and on ways that you can integrate the tasks associated with the thesis into your existing lifestyle.
>
> (Burton and Steane 2004: 99)

The same could be said of writing journal articles.

There are, therefore, many sound strategies you can use in your writing, but if you are hung up on the question of protecting time for writing – to the extent of failing to do it – you will not write. If you are determined to persist with your old habits, you will probably write as much as you do now. Until you make time regularly to put words on paper or screen, you might not know that you can write.

Incremental writing

I'm too busy to publish! This is like the excuse of the manager who is too swamped with brush fires to take a time management course. Time management isn't the problem. Change is the problem. Unless people are ready to alter their lifestyle, they will always be too busy. People like to pretend that they are using all their time wisely. But if you watch them, you quickly become convinced that they are not as productive as they could be. For example, I am missing lunch with my friends to write this article. I don't want to skip too many lunches with the gang because that's fun, but so is publishing.

(Matejka 1990: 9)

A sensible way to become a regular writer is to make small demands on yourself, at any one time. This may require you to plan your articles in different ways.

Incremental writing is the approach advocated throughout this book, involving treating the writing of an article as a design project: think about audience, purpose, scope and structure before you worry about paragraphs and sentences. Chapter 5 shows how to produce the total design of your article. Once you have this, you can write in short bursts. Having a total design means you can write with a certain amount of confidence, since you have decided what you want to say and how you will say it. You can be confident to the extent that not only have you found something to say but you have also thought it through and tested it against your reading.

If you divide writing into small tasks, small increments, you can fit writing into your busy life: 'To overcome fears about writing, I began to write every day. My process was not to write a lot but to work in small increments, writing and rewriting' (hooks 1999: 15).

Regular writing can have the effect of removing the fear. Each increment is small enough to be manageable, rather than daunting. On the other hand, if you do not have an incremental model, you do not experience that sense of gradually, little by little, making progress.

This is one of the 'soft' outcomes that this book is driving towards: the 'hard' outcomes are the outputs, the numbers of articles readers of this book publish in journals, while the 'soft' outcomes are the writing habits they develop along the way, the confidence they feel in their ability to write and the barriers to writing they remove.

'Binge' or 'snack'?

All of them did it by making time to write rather than waiting to 'find' time.

(Cameron 1998: 14)

You might as well wait for time to find you as wait to find time. Making time for writing – for anything – is an active process. One of the most challenging transitions is moving from 'binge' writing – 'I can only do my best work in large chunks of time' – to 'snack' writing – you can write almost anywhere and almost any time. So many new writers resist this suggestion that I have come to assert that the most productive model is 'snack and binge', with the proviso that all binges should be structured. Some have taken issue with the word 'binge', suggesting, instead, the word 'feast', so as to capture the enjoyment that comes with the headlong, seemingly unstoppable, but still controlled, magical 'flow' of writing that does sometimes happen. It is possible to induce this flow state by a combination of regular writing and joining up the writing sessions through detailed outlines, plans and timetables.

While this seems counter-intuitive to many new writers, again, it has to be said that their discomfort with the idea of writing in this way is usually based on what they think about it; in practice, in other words, it often proves less radical, less dramatic a change in their writing practices than they think.

Even if you feel that you will be sacrificing what you feel are your most 'creative' moments (large chunks of time) by carving your thinking and writing into small 'snacks', your brain will be working on your writing project while you are not writing; be ready to note ideas, headings or questions as they come to you at unpredictable moments, to use in your next writing session. Capture these in sentences – rather than notes, bullets or fragments – so that they will be more meaningful – and useful – when you come back to them in your next writing session.

A writing plan

The key point of this section is that while there are general principles for making writing time, you have to create real time slots in your diary.

This means 'matching' your outline to your diary, literally using the detailed outline of your paper-in-progress (see Chapter 5) to map out the writing slots you need to produce text.

Many authors have addressed this question of planning for writing:

How to plan writing time

1 Decide to do it.
2 Decide on your focus.
3 Plan your work.
4 Remember how many things, in real life, get done in the last 10 per cent of available time.
5 Think in terms of small blocks at a time.
6 Open your daily planner.
7 Commit to the schedule.
8 Unplug the phone, close the door . . .
9 Try not to exceed your allotted time.
10 Plan to edit later.
11 Schedule time for peer review.
12 Plan time to celebrate!

(Black *et al.* 1998: 20–1)

However, an effective writing plan must be more specific than this. It has to fit into the time you actually have. I still think that if writing is not in your diary, it is not in real time. This means that you will do things in your diary before you do things that are not there. You will do tasks with a deadline before you do those that do not have a deadline. That is one of the reasons why writing – the act of writing – so regularly falls off the list, has less priority and is difficult to make time for: it wasn't really on the agenda in the first place.

Of course, there are people who can carry this information – tasks, times, priorities – in their heads, and if you are one of them, then this may all seem a bit too simplistic or programmed. Yet this is a model for changing your behaviour, and that may mean changing some aspects of how you normally think about and do writing, particularly for your first few journal articles.

What would a more specific writing plan look like? You put writing tasks and time slots in your diary. You include the full range of writing tasks, not just drafting sections of your article. More importantly, you break your writing goal into sub-goals:

Put your writing goals and sub-goals in your schedule/diary

Week beginning	Goal	Sub-goals	Activity
Monday 1 Oct	Choose target journal	Analyse articles, identify type to write, find example	Copy/print, highlight topic sentences, etc.
	Check relevance of article to journal	Find editor's email	Write four sentences: email
Monday 8 Oct	Literature review	Classify readings	Write overview
Monday 15 Oct	Review articles	Critique Smith paper	Write summary
Monday 22 Oct	Outline my article	Write abstract	Brown's 8 questions (see Chapter 5)

You can do one of these plans for the coming week, or month, or year.

Will this work? Does this tell you when you are going to do your writing? To a certain extent it does, of course, but there is no definition of two key features: time and length of each writing task. How many words in each task? What is the scale and scope of each task? How long is each slot to be, in terms, literally, of minutes or hours? Without time allocations, these are not specific, achievable goals.

While creating your list of goals is important, an effective plan must be specific. What would a specific writing plan look like? It would look like a timetable. You produce this by taking tasks defined in an outline of your article (see Chapter 5) and mapping them onto real time:

1   Take each heading, sub-heading and sub-sub-heading separately.
2   Allocate each one a time slot of its own.
3   Go through your whole outline if you have time.
4   If not, just do what you can in the time you have.

For example, the prompt for a short burst of writing used in Chapter 5 defines the writing task. It specifies one element of the outline as a writing instruction, using a verb to define the type of writing required, 'Define', and allocating a word limit:

Define the form of cardiac rehabilitation that involves exercise, as developed in the west of Scotland, over the past 10 years (200 words).

This could fit into a 30-minute slot in the writer's diary. The same approach could be used with other sections and sub-sections, if you have done the 'level 3 outlining' described in Chapter 5. These go into the diary, alongside all your other tasks. If you do not have a diary for planning and monitoring your writing, it may be time to start.

Create your writing timetable

Monday	8.30–9am	Define the form of cardiac rehabilitation that involves exercise, as developed in the west of Scotland, over the past 10 years (200 words).
Tuesday	11.30am–12pm	Overview the different professionals involved in this development (150 words).
Wednesday	12.30–1pm	Describe the role of physiotherapy (100 words).
Thursday	8.30–9pm	Summarize Newton and Thow papers and state how present study takes this work forward (200 words).
Friday	6–6.30pm	Define and justify aims of the study (200 words).

You may wonder at these as headings for a journal article. You may wonder if the word allocations are right. You may even have started to question the purpose of the research this article presents. By this point it will be clear that a lot depends on how you outline your article and on the level of detail in your outline.

In order to make more time for writing in this way you might have to give more time to outlining, as described in Chapter 5. However, the point of this illustration is to show how you can map a detailed outline of an article onto real time slots. If each of your writing tasks does not have a time slot, how will you know when you will be able to do it? By not allocating a time slot are you not more or less planning not to do it? More importantly, if you do not produce something along these lines, how will you work out when – realistically – you can write?

If, in practice, you find, for example, that you fail to write your 200 words on Monday, then move on. Resetting is part of goal setting. Reset your goal.

You may find that you cannot do one of these slots every day. You can, of course, do a longer slot, as long as it is structured around your outline. At the end of the week, take stock: to what extent have you been able to write to your timetable? Can you already tell that certain time slots never work, while some always work? Or is it too soon to say? Should you give this approach another week, or two? Are you able to note – in a separate file – emerging ideas for future articles, using your outline to mark what to leave out of the one you are working on now?

If this seems like just too much planning – time spent planning that could more usefully be spent writing – then, again, remember that the goal is to change an aspect of your writing practice, in order to make more time for writing.

When do you have time to do all this planning? Well, if the outlining is already done, you can work with your diary and be realistic: resist the temptation to do too much in a short time or to run over the end of your dedicated time slot, perhaps creating a new 'catch up' problem.

There will, of course, be times when you have to interrupt your writing schedule, perhaps dropping a time slot for other professional or personal reasons; it is not the end of the world, but in some situations it might point to a weakness in your timetable or outline. For example, maybe it is not a good idea to allocate too many writing slots to Friday afternoon, if you are usually exhausted by then. Or, you might surprise yourself, and find that the sudden onset of euphoria that the prospect of the weekend brings gives you a brief – 30 minutes will not exhaust you – burst of energy. It is possible, for example, to do one of those 30-minute time slots between getting home and going back out again, settling down to relax or taking over caring for the evening or on the train home or in the station café waiting for your train.

Planning your writing times must be integrated with the other work you do on your article. It should include the many different types of writing activity proposed in this book: freewriting/generative writing (Chapter 4), or some version of it, some form of regular focused and unfocused scribbling in short bursts as well as the more structured 'writing-to-the-outline' (Chapter 5) time slots for drafting (Chapter 6) and revising (Chapter 7).

Goal setting

Probably one of the most serious and motivating activities is to set goals. How many articles or books could you realistically expect to get published in the next five years? Add another one, or two, to that total. (Remember you are always capable of much more than you think.)

(Drake and Jones 1997: 52)

Think ahead and develop a long-term writing programme, a body of work. See your work in 'units', rather than trying to fit too much of your work into your first article. For each of your long-term goals, you'll need medium-term and short-term goals.

The following examples illustrate learning to set writing goals and sub-goals. This may take time. Three writers, from a group of about 30 people, wrote out their goals, after an initial discussion of the range of strategies that, I suggested, they should be thinking about and adopting over the longer term.

The point of these illustrations is not to show weaknesses in their planning, since, for many, this was their first formal discussion of writing in a professional context; instead, the aim is to show that while each writer picked up on my suggestions, they did not define their goals, and this is problematic because, experience suggests, they would therefore be unlikely to achieve them.

New writers' over-reaching goals

Writer 1
- Review articles in several journals.
- Decide on target journal.
- Email editors.
- Do some freewriting sessions about ideas for article.

Writer 2
- Clarify topic.
- Identify journal – determine style and preferred article type.
- Request 'notes for authors'.
- Five minutes' freewriting per day.

Writer 3
- Identify a journal.
- Consider what type of article.
- Do five minutes' writing practice daily.
- Organize meeting with someone else for feedback.

They were all picking up on the 'right' tasks, but were in danger of trying to do too much in the time they had, and it was not clear from these goals how they would use their time. In fact, 'time' only featured in two of their twelve goals. When were they going to do these tasks? No matter how small the goal, there still has to be a real – and realistic – allocation of time to do it.

What these examples show is that even when we have discussed what constitutes 'good goals', and even when the group is very experienced and knowledgable in goal setting, having helped patients, for example, set goals for recovery, rehabilitation or health promotion, there could still be a lack of definition. This suggests that, while we all have the knowledge, it is easy to get goal setting for writing wrong. Is that because academic writing is not routinely broken down into its constituent parts? Is it because academic writing is conceptualized as a completely different task – different from all other tasks – to the extent that goal setting is not seen as appropriate? Or it seems reductive? Or over-simplistic? Or unrealistic?

Contrary to the quotation at the start of this section, therefore, the best advice might be to do *less* than you think you can. If you admit that you are still learning about setting writing goals that work, you can start by changing your perception of what is 'enough'. Do less. Do much less than you think you 'should' achieve in the small amounts of time available for writing. Make the sub-goals as small as possible. An expert in this area recently encouraged us to make our goals 'stupidly small', so that they are genuinely feasible, and so that we experience success – which is key to motivation.

Realistic goals: do less than you think you can

How long is that section to be?	800 words	
What is the content?	Literature from 2000 to 2004, UK and US	
How to structure it?	Option: As a debate/two schools of thought/three main approaches/as a narrative/chronology/ two main groups of researchers	
How many sub-sections?	Four	
Length of each section?	Section 1	100 words
	Section 2	200 words
	Section 3	200 words
	Section 4	400 words
What is the story of each?	Section 1	Overview of . . .
	Section 2	Summarize work of X, Y and Z
	Section 3	Evaluate . . .
	Section 4	Demonstrate need for . . .
When will you write it?	Monday 3–4pm and Wednesday 7–8pm	

Unless your writing goal is defined to this level of detail, there will be problems achieving it. If the sub-goals are not small, they cannot be achieved in small amounts of time. Only large amounts of time will do, and if large amounts of time for writing are not available, then you have a model of writing that is dysfunctional.

Goal setting will work if you join up your small sub-goals, that is, if you connect the work of one session, Monday 3–4pm in the above example, with Wednesday 7–8pm. You can do this in less than a minute at the end of each writing slot, by writing yourself a 'writing instruction':

Write yourself a writing instruction at the end of every writing slot

- My next writing task is to define . . . in X words . . . in Y minutes.
- The next section will summarize . . . in X words . . . in Y minutes.
- My next 30 minutes will be for describing . . .

The purpose of these is to make sure you know exactly what you have to do when, after a gap of a day, a week, or a month or more, you come back to your writing with only a vague memory of where you were last time. Instead of re-reading what you wrote then, your goal tells you how to get straight on with the next bit. Instead of getting bogged down in revision – although revision is also an important step, with its own time slot in the diary – you take your article a stage further. In this way, instead of feeling that you are starting from scratch every time you go back to your article, you feel that you are moving it forward. This is crucial for your motivation, as much as for actual progress with your article.

This is not to say that goal setting replaces thinking; goal setting for writing involves a lot of thinking. So much thinking is still to be done; thinking and writing occur simultaneously. No wonder people report that it takes them so long to get started. No wonder they feel that they must have time to think before they write. If they have not designed the task, then of course they need thinking time. Thinking and designing time will also have to be timetabled.

In discussions about this approach to writing with various groups of academics, researchers and professionals, I sometimes get the impression that they see goal setting, at least initially, as behaviourist and perhaps not entirely appropriate for research and writing. Some say they worry that this will constrain their creativity and cramp their style. I wonder if some of them see goal setting as a kind of lower-order skill that they feel they should have moved beyond, even though many admit that they have not yet developed effective practices or alternatives to this approach. This may be exactly the problem with academic writing: it is positioned apart from other forms of writing – when, in fact, it has much in common with those other forms.

30-minute slots

If, after reading the previous sections, you are still not convinced that this short-burst approach works, then it is time to try it for yourself. If you have tried it once or twice, then I would suggest that you persevere, since this 'snacking' approach constitutes significant behavioural change.

If you agree with Zerubavel (1999) that you must always take 15–20 minutes to start writing and are sure that you would find the idea of 'snack' writing for 30–45 minutes frustrating or useless, note that there is research to show that academics and professionals can start writing more quickly than that and can make use of these short time slots to progress academic writing (Murray 2015).

Write for 15 minutes. Do it twice. Count the number of words you have written.

Write for four sets of 15 minutes. Prove to yourself that you can write 1000 words in one hour. The aim is to generate text – try to forget/delay the question of quality. You can use any topic at all, but it might make more sense if you used some of your prompts (see Chapter 4). Remember to 'top-and-tail' your writing sessions: as you end one session, define your writing task for the next one.

The word 'write' may not define your writing tasks and sub-goals: what kind of writing do you want to do? Reviewing? Summarizing? Analysing? Reporting? See other examples in other chapters.

If, after all that, you want further evidence or theoretical underpinnings to make the case for this approach before you invest any time in it at all, see Murray (2012). That article complements this chapter, in the sense that while this book is a collection of materials and writing activities developed in workshops, seminars, conferences and, above all, discussions with academics, researchers and professionals who write articles, my own articles provide evidence and theorizing for this approach.

Monitoring progress

> People who write a lot typically do some kind of monitoring. There are different ways to do this . . . when I tell people about my system they give me an odd look, as if I had just said that I make quilts out of Bernese mountain dog hair. The system sounds nerdy, obsessive, and weird, but it helps me stay focused.
>
> (Silvia 2007: 40)

You can monitor your progress, in terms of output, as you go, looking back to take stock and looking forward to set new goals. This could be a further variation on your 30-minute meet-to-write session (see Chapter 8):

30-minute monitoring meetings

1 *Five minutes' writing: taking stock*
   What writing for this article have you done since the previous meeting: amount of time spent writing, number of words written, topics covered?
2 *Ten minutes' private writing*
3 Write about the theme/sub-theme/sub-heading that is next on your outline/plan.

4 *Ten minutes' discussion of your ten minutes' private writing with a partner*
   Five minutes focusing on each person's writing.
5 *Five minutes' private writing on your next sub-goal*
   What writing do you want to do next? Headings? Time slot? Number of words?

This is useful for calibrating your motivation, checking that you are not trying to do too much and acknowledging that you – sometimes – have done more than you thought you had.

In practice, again and again writers turn up to monitoring meetings and, after reporting that they have not done much since the previous meeting, reveal that they have, in fact, done more than they had planned to do, but feel they have not done 'enough'. What is that about? Over-reaching? Setting unrealistic goals? The frenzy of academic and professional lives causing them to lose sight of what is 'enough'? The answer to this question is probably quite individual, but it is as well to look out for this pattern and to have a way of seeing your actual journal article writing progress.

Creating a place for writing in your life

Although some writers feel that they need to write in the same space, the same physical space, it may be more productive, and worth trying, to write any time, anywhere: 'in your dentist's office, on an airplane, at the train station waiting for someone else's commuter train, between appointments at the office, at lunch, on a coffee break, at the hairdresser's, at the kitchen table while the onions sauté' (Cameron 1998: 14).

In recent research on academic writing, finding time and space come up so often as the absolute barriers for those who want to write journal articles. Is there a connection between creating space in your life and finding space for yourself in the published world? Is it impossible to create space for your writing while you see no space for yourself in writing? Do we have to invent a writing self before we have published? Or are we trying to invent a published self when what we need is a writing self?

Perhaps it is not until you are finally part of the published world that you can legitimize your time and space for writing, to yourself and to others. Perhaps this is because being a new writer means not yet being in an environment to write and perceiving writing environments and behaviours as 'other' or 'out there'. Perhaps there are just too many demands on your time and space: 'Rare is the woman writer of any race who is free (from domestic chores or caring for others – children, parents, companions) to focus solely on her writing' (hooks 1999: 167) – is this true for men writers too?

Limiting the time for each writing activity – in the ways described in the above sections – can bring sharper focus to writing, and having limited time in one place, for example when you are travelling, can work well for these short bursts of writing. The trick is to 'make writing time in the life you've already got' (Cameron 1998: 16). Trying to create new time creates more pressure.

There is a wellbeing issue here. Making regular time for writing should not necessarily involve giving up your personal time, which is where writing is most likely to be found, according to reports gathered from academic and professional writers in interviews and workshops. Even those who enjoy writing have to be able to 'manage the mania' (Murray and Moore 2006) and pace themselves. Writing regularly does not involve writing all the time. It should not involve giving up evenings and weekends to writing; in fact, the approaches covered in this book should make that unnecessary. A further deterrent to writing for hours at a time is the research on the serious risks to health of sitting for long periods. For example, 'Television viewing time and mortality' (Dunstan *et al.* 2010) reports that sitting for five hours increases cardiovascular risk factors by 80 per cent:

> These findings indicate that television viewing time is associated with an increased risk of all-cause and CVD [Cardiovascular Disease] mortality . . . our findings suggest that reducing time spent watching television (*and possibly other prolonged sedentary behaviours* [my emphasis]) may also be of benefit in preventing CVD and premature death.
>
> (Dunstan *et al.* 2010: 389)

The longest we should sit continuously for is one hour. (Google 'killer chairs' for more information.)

So, if you have been sitting reading this book for an hour or more, stand up for at least two minutes now. You don't need to keep standing, just stop sitting.

Becoming a regular writer

> Habit . . . functions in human life as a flywheel functions in a machine, to overcome temporary opposing forces, to keep us behaving for a time in a particular way, according to a predetermined pattern, a general rule . . . habits function to help us avoid making decisions on a case-by-case basis, to commit us to decisions made earlier, and to reap the benefits of following abstract rules rather than particular impulses.
>
> (Rachlin 2000: 7–8)

Rachlin (2000) argues that this is not – in spite of popular belief – an internal battle only; external factors, particularly social environment, play their part. This raises the question of why we need to develop 'harmonious patterns' (Rachlin 2000: 8): harmonious with what? With our ambitions? Aspirations? Family? Friends? Colleagues? Our personalities? How are these patterns created? By developing good habits specific to writing? Do we know enough about the literature on self-control to do this? We think we do, then we fail, then we blame ourselves. Alternatively, we could decide to learn more about how to establish 'harmonious patterns', experience more success, and achieve what we want to in writing.

. . . the more I write the easier and more joyous a labor it becomes. The less I write the harder it is for me to write and the more it appears to be so arduous a task that I seek to avoid it.

(hooks 1999: 168)

There is no mystique to it, and there are many strategies to try. The key possibly lies in the social dimension (Murray 2015): can you find others who are trying to become regular writers with whom you can work as you move towards this goal? Trying to make and sustain all these changes alone, separate from the rest of your professional and personal environments and without social support, may be more difficult. It may take longer to make changes you want to make.

From process to programme

For new writers particularly, it might be helpful to think about how to integrate all the strategies described in this book in real time.

If you are not only aiming to write a draft of your article, but also to develop your academic writing practices, you should be careful to pace the different activities over a realistic period, such as six months. Think about when to use which strategies, whether you will use some at one stage, but another one later, or whether you might use different strategies in different ways, at different points in the writing process and at different times in your working/writing days. What works one day, in one way, may not work every day in the same way.

For this programme to work, you may need to insert the essential element of feedback at each stage. It will help if you plan milestones, in terms of specific

Creating steps in the writing process

	Generate text	Focus	Target
Step 1	Freewriting	Write to prompts	Choose target journal
	Generative writing		
			Email initial enquiry to editor
	Intrinsic motivation for writing		
Step 2	Freewrite regularly	Draft abstract	Calibrate abstract with journal
	Write in short and long time slots	Set sub-goals in specific time slots	Revise abstract
	Decide focus of article		

Step 3	Write prompts	Create detailed outline	Analyse published articles
		Add prompts to outline	Revise abstract
		Calibrate abstract and outline	Check against journal
Step 4	Draft sections	Use prompts and outline	Check against journal
Step 5	Do multiple revisions	Check against abstract	Check against journal

outputs, along the way, for taking stock, calibrating sub-goals and coordinating your writing as you move towards your deadline.

Time-saving digital tools

There is now a host of digital tools which can help you in planning and executing your writing plan. This might include using your digital device (smartphone, tablet, laptop) to diarize your writing time, for example, or to set reminders of your milestones and the outputs you expect to deliver at each stage. Smartphones, tablets or other devices can also of course help you to make written or audio notes on the move.

To round off this section about planning, a final house-keeping note. There are other digital tools available that may also save you time as you write. For example, you might decide to use bibliographic tools such as Endnote, Mendely or similar packages. They can enable you to search sources online, record your references as you write, and automatically create and format bibliographies. Once you are familiar with these tools they can help to establish good record-keeping habits that allow you to focus instead on the real business of writing.

Writer's block

Our minds are powerful instruments. When we decide that something is true or beyond our reach, it's very difficult to pierce through this self-created hurdle.

(Carlson 1997: 119)

> You can ask yourself what scares you so much; try writing down the answer, and pay attention to what you've written.
>
> (Bolker 1998: 93)

> If you're stuck on a difficult scene [or chapter], write it anyway. Write it badly, obviously, burdened with clichés.
>
> (Palumbo 2000: 35)

All the strategies covered in this book are tried and tested. They do work. However, every so often there can be a blip in even the most organized and fluent of writing processes. I have written about writer's block elsewhere (Murray 2017a: 191–8) and recommend Palumbo as one of the most thorough treatments of this subject. See also Hjortshoj (2010).

What is writer's block? In its mild form, it is often about not being able to face writing or not knowing where to start or how to start. In its more extreme form, it may be an inability to write anything at all. Does that happen overnight? Or is it more likely to be the end of a longer process? If so, what are the warning signs we should watch out for? Clearly, increasing anxiety related to writing and low levels of writing activity will be part of the picture. However, some say that it is natural or normal to be anxious about or when writing journal articles. But should it be? And might that view head us off in the direction of writing blocks, when we find the anxiety unbearable or exhausting? In any case, we have established that there are ways to contain writing-related anxiety so that it does not inhibit or stop writing (MacLeod *et al.* 2012), and there are ways to increase regular writing in small increments.

Why does it happen? It is because of pressure to publish? Competing tasks? Conflict between what you want to write and what journals seem to want to publish? Or is the problem with the writing process itself: is it about not writing regularly, thereby making writing more difficult and even overwhelming? Is it in response to a rejection or a snide comment from a reviewer? Is it about fear of reviews? Fear of failure? How far do we want to go with this analysis, and how quickly can we turn it around to do something we want to do, that is in our interests, that has meaning and brings pleasure and satisfaction? How often do we use these terms in relation to our journal article writing? Isn't that part of the problem? If so, what can we do about that?

Let's assume that the pressure to publish will not go away and that the problem of finding time to write regularly will not be resolved by anyone else. Let's assume no one is going to step in and get the blocked writer unblocked; no one is going to be looking for the warning signs and making some kind of constructive intervention. So it's up to you, the writer. What you can do is 'write scared' (Bolker 1998: 93), 'write it badly' (Palumbo 2000: 35), even write blocked: write words rather than sentences, combine words, throw in some verbs, write down exactly what you think of this suggestion.

How can you avoid a block? I think one of the main problems is isolation, and one of the best solutions is writers' groups (see Chapter 8). This has been the focus of my research (Murray 2015), which shows benefits in terms of increased writing and decreased stress. We don't see writer's block so much in these settings – which is not to say that it'll never happen, but it does suggest that those who use the group writing mode – in various forms and combinations – are less likely to experience writer's block.

To return to the first quotation at the start of this section, writing in spite of a block – rather than stopping because of it – may be as much an acquired mindset as a writing strategy, but this is one of many facets of writing where it is difficult to separate writing and thinking, and it might even be unhelpful to try – maybe that is part of the problem. Maybe it's also the solution.

Checklist

- Combine this chapter and Chapter 5: make a programme of writing tasks. Use your outline to define your writing tasks. Create a real-time writing slot for every section of your article.
- Since this is a change process, your new programme may fail initially – persevere. Sustaining change is easier with social support. Recruit others to write with, at least some of the time (see Chapter 8).
- Monitor your progress in terms of achieving your *sub-goals*, not just your goals. See making regular time to write as an achievement in itself – that is, after all, the goal. Make it a goal.
- Defer the 'quality question' – it is not helpful, motivational or even appropriate to judge the quality of writing you produce in these regular writing slots. It is, at best, a draft. You will improve it in a series of stages – further real-time goals. Define quality as a set of components – coherence, grammatical correctness, structure, clarity, etc. Make some of these – not all – part of your goal.

Further reading

Acker, A. and Armenti, C. (2004) Sleepless in academia, *Gender and Education*, 16(1): 3–24.

Hey, V. (2001) The construction of academic time: sub/contracting academic labour in research, *Journal of Education Policy*, 16(1): 67–84.

MacLeod, I., Steckley, L. and Murray, R. (2012) Time is not enough: promoting strategic engagement with writing for publication, *Studies in Higher Education*, 37(5): 641–54.

Murakami, H. (2009) *What I Talk About When I Talk About Running*. London: Vintage Books.

Murray, R. and Moore, S. (2006) *The Handbook of Academic Writing: A Fresh Approach*. Maidenhead: Open University Press/McGraw-Hill.

Murray, R., Thow, M., Moore, S. and Murphy, M. (2008) The writing consultation: developing academic writing practices, *Journal of Further and Higher Education*, 32(2): 119–28.

Zerubavel, E. (1999) *The Clockwork Muse: A Practical Guide to Writing Theses, Dissertations and Books*. Cambridge, MA: Harvard University Press.

Chapter **4**

Finding a topic and developing an argument

Finding a topic • The literature review • Conference presentations
• Thesis • Freewriting • Generative writing • Writing to prompts
• The writing 'sandwich' • Finding readers: critic, mentor, buddy and
others • Finding a voice • Finding an argument • Formulating a
hypothesis • Constructing an argument • The quality question
• Calibrating your topic • Writing a working title • Checklist
• Further reading

The first part of the title of this chapter may sound odd – surely everyone
knows what their topic is? Topics are obviously to be found in your work and
research, so you already know what you are going to write about. Not always –
in some disciplines, research does not automatically translate into topics for
articles, and even when you have topics to write about, you still have to develop
an argument.

The purpose of this chapter is to suggest ways in which you can (a) shape
your ideas into topics for articles – this is particularly aimed at those who have
not already done so – (b) develop your idea beyond just thinking about it, and
(c) start writing.

If you are new to journal article writing, there are strategies for starting
from scratch. If you want to 'translate' your other writing into journal articles,
there are strategies for reusing and reshaping. If you published in the past and
are looking for a way back to writing, or are mentoring new writers, these
strategies can help.

Finding a topic

If you have not written for publication before – or if you have been unsuccessful in your submissions – you may feel that you have to do more reading before you can think about writing a paper for an academic journal. However, you can start to write with what you have already:

Finding a topic

- What I am interested in is . . .
- I did a couple of small studies that looked at . . .
- I could do better than . . .
- That paper on . . . by . . . is exactly the type of thing I'd like to do.
- I'd like to write about . . . but that's already been done by . . . who . . .

In many disciplines these are topics for writing, not just for continuing to mull over. For new writers, some of their new topics, like the last in this list, are accompanied by their familiar barriers and fears. All the more reason to start writing, to get the ball rolling.

You have something to say that you think needs to be heard, something that will improve things in some way. You not only have to argue your case for your idea, you also have to make the case that your idea was needed in the first place. You may have to make the case that what you see as a 'problem' or 'issue' to be addressed is, in fact, a problem: why is it a problem? How did it become a problem? Who else thinks it is a problem? Who would disagree? In order to say what you want to say about the subject of your paper you have to connect with what has already been said by others.

This does not mean demolishing the work of those who are already in print – as many new writers do, at first – but making the case that aspects of your topic 'remain in dispute. . . [and] still invite contention' and that you have identified an area that 'has not been sufficiently explored' (Selzer 1981: 70–1).

There may also be a need for an important reorientation: rethinking your work in terms of potential papers. Some people see this as mechanistic, but the intention is to prompt you to think differently about your work, and that is certainly not mechanistic:

1 What are your topics?
2 How many can be made into papers?
3 Can any of these be subdivided to make more than one paper?
4 Which one could be developed most easily/quickly?

This approach involves not looking for topics in the literature, but starting with what you know, developing topics from familiar subjects. In a sense the topic is already there, before you start. Based on what you already know, experience you already have and reading you have already done, you can write a paper for an academic journal, if you find the right journal for your topic.

This will probably mean adjusting your topic to achieve a good 'fit' with a target journal. Rethinking your topic for a particular, high-level, academic audience is the work of this stage in developing topic and argument. The aim is to find focus by writing, rather than through more reading.

The literature review

But, 'surely you have to immerse yourself in the literature before you write?' Some will tell you that you should not be writing at all until you thoroughly know the literature; this is, potentially, a recipe for you to defer writing. Of course, every researcher knows the importance of the literature. It is not just a game of who cites whom and mentioning all the big names. It is difficult conceptual work to link your writing to that of others, particularly the first time you do it for publication. But the importance of literature in your field should not develop into dependency. The literature provides a scaffolding, or structure, on which to build your work.

Of course, you have to contextualize your work, for the purposes of your paper, in the literature, but this means your writing task is to produce a highly selective piece of whatever length your target journal likes literature reviews to be. You can write the overview piece of your literature review now, since you know the 'big names' already. Drawing on memory, write answers to these questions:

- Who are the key researchers in your field?
- What are their key projects and publications?
- Which of these is relevant to your article?
- In what way do you challenge some of their work?
- What do you say that confirms some of their work?

You can top that up with their more recent work in due course, if need be, but the topic of your paper is likely based on work you have completed and reading you did before doing that work. Only add more recent references if more recent work is directly relevant to your paper.

Then check the literature review sections of articles in your target journal:

- Is there a section called literature review?
- Or is it blended into a section called 'Background', for example?
- How long are these sections, usually?
- If they vary, decide how long your literature review will be – how many words?

Then think about structure for your literature review:

- Start with chronology – do you see stages?
- Can you create stages? Is there a progression?
- Or are there groupings?
- Or can you structure your writing around themes in the literature?
- Or methods?

By writing answers to these questions, you will sharpen focus and produce text for your article.

Conference presentations

You may think that even your most recent presentation is out of date. You may think the presentation you gave to your faculty or department is too small-scale. You may not even have thought about these as potential topics for papers.

You may be right, but the fact remains that for any presentation you put in a fair amount of work, developed the idea, gave it structure and brought closure to a piece of writing about it. More importantly, you had feedback on it. It could be a draft paper.

If you have a conference presentation coming up, see if you can miss the session after yours, and take that hour to write notes on participants' responses and feedback.

Writing at a conference

1 Write down all the questions and responses from the audience.
2 Write down your responses.
3 Copy and paste your presentation into a new file.
4 Keep a copy of the paper for conference proceedings, if requested.
5 Reformat the text to 12-point font.
6 Fill in your oral comments, as you gave them in your presentation.
7 Do a word count. Check your target journal's requirements.
8 Estimate the lengths of sections of papers in that journal.

Adapt your format, layout, style, headings, title and so on to suit the journal. If you find it difficult to make a connection with the journal's agenda, you might be able to make this struggle part of the paper. You may want to adapt the focus and key words of your paper – which were explicitly linked to the conference theme – to the journal's style and current agenda. You may feel that you have to develop a whole new outline for your paper, but that may not, in fact, be necessary.

In some disciplines, where the requirements of structure are more defined, this will be more straightforward, and you could have a draft of an article to send to colleagues for feedback by the end of the hour or at least before you return from the conference.

Check the word count again. How far short are you of the journal's requirements? Is that including references or not? Do you have figures, diagrams or tables? Plan the additional writing you have to do section by section: for example, how many more words do you have for your introduction, methodology/approach and so on? Or are you over the word limit? What can you cut?

Try not to spend all your time in this post-presentation writing session outlining or reading articles in the target journal. Perhaps this implies that you could usefully be reading articles from the journal on the way to the conference, or browsing abstracts in that journal at a coffee break or writing during a presentation that you have lost interest in. While some of your attention and time should go on outlining, the emphasis here is on using specified tasks to start writing the article:

Write for five or ten minutes (in sentences) on:

- Questions asked during/after your presentation.
- Discussions you had with people who are interested in your work.
- The key message of your journal article.
- The key themes you will develop in the sections.
- Other references mentioned by participants – do you need them?
- A paper published recently in your target journal – can you cite it?

If, at the end of your hour's 'time out' from the conference, you have a detailed outline, but no writing, take another ten minutes to write in sentences. If you have done two or three short blasts of writing, you will probably have both a decent outline and between 500 and 1000 words of text, in addition to the headings from your presentation and your notes on what you said about them.

Counting the number of words is – or is not – important, depending on where you stand on the issue of what constitutes a useful writing goal and, equally important, how you measure whether or not you 'achieve' anything in writing sessions. Setting yourself a goal to write for a fixed amount of time and to produce a certain number of words strikes some writers as simplistic, but it can be an effective antidote to the impression that you have not achieved much. If you complete all the tasks suggested in this section during that hour after your presentation, you can be justifiably pleased with yourself. Time for a rewarding coffee/drink/workout/swim/phone call/visit to the bookshop.

If you have not already done so, contact the journal editor while you are at the conference. If appropriate, send an initial enquiry. (See Chapter 2 for guidelines on what to say in your email.) An editor's response may help you further focus and develop your paper.

Take this time, while you are away from other commitments, as writing time. If you leave all this until you get back to your workplace or home base, you know what will happen: you will quickly be swept up in a wave of catchup tasks. The priority you give to writing may be highest when you are presenting. The energy and enthusiasm you have for your ideas may be at their highest during and just after your presentation. The trick is to capture this energy and focus and channel it into writing.

Just as important, of course, is to plan your next writing session: when will you be able to spend another hour on this paper? The secret to connecting up your writing sessions is to write an instruction for yourself, so obvious that you will know exactly what to do when you come back to this paper next week or next month, such as 'My next writing task is to summarize the research of Brown, Jones and Hoolihan in 300 words. I'll do that in 20 to 30 minutes. My prompt for starting is "Brown argues. . . Jones confirms. . . Hoolihan combines. . .".' If your writing instruction is specific, in terms of content, scope, word length, time and prompts, then you will know exactly how to start where you left off, rather than going back through what you have already written. Joining up your writing sessions is one of the ways to become a regular writer, even if you do not have regular writing time at the moment and do not envisage having it when you return to your workplace.

Thesis

The same applies to a thesis as for conference papers, only more so. If you have already completed your PhD, you may be able to work material from your thesis into a paper. A note of caution: you should not aim to cram your entire thesis into a paper of around 6000 words. However, there may be aspects of the thesis which could form a paper (or papers) in their own right.

Even the review chapter could be an important paper, since you are up to date with the literature, your work is at the cutting edge of your area and you are well positioned to give an educated guess about possible future directions of research in your field. Clearly, you will have work to do to 'translate' a chapter of your thesis into a paper for a journal, but you can follow the steps outlined in this chapter. Start with the strategies in the next three sections.

If you are a practitioner or an early career researcher who has not yet completed a PhD thesis, there are many other ways of developing your research interests into papers for publication by applying these strategies.

Freewriting

Freewriting is a technique developed by Peter Elbow to help students unlock their thinking and writing. He found that regular freewriting increases fluency, meaning the ease with which writers get their ideas or thoughts down on paper or screen. Freewriting involves writing about anything for 15 minutes.

I adapted this technique and developed a new form of freewriting for academics and professionals.

How to do freewriting

- Write for five minutes.
- Write about the potential topic of your article.
- Explore different ways in which you might write about it.
- Write without stopping.
- Write in sentences (without worrying about grammar, punctuation, etc.).
- Write for no reader.
- Write without structure of academic writing.

If your response to the idea of doing any writing – let alone freewriting – is that you have nothing to write about yet, then these could be the very words to start a session of freewriting: 'I don't have anything to write about yet. I don't feel ready. I don't see how this leads to writing a paper anyway. This is not how we write papers in my area', and so on. Start writing.

By starting in this way, new writers are often freer to generate ideas and possibilities, without evaluating them. You start to write, even if you are, in fact, not sure about where the writing is going. Even your reactions to writing are legitimate subjects for writing. Writing about writing can help to get into the writing habit while also identifying writing barriers and motivations.

There is a cliché that you should 'write about what you know'. For the purposes of academic writing, 'what you know' may be an accumulation of your experience, education, experiments, reading, worries, feelings, conversations and teaching. This may be constituted as a solid body of work or as something that seems to you to be more transient and intangible. The point is that you can write about it in any form; it is not necessary to wait until you see it taking some kind of 'academic' shape. As a writer, you actively give it shape, perhaps even reshaping your work as 'academic' or as 'research'.

This cannot be done in one easy step, which is where freewriting comes in, since it lets you write from where you are now:

> Freewriting was good. I normally write in a more structured format, but this gave me a chance to just get what I needed down on paper.
>
> (Writing course participant)

If you are further down the line towards academic writing, or work in a discipline where connections between your work and academic writing are obvious, freewriting has two uses: (1) as a bridge between experimental work and writing, and (2) to make the step from your outline to writing.

Writing without stopping helps you to silence your internal editor. You might think this is a mistake, since that will stop you applying the criteria for academic writing, but writing without stopping can help you produce writing by not letting you cut content for the sake of grammar or punctuation. This does not mean that you ignore grammar and punctuation, which might be impossible in any case, but that you can ignore those writing choices for a few minutes in order to focus on content.

Writing in sentences can help you to make connections and, paradoxically, to persist with writing when you do not see any connections. Freewriting sometimes produces new connections. You may prefer to work with a list of bullet points. Many do. Yet this will not produce the same benefits. It is not that you should never use bullet points; instead, do 'writing in sentences' for your article-in-progress every day.

You may feel that you write best when you have a plan first, rather than just 'diving into' writing. Again, the point is not that you should abandon all planning activities; instead, combine planning with freewriting in order to get into the writing habit and thereby improve your writing.

An even greater challenge in freewriting may be the 'snacking' approach; many writers insist that they can only write in large chunks of time. Freewriting takes only small chunks of time and this, too, seems counterintuitive to those who think that they need plenty of thinking time *before* they can write.

The potentially unstructured, possibly even disjointed, nature of freewriting is also a challenge for academics and professionals. Yet much of our thinking and research is not laid out in the linear structure required for papers in our journals. Freewriting can help us to capture some of the different types of analysis and reflection that do not immediately seem to fit the paper, yet which we can transform into academic writing at a later stage.

In fact, the 'quality' end product you are striving for, or even your topic, will not always emerge immediately. Ideas you have been thinking about for some time do not necessarily constitute a topic for a paper. They are perhaps only the starting point. What do 'topics' look like? Presumably they can take all sorts of forms, at different stages in the writing process: for example, what form do they take, and what types of words are used, at the working title, rough title and final title stages? In the context of your discipline, you will know what they look like in their final, published form, but that tells you nothing about what the topics looked like at the earlier stages.

Freewriting may serve different purposes at early and later stages in your writing project. It may also serve different purposes early and later in an academic writing career. There is further unpredictability of outcome: will you use your freewriting text or not and does it matter? You may develop your thinking through freewriting, but not produce text you can use.

Once you have started, freewriting is habit forming. It requires a tiny amount of your time – five minutes – but a change in your behaviour. Try regular freewriting: for example, writing for five minutes two or three times a week. Then assess its effects.

As you do this, it is probably as well to decide on a purpose that is meaningful to you, even if you are writing without a topic in mind. Over the years, in workshops with academics and professionals in many disciplines, we have generated a range of potential uses for freewriting:

Using freewriting for academic writing

- As a warm-up for academic writing
- To overcome procrastination
- To start writing
- To develop confidence – that you can write
- To develop fluency – ease of writing
- To write your first draft
- To clarify your thinking or your argument
- To stop yourself editing and getting bogged down
- To generate topics for your papers and sections
- To start developing the habit of writing in increments
- To develop 'snack' writing

Those who persist with freewriting, twice a week for ten minutes, find it benefits their thinking, writing and, in some cases, wellbeing. Many writers report that free-writing lets them produce text that they can then work on for their papers.

While responses to freewriting may be discipline-specific, academics and professionals are able to analyse what is going on here and to extrapolate potential uses and even to observe immediate effects on their writing and thinking. They can also see potential uses and effects that are arguments for continuing to use freewriting over the longer term.

What academics, professionals and researchers say they use freewriting for

- For 'self-discussion', thinking about both sides of the issue
- To think through alternatives to your own view
- For linking different ideas
- Developing the writing habit
- Thinking through ideas
- Breaking through rigid or established ideas that do not fit the outline
- Doing the first draft
- Getting initial thoughts
- Generating ideas – it's OK to abandon one idea and go back to other work
- Preparing the analysis
- Emotional expression
- 'Ventilating' feelings and ideas
- Thinking beyond your patterns
- Breaking free of existing structure in your thinking and your discussion
- For notes, revision or confirming your understanding
- Summarizing knowledge

What is striking about this list is the number of references to what I would consider intellectual development. This is surprising, given the wide disciplinary mix – academics and professionals in the sciences and arts. This list suggests that freewriting has the potential to bring many different types of benefit to many different types of writer.

Some of these – for example, 'thinking beyond your patterns' – are creative, not in the sense of 'creative writing' but in terms of finding new ways to think about your material. Some find that freewriting fulfils many different functions at once – for example, 'notes, revision or confirming your understanding'.

Oddly, you may think, some find it useful to have a writing activity that is completely separate from their academic writing; although it assists academic writing, it sits apart from it in some way. Scientists may be thinking at this point that it is patently obvious why freewriting sits apart from academic writing. Yet the above list shows how it can also be connected to both academic thinking and writing.

For me, and for the purpose of this chapter which deals with how papers get started, the main benefit of freewriting is that you can start to write, using writing to develop potential topics:

What are you going to write about?

1 What is your area of special interest?
2 Can you combine two or three of your areas?
3 What are all the possible angles for writing about it?
4 Write about two or three of these in a little more detail.

This approach is like brainstorming in sentences, as you generate topics, make connections, establish distinctions and change your mind.

Over the long term, the key benefit of freewriting is that it lets you have your say, say what you think and, perhaps, achieve both quickly. In the process of accommodating your writing in the on-going debate, the mountain of knowledge and the phalanx of experts in your area, it is easy to lose sight of exactly what you want to say or why you ever thought it was sufficient to make some kind of 'contribution' to your field. You can say exactly what you think in freewriting. You know full well this will have to be modulated for your paper, but it can help you to find and focus on your key point.

This effect may be related to the impact of freewriting on writers' motivation: it gives you a space to voice your commitment to making a contribution, however small, about your topic. If you lose this commitment, writing is much harder. As research or publication audits of one kind or another begin to bite, paradoxically, for some people they undermine the motivation to write. Some people love targets, but others do not find them helpful. Wherever you are in this debate, it is important that you have a way of getting back on track with your own interests.

You can also use freewriting in your teaching role, since that is what it was developed for in the first instance, and this is another way to create time to write: as your students do their freewriting in the classroom, you can do yours; in the midst of a supervision session, you and your postgraduates can do some freewriting, thus building writing into supervision and, possibly, supervision into writing. This may make for a talking point in itself, and students and novice professionals are often intrigued to find out that academics and experienced professionals face the same challenges they do in writing.

If this whole argument has passed you by: you tried freewriting and hated it; you know that might mean something, but you frankly cannot see the point of working out what it is; if freewriting is just too 'unacademic' for you to even want to begin to make sense of it, even though you know you need something new in your writing, then you are not alone:

Why some reject freewriting

- It bears no relation to the 'real thing' – academic writing.
- It is a waste of time.
- They are afraid of it (some say).
- It produces 'bad writing'.

It is, of course, important to question any new approach. Ideally, you would go back to the original source, Peter Elbow, and read his books, check his website for current publications and read his papers for evidence of impact.

At the very least, you can use freewriting as a warm-up for other kinds of writing. All that time you spend getting ready to write – some people say they cannot do any writing in five minutes because it takes them half an hour, some even an hour and a half to get started. This makes getting started so time-consuming that you really do need a fair amount of time, or it will not be worth it. This can be another reason not to write. Freewriting can help you to get started without delay or delaying tactics.

Even if freewriting is ephemeral – like the newspaper, you discard it when you are finished – it is still writing. If writing is a skill – without wanting to get into a great debate about skill acquisition and maintenance – you need to practise it. If you do not practise, the skill is much harder to perform. The standard of performance in the skill may fall. This is not simply a metaphor for writing; there are, for some, very real benefits from regular short bursts of writing, even if only as a warm up:

Subjects for writing warm-ups

- I really do not feel like writing now because . . .
- I really want to watch the football/soaps/film/clouds in the sky . . .

- I really want to spend time with my partner/kids/volleyball team/TV . . .
- I know what I want to say, but can't be bothered . . .
- I have no energy right now for writing about . . .
- This is all such a big game anyway . . .
- I am bored with my paper because . . .
- My methods section needs more work than I have time to do . . .
- The feedback is just too much to . . .
- I am not looking forward to the reviewers' comments on . . .
- There is little chance that this will be published because . . .

The list of potential negatives is endless. The point of the list is to illustrate that even strongly negative feelings about writing and actual weaknesses in your paper can be the subject of a five-minute warm-up for writing. For some, the person they have to work hardest to convince that they have something to say that constitutes a contribution to the literature is themselves. If this is true for you, you have to attend to that internal critical voice in some way: define the weaknesses – we all have them – assess their seriousness and address them in your paper, as appropriate. Alternatively, cut them. The internal critic can, if handled properly, help to strengthen a paper. You can literally address internal critique by writing about it.

Whatever your current thinking about your paper, you can write for five minutes on that. Many people surprise themselves by coming up with a solution to a problem in the paper. If that sounds just too good to be true, then I can only repeat my suggestion that you try it before you dismiss it. I can accept that if you have never written in this way, or never used writing itself to solve a writing problem, it seems unlikely, and I have had hundreds of conversations where I tried to point out the potential value of freewriting. At the end of the day, all my cognitive persuasion will have no effect; you have to do freewriting to see the benefits.

You can use freewriting to vent feelings or thoughts that might be stopping or inhibiting your writing. In 'ventilating' you sometimes see a way to reframe your writing. You might simply calm down. Some find they relax into their writing in this way. This is probably a very different process from simply discussing your writing, or talking to someone about one or more of the items on the above list. You could engage in lengthy speculation about why that might be so – what is the mechanism? – or you could simply use it for the benefits you know that many others, in many disciplines, have observed quite soon after they started to use freewriting.

Finally, freewriting is a way to force writing and stop procrastinating. You can write even when it is the last thing you want to do, even when you are tired. This is not to say that it is right or fair that you should have to write when you are tired, but it is useful to have a way to get a certain amount done in a limited time and on low energy or motivation. In fact, if you do not expect too much to come out of your freewriting, so much the better, since you have lowered the stakes, and this can make writing, and thinking about writing, less daunting and draining.

This may be why freewriting, or some variation of it, is the perfect solution to the new writer's lack of confidence in writing, lack of time for writing and potentially crushing uncertainty about the value of their writing – even before they have done any – to any reader. Fears of writing build up over many years; they are not going to be easily dismissed. Freewriting is one way to start to unravel fears and bad habits and to become more productive.

Writers who use freewriting report that writing is a completely different experience when they know that no one is going to read it. Then, when they look at their writing again later, they are surprised at how good it is, or at least useable. They feel great relief in knowing that they can get on with their writing, get something down on paper and work on it later. Freewriting, therefore, seems to work well in staging writing, breaking a complex process into a series of manageable steps.

Generative writing

Robert Boice (1990a) developed generative writing as a technique for increasing writers' productivity (although the term 'generative' is also used to describe all writing strategies for producing text).

Generative writing is the same routine as freewriting but with a couple of differences that generally appeal to writers, apart, that is, from the last feature in the following list:

How to do generative writing

- Write for five minutes
- Without stopping
- In sentences
- Without structuring
- Write about one part of your freewriting or the subject of your paper
- Let one other person read it

Generative writing can be combined with freewriting. Some prefer it. Some decide that their freewriting was actually more like generative writing anyway, because they are used to writing with a topic in mind. If you find this, it could be a moment to pause and think about whether you have to stick with your current writing practice: rather than adapting this activity so that it resembles how you 'normally' write, could you not, instead, try this different practice to see what it does?

In many academic writing workshops, some find that knowing one other person will read their writing immediately changes it in ways that you might be able to predict: some say they are more hesitant in their writing; some feel they have to provide more explanation and definition; some write more, others much less. Asking them to show such early pre-rough-draft writing to a colleague seems to some unfair and unhelpful. Yet if the writing is at an early stage, your colleague will lower his or her standards accordingly. In addition, they know that they can ask you about anything that seems unclear, and you can fill in the gaps.

The purpose of including reading is, of course, to introduce discussion and feedback – so important, even at this early stage – and, if need be, to lessen the fear of peer review. In fact, the idea is to get into the habit of showing writing to others at various stages, not only when you have a full, revised draft of your article. In this way, you develop the skills of giving and receiving feedback on writing.

A productive writing process will probably involve both freewriting and generative writing, and you can probably see that the combination of the two could establish a progression in your writing, as you gradually, step by step, move towards more structured and 'academic' writing.

Writing to prompts

The downside of regular freewriting is that, if it's the only type of writing you're doing, you can feel you're drifting, not focused, and even wasting your time. You may have no sense of moving towards your goal of structured academic writing. As an alternative, writing to prompts is the best of both worlds: you can engage with a topic, perhaps in academic terms – or a writing problem – without the constraints of building an argument at the same time.

It involves writing questions or fragments – incomplete sentences – that prompt you to write more, but with a focus on your main points.

One of the most effective prompts, in many different settings, is one of the simplest:

Starter prompt

What writing for publication have you done and what do you want to do in the long, medium and short term?

If you have not done any writing for publication yet, what is the closest thing to it that you have done? Write about that.

With this prompt everyone has something to write about. It always generates text. It actually gets people starting their papers. There is no more beating about the bush, no more delaying. It is probably important to use the word 'want' rather than 'must' in this prompt, as that is more likely to focus you on what motivates you.

As a next step, you can follow this up with freewriting and/or generative writing. Or you may prefer to do freewriting and generative writing first and follow them up with writing to prompts. The key point is to try all three strategies, perhaps in different combinations, perhaps for different purposes in your paper-writing process.

If, in practice, you find that your prompt does not actually, literally, prompt you to write, there may be something in it that stops you from starting. Rather than seeing yourself as failing at this task, change the prompt. Perhaps you chose too big or too wide a topic to cover in one block of writing – perhaps, instead, you should plan two or more blocks. Perhaps, as in the above starter prompt, you had two prompts in one – separate them out and write about one at a time. Perhaps your prompt is written in an academic style, and that is inhibiting the flow of your thinking and writing. Change the style: use personal pronouns, simple language and short questions or fragments.

Try using different forms of prompt:

Fragment	Question
What I want to write about next is . . .	What do I want to write about next?

You may find that prompts in the form of a question lead to open exploratory writing, as you generate several possible answers, while the fragment form keeps you more focused and produces one sentence. Alternatively, you may find the opposite is true for you in practice. The point is to try them both. Otherwise, how would you know if they work and how?

This particular prompt is, of course, one that you can use again and again. It can help you to take stock, noting your writing achievements or outputs so far, and look forward to your next writing goal or task. Because of this it works as an effective warm-up activity, enabling writers to focus on the task in hand. Instead of taking an hour to 'get started', therefore, you only need five minutes.

These are not the only prompts you can have. It is interesting to study internal prompts that you already have, some of which may be neither positive nor productive:

Internal prompts that can inhibit writing

- I had better do more reading first.
- The reviewers are not going to like this bit.
- I should have had more done by this point.
- I said I would submit this by the end of last month.

It is likely that you will have to learn from practice – from what works and what fails – how to write good prompts for yourself. For example, you will find out whether the question or incomplete sentence form works best for you. Does the academic or informal style prompt writing best? Or is there another style that you can develop?

It may also be important to keep the informal style for some of your writing, or, more importantly, to frame your prompts differently:

Poor prompt	Effective prompt
What literature is there on this subject?	Where do my ideas come from anyway?
Who has researched/written about this?	Who has influenced my ideas?

The so-called poor prompts can lead writers to be overwhelmed by the literature – a common complaint among new writers – whereas the effective prompt leads to a relevant and manageable selection of the literature, and perhaps of particular works by a few authors. In this way, you can write prompts that help you to do some of the thinking for your paper. You can also, of course, write prompts that are much more specific to your target journal, and use them to produce writing.

You are your own 'prompt writer'. It is up to you to tackle poor prompts and to create productive ones. It may help to write these down, so that you can consider them, analyse them and, if need be, revise them so that you have ones that work.

As time goes by, and as you are successful and published, you may find you no longer need to write your prompts down because you have internalized them. As more time goes by, and perhaps you become head of department and put writing to one side for several years, you may find it useful to revert to the tactic of writing down your prompts, creating ones that actually generate writing. With freewriting, generative writing and writing to prompts, you always have strategies for producing text.

The writing 'sandwich'

The idea is quite simple: you combine writing and talking in a kind of 'sandwich', with layers of writing and talking:

Step 1   **Writing** in a short burst, for example ten minutes' private writing.
Step 2   **Talking** for ten minutes with a peer, 'writing buddy' or writers' group participant about what you both wrote, five minutes each.
Step 3   **Writing** for five or ten minutes, building on what you discussed.

The challenge of this activity is to make time for discussion – that is, to stop writing, even if you feel that you could go on writing for another five minutes or even for longer, since that is, usually, what writers do. The point is to use the five minutes to set out, in writing, the main point of your paper – and, it has to be said, sometimes just to see what comes out in your writing – and to use the very short deadline to force you to focus. The argument for this is that if you had more time you might range more widely in your writing. Not that this is a bad thing, but the focus that the five-minute deadline brings can sharpen thinking.

The most important feature of this activity is to do more writing after your discussion. At first, you may find that you end up talking for much more than ten minutes; in time, you will have to make sure that you are able to cut that short, at least some of the time, if the purpose is to increase writing time.

In order to find someone with whom you can do this – if you are not already in a writers' group, and perhaps even if you are – you will, of course, have to discuss and agree with your colleague(s) what you are trying to do, that this has purpose and how exactly you are going to manage your time. You will have to agree to just try it and to learn about how to manage this kind of session as you go along. It is not a complex process to manage. You just need someone to keep an eye on the clock so that you do move from writing to talking and back to writing.

There is a temptation in many of these group and peer activities to spend much or all of your time talking about writing, promising each other and your-selves that you will actually do the writing later. This is to miss an opportunity to get some writing done and, more importantly, to get some of the essential thinking done.

The value of this way of working is that it captures the positive response of your peer discussion and lets you use its impact to motivate you to write more. These discussions often throw up other subjects for your writing, and you can capitalize on your writing time by doing it right away, rather than trying to remember what you wanted to write about later. In addition, you are rehears-ing your arguments, and verbal feedback can help you to sharpen them. For example, subjects for further writing that can be prompted by such discussions could include:

- I have to define this more carefully . . .
- I need to add a bit on . . .
- I can move on to write the bit on . . .
- I have to elaborate on what I wrote about . . .
- I have made a bit of a jump here, the connection is . . .

These new writing topics are not just responses to your peer's comments; they arise from the thinking about your writing that carries on while you are talking or listening. This does not mean that you should direct your writing towards your peer – you might have to watch out for that – unless he or she actually reads your target journal and is, therefore, part of the audience for your writing and is prepared to respond appropriately. Instead, you use him or her – and he or she uses you – as a sounding board, not only for your ideas, but also for your writing practices. By doing this you are opening up the many stages in academic writing, often left unspoken in academic and professional environments, revealing your on-going choices, decisions and uncertainties.

The more you work with other people who want to do this, the better your understanding will be of what you are both/all trying to achieve.

Peer discussion is also important for motivation to write. Mutual encouragement can be motivational, as you are helping someone else to get on with their writing. In these short discussions, there can be valuable consolidation of work that you have already done, thereby preventing you from getting bogged down.

These discussions also provide feedback on your writing. You can use them as an early form of peer review. You can discuss the types of feedback you are looking for – structure, content, style, 'contribution', focus and so on – and can make it as 'hard' or 'soft' as you want at any given time.

In fact, the writing 'sandwich' structures feedback into your writing practice. Rather than waiting until you have brought your paper to a stage of completion, and you are ready to submit it, you get feedback at much earlier stages, and from someone who knows what you are trying to achieve in your paper, and who is, therefore, potentially well placed to tell you whether or not you are achieving it. These regular discussions of on-going writing projects can help you to be realistic and positive about your developing paper, not just in an emotional sense but also in an intellectual sense.

The 'writing sandwich' is another strategy for getting into the writing habit. In such 'sandwich-structured' meetings you are building writing into work time, and not just giving up your personal time. Perhaps more significantly, you are bringing writing into peer interactions. Workplace discussions that might previously have been limited to teaching, marking and meetings can now also include your writing. Initially, you might want to share this with the select few with whom you work in this way, but later you might alert others to the fact that you are actively writing.

For example, it might be politic to remind your head of department of what you are doing – and how much you are producing – in these 'sandwich' meetings, even if you do not use precisely that term in such discussions. You can tell your head of department exactly what you are writing about, which journal you are targeting, and when you intend to submit. If your paper was developed out of a conference presentation funded by the department, say that too. Mention your progress towards your goal of submitting your paper the next time you see him or her. Later, happily report submission. Do not worry if the response is complete indifference; the purpose of that conversation is to give information, not to seek reinforcement. On the other hand, you may actually pick up a tip or two about the journal that will help you to target it more effectively, although if the information provided is liable to take you down a completely different tack in your paper, get a second opinion.

Above all, in the sandwich meetings you are protecting time by putting writing, cloaked or disguised as a 'meeting', in your diary. If these meetings are not in your diary, they are not in real time, and it is highly likely that they will be displaced by one of your other responsibilities or tasks.

How often you do this 'writing sandwich' will, of course, depend on a number of factors, but if you feel that it has to come last in a long list of other tasks, then either you might be on the way to deciding not to do it at all before you have really given it a proper chance to work, or you might make the sensible decision to meet once a month at first, if that is all you can manage. Once a week sometimes seems too often. Once every two weeks may be best.

How long you meet for can vary in the same way, but you should probably set aside an hour, knowing that you can get through the writing sandwich process in 50 minutes. Over time, with practice, you can develop your meetings:

- Try quick taking-stock meetings of 20 minutes over the phone/Skype, if you do not have time to meet face-to-face.
- Try using more of the 50-minute meeting to do writing, trimming discussions of writing goals at the start and end of the meeting to five minutes.
- Try building up to using the whole session (e.g. an hour or 90 minutes) for writing, starting where you left off at your previous meeting (at which you wrote yourself a writing instruction for your next task, so you could start quickly at this one).

You do not all/both have to do the same task at each session. The above list gives you options to try at different times. You will also come up with others. As long as you stick to the time limit you allocated yourselves, then you will manage your writing, rather than letting it run over into other task-times, and, potentially, creating problems in other areas of your lives.

What can go wrong? What is most likely to undermine your good intentions to use the writing sandwich is that you meet and decide that you do not really need to do any writing there and then, and that you will instead just talk about it. This means you postpone writing, rather than progress it. To avoid this, arrive at any writing meeting feeling that you want to seize any opportunity, any time slot – however small – to write. Another problem might be that one of you has to cancel the meeting, meaning that you both lose out on the potential benefits of the interaction, at least, and, at worst, you fail to write. To avoid this, have an alternative up your sleeve: if your colleague cancels, you can still use the room you booked. You can still write. Keep your eye on your writing goal.

If this is all beginning to sound just a bit too 'scheduled', then you can reflect on why it is that stages in a writing project are not routinely scheduled in this way, or, if they are, why no one talks about it. Other professional tasks are usually scheduled. This is not to say that we should bureaucratize writing, but that not having some form of timetable for writing is one way of making sure it does not get done. Not having deadlines and interim deadlines for writing means you are likely – rightly – to do those tasks that do have deadlines and risk not getting to the writing at all.

To sum up, there are many potential benefits in progressing your writing in this way:

Benefits of the 'writing sandwich'

- It's quick. It doesn't take up much of your time.
- You have a real audience who gives you a real response to your writing.

- You get immediate feedback, often positive.
- You can respond to it immediately, in further writing for your paper.
- Each meeting becomes a writing deadline.
- The writing meeting may be your only writing time.
- The discussion usually stimulates more writing.
- It stops you biting off more than you can chew – i.e. helps you set realistic sub-goals, stick to them and/or reset your sub-goals for stages in your writing.
- It can make you more aware of what you have achieved already.

If/when you find that you tire of this way of writing, move on: have longer bouts of writing, work with other partners, bring together a writers' group, use the five-minute writing slot as a warm-up only, then do academic writing. As your paper takes shape and as your structure becomes fixed, you can probably write straight from your outline, using it as an agenda for writing.

A key to the effectiveness of this strategy – which people often struggle with both conceptually and behaviourally – is the importance of keeping these interactions short and focused. Any time you sit down to write, try to design the writing slot in terms of time, content – specifically in terms of verbs that describe the type of writing you want to do, such as 'describe', 'define', 'analyse', rather than in terms of the non-specific 'writing' – and the number of words required for the section you're writing.

As writers who attend writers' groups or retreats begin to develop an incremental writing strategy, using the 'snacking' strategies, some report that they write regularly for three months after a retreat and then stop. However, thanks to the strategies they learned at the retreat, they knew how to get back on track. Sometimes there is benefit in a refresher course or meeting, which is an argument for repeat retreats or regular departmental writing days away (see Chapter 8).

Unless you have some way of dividing up the writing task, in terms of small sub-goals that you can do in small amounts of time, then it is difficult, and at times impossible, to fit writing into smaller blocks of time. There may, at certain points in the working year, be no large chunks of time available for writing at all.

For new writers, the strategies in this chapter involve repositioning yourself as writer: for example, you can email an editor and say that you missed your end of the month deadline, but could have your paper in by the end of next week. In other words, create a new deadline and externalize it, rather than wasting any more time and energy worrying about whether or not they will still want it or feeling guilty about having missed the first – or second or third – deadline.

Writing in these ways can show up gaps in your thinking, and sometimes that prompts you to read more; yet a gap in your writing does not necessarily represent or signal a gap in your reading. In fact, reading more can create new gaps – or the impression of them – in your writing. Any developing argument has gaps, gaps that require further writing, not just reading. The writing sandwich process can help you to develop further writing to fill the gap.

Finding readers: critic, mentor, buddy and others

A writing mentor is someone who actively helps you to develop and achieve as a writer. Think about what you are looking for and listen carefully to anyone who appears to give this kind of support. Clearly, you can determine the role in a number of ways, or you may find that you have to take what you get.

The mentor role might be formally or informally instituted in your department. You and your mentor might have to negotiate how you want to work together within certain parameters, such as the frequency of your meetings and the production of publication targets.

The following note was developed to guide those who want to take on the writing mentor role and encourage colleagues to use strategies described in this chapter.

Note for writing mentors

This note provides an initial guide to the role of writing mentor. Its purpose is to prompt discussion among those learning this role, those who are already writing mentors and those being mentored.

Remit

The remit of the writing mentor could be defined as follows:

- To support the development of specific, achievable goals and sub-goals and maintain the writer's focus on them
- To maintain contact with writers
- To provide support and specific advice to writers as required
- To monitor the writer's progress towards achieving specified goals
- To monitor 'study buddy' and other mentoring relationships
- To follow up on lapses, delays and failure in writing.

Experience suggests that different writers require different forms of support at different times; i.e. all of these will not be required by all writers. Furthermore, the role can be customized by writers and mentors.

Tasks

The mentor's activities could include the following:

1 Weekly email contact with writers
2 Occasional one-to-one discussions as required
3 Occasional discussions with groups of writers, as appropriate.

Time

One hour per week/month maximum, as agreed between mentor and writer.

In my former staff development role, I advised writing mentors, because they said they also needed support, particularly in finding time to support writers while still having time for their own writing.

Not everyone is a natural mentor. Many are willing to admit this and seek advice on how to play this role. Some do not feel that they are experts with sufficient authority, perhaps even lacking a credible body of publications themselves. Some mentors, therefore, will provide expert help; others might provide general support, which can be equally important. If you are writing your first paper and the resident experts seem intimidating, or simply never make time to give you the benefit of their knowledge and experience as writers, then you will have to find some other form of mentoring, and for some this works out even better in any case.

Finding a voice

The paper will achieve a far wider readership under my name than under the name of an unknown. Surely these considerations are more important than mere personal vanity?

(McCall Smith 2003: 31)

It is not simply 'personal vanity' that makes us want to have our say, in our own voices, and to be acknowledged for that.

Would voice-activated software or talking into a Dictaphone help you to find a writing voice? Some people wonder if this would help them to become more fluent in their writing, helping them to record ideas and rehearsals of text as they think of them; others find it a useful way to capture ideas quickly, particularly if they are engaged in another activity, like driving, for example. If you do not have typing skills, recording your speech has obvious advantages, and speaking may have an important role in writing (Elbow 2012). In due course we may all use our voices for many tasks, not just writing. Try these strategies and see what happens.

However, it may be that discussing your ideas and writing with others is a better, quicker way of developing your writing voice; doing regular writing, in a variety of modes, will help you, over time, develop your writing voice.

Finding an argument

There is nothing more to be said on this subject. Nothing.

(McCall Smith 2003: 11)

Writing about the connections and distinctions between your work and others' may reveal that you do not really know what they are, have not clearly worked out what precisely the main ones are and/or what exactly constitutes a viable argument in your field at the time of writing.

Use this issue as a prompt for writing, to hone your argument:

• What are the connections between your work and the work of other scholars and researchers?

- What are the distinctions between your work and theirs?
- What is the main connection between your paper and their publications?
- What is the main distinction between your paper and theirs?

Make a proposition:

> Propositions are interesting or uninteresting only in relation to the assumption-ground of some audience.
>
> (Davis 1971: 328)

Asserting a proposition is a legitimate way of writing for publication, but for it to work you have to contextualize it. You also have to include the debate around your proposition in what, to borrow a term from Davis (1971: 331), could be called an 'internal dialectic':

- What propositions have been generated about your subject?
- Which of these have become 'taken for granted' assumptions?
- What new proposition have you generated?
- How does your argument relate to established propositions?
- How does your argument relate to current assumptions?

This is not just a matter of including both sides of the debate, but about ensuring that your set of assumptions stands up against others' in a way that shows the sense of yours.

Formulating a hypothesis

> Some writers on research methods treat hypotheses as a necessary part of research. . . However, this is an unnecessarily limited view of research. It fits well with a situation where there is an already well developed body of knowledge – that is, established theory from which hypotheses may be derived – but is less appropriate where the research is more concerned with developing our understanding of a relatively new field of study, that is, where the need is for theory building more than theory testing.
>
> (Burton and Steane 2004)

> Scientific research begins with a problem . . . Problems are tackled by the method of investigation, in an attempt to obtain evidence related to a hypothesis. If the problem is stated as a question, then each hypothesis is a possible answer to the question or a possible explanation.
>
> (Barrass 2002: 2–3)

A hypothesis is a general proposition. It is often taken as a principle on which an argument is based. It is a premise from which to draw a conclusion or, alternatively, the basis for action. The hypothesis tells us that certain things are known and that we can base future action and thought on these. In science it is used as a starting point for further investigation.

These definitions raise questions for your writing. If you are to include a hypothesis:

- Which type of research have you done – in a new field or in an established one?
- Were you testing or building theory?
- Are hypotheses used in journals in your field?
- If so, what do they look like?
- How exactly are they written – in what terms, using which words?

Develop a journal-specific understanding of hypotheses, if they are appropriate at all, by studying papers published in your target journal. Yes, you know the journal well, but scrutinize how research problems are defined – analyse that.

Constructing an argument

An argument starts by establishing a problematic, which is an argument in itself: how is this done in your target journal? List and analyse published authors' ways of referring to the literature and/or to the published work of others.

How is the research gap defined? How is the literature defined?:

- deficient;
- open to debate;
- incomplete;
- missing certain components;
- narrow.

When you problematize your issue in the literature – that is, when you make the case that you have an issue worth writing about – you do not have to problematize the literature itself.

A good technique for modulating the problematic is to refer to or quote someone in your field who has been even harsher or more radical than you want to be in his or her critique of research or others' articles. This works particularly well if the harsh critic is widely respected in your field.

The process of contextualizing your ideas in others' work – reviewing the literature – is not just a means to an end, going through the motions of mentioning the great, the good and the not-so-good who still have authority; it is a way of honing your ideas and your thinking processes. You may feel that the end result is that you have blunted your original idea, when, in fact, you are likely to have sharpened it.

How you actually produce the type of sentences that are required, the type of academic writing you need, will be shaped by your target journal. Examples of academic arguments are analysed in Chapter 6 to demonstrate some of the key techniques.

You can also think about which type of argument you are constructing: is it a proposal (Fahnestock and Secor 1990)? Evaluation? Refutation? Analysis? Comparison and contrast? Definition? Or are there elements of more than one of these in your article? If so, what order should they be in for your article, and what is your main line of argument?

The quality question

This chapter has introduced three strategies for generating text: freewriting, generative writing and writing to prompts. This means you have three ways to force yourself to write, even when you least feel like it and even when you are most uncertain about your topic and your ability in writing.

You can use all of them to write in short increments of time, a key feature for overloaded academics and professionals. Being able to produce text on demand is reassuring and builds confidence. These are important outcomes for those who want to become regular, productive and successful writers.

For every research task, there is a writing task. The writing strategies covered in this chapter are primarily about getting new writers started. At some point, you know you have to address the question of the quality of your writing, but, it has to be emphasized, this does not mean that you should stop using these generative strategies and move into a stage of revision (see Chapter 7). The emphasis of this book is on the value of generating text that you can then work on, improving it gradually. If you don't generate text . . . [do I need to complete this sentence?].

The quality question means attending to the structure and style of your text, and your ability to do this may depend on how much effort you put into analysing articles in your target journal. Quality is defined in a particular way for that particular journal. In addition, you can find out more about academic style and define 'quality' quite precisely (Sword 2012).

Think of quality as a set of components. Define what 'quality' writing means, e.g. coherent, well structured, grammatically correct and so on. It means many things. It is not always possible to produce all the components of quality in a first draft. Therefore, you can define which components of quality you are aiming to achieve in each writing task (and which ones you will not set out to achieve in that task). In other words, decide to produce certain components of quality. It's part of your writing goal.

Calibrating your topic

Once you have (a) developed your topic, (b) started writing about it, (c) discussed it with your trusted peers, (d) topped up your reading and (e) had some pre-peer review – perhaps not exactly in that order – you need to check that your paper is still aligned with your target journal.

Assess the extent to which you are still doing what you set out to do:

- Are you doing what you said you would do in your email to the editor?
- Go back to your profile of the journal: does your paper fit it so far?
- Scan a couple of recent issues of the journal. Read a paper of the type that you are writing. Then review your own paper.
- Ask someone who reads the journal to read your writing so far and/or to discuss your ideas with you to assess how they 'fit'.
- Better still, if you know and trust someone who has been published in your target journal, and if they have time, ask them to read what you have written so far. Don't wait till it's finished.

Use the feedback you get as prompts for further writing, developing your topic and perhaps even planning some of your sections. Write your development points in sentences – rather than notes – so that you think them through and work out whether or not you need them in your paper at all.

It is perhaps worth repeating that this does not involve you 'cloning' yourself to the journal; instead, this is one of your focusing devices. It is another activity that you can bring to your writers' group.

Writing a working title

As you are thinking about writing or revising your working title, you might want to consider Sternberg's (2000: 37) take on titles in academic publications ('Titles and abstracts: They only *sound* important'): 'Whether your article will be read by many people, few people, or virtually none at all . . . can be largely a function of the title and the abstract'.

A working title can be a useful focusing device as you write. It stops you straying from your line of argument. It gives your paper a name – distinguishing it from your other projects – with which you can refer to it over the weeks and months of planning, researching, writing and revising.

- Have you identified your key words?
- How will you fit them into your title?

Having scrutinized the journal, you know what types of title they like to see:

- Is it the catchy buzzword?
- The contentious statement?
- The main catchy title – colon – then descriptive title?
- Is it a question?
- A question and an answer?

Your title is an important starting point in catching the reader's interest, but since your first reader will be the editor, model the style and content of your title on the range that appears in the journal. Remember to put key words in the title that will bring up your paper in searches.

Checklist

Look for topics for your writing in what you already do, know, think, teach, like to talk about regularly and/or are interested in.

- Use regular 'snack writing' to produce text quickly and often. Freewriting and generative writing are tried and tested techniques. My 'writing to prompts' strategy builds on these. Try them all.
- Define what 'quality' academic writing means for each writing goal.
- Learn about the 'genres' of academic writing.
- Learn about the structure of academic argument – see Fahnestock and Secor (1990) and others – and work out how it applies to writing in your discipline. See examples in Chapters 2 and 6.
- Do your own analyses of the structure of arguments in your target journals. Write about that too.
- Discuss your writing with others, show it to them and get feedback in the early stages.

Further reading

Boice, R. (1990) *Professors as Writers: A Self-help Guide to Productive Writing*. Stillwater, OK: New Forums.

Elbow, P. (1998) *Writing with Power*, 2nd edn. New York: Oxford University Press.

Elbow, P. (2012) *Vernacular Eloquence: What Speech Can Bring to Writing*. Oxford: Oxford University Press.

Fahnestock, J. and Secor, M. (1990) *A Rhetoric of Argument*, 2nd edn. New York: McGraw-Hill.

Gill, R. (2010) Breaking the silence: the hidden injuries of the neoliberal university, in R. Ryan-Flood and R. Gill (eds) *Secrecy and Silence in the Research Process: Feminist Reflections*. London: Routledge.

Greenhalgh, T. (2019) *How to Read a Paper: The Basics of Evidence-based Medicine and Healthcare*, 6th edn. Chichester: Wiley-Blackwell.

Lillis, T. and Curry, M.J. (2010) *Academic Writing in a Global Context: The Politics and Practices of Publishing in English*. London: Routledge.

Murray, R. (2010) Becoming rhetorical, in C. Aitchison, B. Kamler and A. Lee (eds) *Publishing Pedagogies for the Doctorate and Beyond*. London: Routledge.

Swales, J.M. (2004) *Research Genres: Explorations and Applications*. Cambridge: Cambridge University Press.

Thomson, P. and Kamler, B. (2013) *Writing for Peer Reviewed Journals: Strategies for Getting Published*. London: Routledge.

Chapter  5

Outlining

Level 3 outlining • Allocating word lengths • Writing a 275-word abstract – Brown's 8 questions • Writing a 375-word abstract – Murray's 10 prompts • Calibrating your outline • Checklist • Further reading

> It would be foolish to maintain that all writing must be planned. But it does not seem unreasonable to assert that good writers must be able to plan.
> (Bereiter and Scardamalia 1987: 192)

This quotation is itself a model of good academic writing: the authors use the device of starting with an overstatement and then distance themselves from it, not only making it clear that they do not intend to go that far, but also making their position in the to-plan-or-not-to-plan debate seem reasonable. They also make subtle, persuasive use of the double negative in the proposition that follows: how different is the effect of their chosen expression, 'it does not seem unreasonable to assert', from 'it seems reasonable to assert' – more effective in the context of academic argument, much less likely to provoke instant refutation.

As a result, for all that every single writer will already have formed his or her own views on the value of planning in academic writing, the authors have eased themselves into the debate without immediately drawing too much fire – cleverly done. They must have thought carefully not only about the subject of their writing – how planning and writing interact – but also about how they could make their case persuasively in the context of on-going debates.

We can agree that it is a good idea, in principle, to produce plans for our writing, but not everyone routinely puts it into practice, and some will argue that they have to know what they want to write before they can outline an article:

> On my list of maladaptive practices that make writing harder, Not Outlining is pretty high – just above Typing with Scratchy Wool Mittens, just

below Training My Dog to Take Dictation. Outlining is writing, not a prelude to 'real writing.' Writers who complain about 'writer's block' are writers who don't outline. After trying to write blindly, they feel frustrated and complain about how hard it is to generate words. No surprise – you can't write an article if you don't know what to write.

(Silvia 2007: 79)

Others see planning as interfering with writing: '. . . trying to follow a written plan can interfere with the generation of ideas through writing' (Torrance *et al.* 1991: 46).

This idea is supported by Elbow (1998), but others argue for using both planning and writing, but this too takes skill and, perhaps, planning:

Elbow [1973] . . . suggest[s] that, as an alternative to constructing a plan, writers should simply start to compose in full text, allowing thought and inscription to run concurrently. This, they argue, may facilitate the generation of ideas in a way that is not possible when the writer is constrained by a pre-determined plan. Similarly, Scardamalia and Bereiter (1985) argue that writing strategies that permit an interaction between idea generation and inscription will produce text that is richer in both content and expression. However, they also observe that the skills required to manage such an interaction effectively are underdeveloped in many writers.

(Torrance *et al.* 1991: 53)

While this study was conducted on undergraduates, it would be difficult to argue that it has no relevance whatsoever for academics and professionals, since the undergraduate years are, for many, the final opportunity for learning about writing. (At the doctoral and post-doctoral levels it is, I think, assumed that writers know what they need to know about writing.)

Perhaps the most contentious sentence in this quotation is the last one: 'writers' – which must include some academics and professionals, perhaps particularly new writers – will not necessarily have developed these skills. This is not to say that they cannot do so; if there is a barrier – to writing and development – it may exist among those who think they do not have to develop their skills.

Even those who 'plan' their writing will be using different approaches and, it's safe to say, some will be doing more planning than others, and some will be using their plans more than others. The purpose of this chapter is to make the case for more outlining: while we all do some outlining, there is value in making our outlines more detailed.

The question is how to go about it when you are writing a paper for an academic journal: how much outlining am I talking about, in what form, what should an outline of this type of writing look like, how do you know, and how will you use your outline as you write, if at all?

The specific skills needed may not be what are often referred to as technical skills; it may be much more important that you develop the skills 'to manage

[the] interaction of "idea generation" and "inscription". Planning, or out-lining, can be a separate process, but it is not a good idea to stop writing while you plan, nor can you expect your writing to flow just because you have a detailed outline, nor will your best outline remain intact throughout the writing process.

Outlining, therefore, whatever it means in practice, involves many very different thinking processes.

The purpose of outlining

- 'idea generation'
- forming a structure
- linking ideas
- clarifying a contribution
- creating coherence
- sifting and eliminating ideas
- finding direction
- contextualizing your work

Finding a way to do all of these at once may not be an achievable goal, or it may be a long-term goal, the by-product of multiple publications. What is feasible, even for new writers, is combining outlining and regular writing. Since this may be easier said than done – given the research referred to earlier – examples of frameworks and suggested writing activities are included in this chapter. The key point is that although the subject of outlining is treated here in a separate chapter, as if it were a discrete step, the activities described in other chapters are to be used here too.

> . . . planning encompasses more than the cognitive process of determining
> 'what to say' and 'what to do' in the text to be written.
>
> (van der Geest 1996: 9)

Drawing on earlier important work by Flower and Hayes (1981), this identifies three different but related processes involved in the planning or outlining stage: '*setting goals* for the execution of the writing task, *generating ideas* for the content of the text, and *organising the ideas* generated in a particular text structure' (van der Geest 1996: 14–15, emphasis added). This helpfully defines the different tasks: setting goals, generating ideas and organizing them, each of which might involve a different writing activity. Yet, if it is also true that 'separate tools for planning . . . and reviewing . . . will be experienced as drawing an artificial line between two activities that are intricately related' (van der Geest 1996: 21), then the collection of writing tasks that make up outlining could be experienced, by the writer, as quite 'messy'. Perhaps this is a problem that writers who get bogged down fail to solve: yes, there are many different tasks to be done, but not in any fixed, linear order. Even when you have a linear outline, you might find yourself changing it and subsequently losing your way in your writing if you keep changing it too much.

Analysis of the above quotations from research on writing shows how carefully you need to think about your audience while you are outlining your article – not just while you are 'writing' it. Outlining is part of the writing process, after all. Your sense of other positions in the debate, as represented in the readership of your target journal, will, of course, shape what you write and how you write it. You can anticipate where opposition to your argument will come from. You can modulate your arguments accordingly.

In other words, the outlining stage may involve some writing, while the writing stages may include some revision of your outline. In fact, it may seem artificial to separate outlining from writing, but the point is to introduce in this chapter several strategies for outlining. Each is described in a separate section, but you can continue to use strategies for regular writing covered in other chapters, so that you develop an integrated writing process. You can develop a set of techniques that you know work for you. This – together with your experience of submitting/publishing your first paper – should make production of your second and subsequent papers more fluent.

This chapter defines and illustrates strategies for outlining your paper in different ways: answers to lists of questions, headings, sentences, abstracts and graphics. All of these are important steps in the writing process; they all constitute 'writing' tasks to maintain the focus of your paper as you write it.

You may be sceptical about some of these strategies: for those who say they can only write an abstract once they have written the paper, writing an abstract is presented here as an important step in the process of designing your paper. There are also implications for your actual writing practices in this approach: the argument is that you also need a detailed design for writing before you can allocate time slots to actually getting it done. Without such a detailed design, it will be difficult, perhaps impossible, to do the snack writing described in previous chapters that is so productive. This is because large, semi-defined writing tasks (3000 words) require large chunks of time, while smaller, well-defined writing tasks (500 words) can be done in short sessions.

Moreover, a draft abstract or summary gives you text that you can email to an editor or give to colleagues to read, in order to elicit early feedback. Feedback is crucial at this early stage, not just at later stages when you have a draft that you are relatively happy with. Early feedback can stop you wasting time by, for example, going off on a line of argument, or presenting what you think are all your significant results or detailing your specific methodology, when none of these is what the audience of your target journal will find most interesting in your work at this time, as judged by the editor, as expressed in his or her response to your 'initial enquiry' email. A further benefit is that discussion with subject experts and others at this stage can accelerate your writing/revision.

How much time should you spend outlining? It has been argued that you should spend 90 per cent of your time outlining and 10 per cent writing

(Reif-Lehrer 2000). Whether or not you agree with this calculation, it does raise the question of how much is 'right' or 'enough' time: what proportion of the whole writing process should we dedicate to outlining? Most of us probably spend less time outlining and more writing and revising. If we spend less time outlining, we have more decisions to make as we write. This makes writing more complex. Structural decisions – about content, sequence and proportion or emphasis in your article – involve deciding what to put in your paragraphs and sentences.

Without a detailed outline, writing is a more complex process in the sense that you have several different levels of decision to make at once: deciding on content, sequence, style, level of detail, references to other work, coherence and so on – all at the same time. And all of these decisions have to be made 'in sync' with each other. This may be one of the reasons why people rebel against the 'snack' writing mode: it is more difficult, perhaps impossible, to write in this way in short bursts, as such complex writing requires constant sustained concentration for keeping focus, and the dedicated writing time needed for sustained concentration is difficult to come by in many workplaces.

Yet, if you learned to write using sketchy outlines, and if that is how you see the outlining process, you may be wondering if it is possible to do a 'total design' for your paper. Certainly, the value of doing so is not difficult to understand, but it does require sustained concentration in the outlining stage and, if you remain sceptical, it can be difficult to put into practice. The frameworks suggested in this chapter are there to help you try a new outlining practice. They have been tried and tested in many writing workshops among academics and professionals, in various disciplines, in many parts of the world, which suggests that they are in a form that you can use as of now.

The proposition, therefore, is that you spend more time than you usually do in the outlining stage. This may save you a significant amount of time later in the writing process, as you are able to write well, in a focused way, in your first draft. In fact, your first drafts may improve.

However, the route to being able to do that is, paradoxically, through regular writing; if you do not write regularly, your writing time may be just as long as it ever was, no matter what you do at the outlining stage.

As you develop an outline, therefore, keep writing in sentences. Use the writing strategies described in other chapters. You also have to 'calibrate' your writing at all these stages with your target journal. Targeting your writing continues to be critical.

There is another good reason for spending more time than you currently do on the outlining stage: 'Use the word processor to type the outline and then convert the outline to prose when you are completely satisfied with the content and logical flow' (Reif-Lehrer 2000). The important words here are 'completely satisfied': you may wonder whether you will ever use these words about your writing, but the point is that you have a chance, in your outline, to create a momentary satisfaction. Because the ultimate – and you might say 'real' – satisfaction of writing only comes when your paper is (a) accepted and (b) published, complete satisfaction with your writing can be deferred for a year or two. You therefore have to manage your levels of 'satisfaction' with work-in-progress by creating small satisfactions with what you have already done. The satisfaction that comes with a completed outline derives from having a clear goal and a clear output: you either have an outline or you don't. Having an outline is the goal.

A more important question might be, how will an outline drive your writing? This question is addressed in the next section, where 'level 3 outlining' is suggested as a mode of outlining a paper, integrating strategies for productive writing dealt with in earlier chapters, such as writing to prompts.

Do not wait for writing to 'come to you'; your outlining practices should still involve regular, short-burst writing, in which you write regularly. This means that while the outlining stage is about you making your writing linear, there are still non-linear – or perhaps parallel – processes going on. There is no need to attempt to stop this happening, and it may not be possible in any case, but you do need to have a way of capturing and filtering ideas and sentences as they pop up. This is not to say that they 'pop up' at random, since your brain will be working on your paper even when you are not actually writing it. Create a way to capture these sentences, since they do not always appear when you are sitting at a keyboard.

As you do all this outlining, you may find that whole sentences or paragraphs come to you, apparently at random. Write them down. If you know exactly where they fit in your paper, write them in under the appropriate heading, without worrying about how you will make the text around them 'fit'. If you are not sure where they go, or wonder if they even belong in your paper at all, save them in a separate file and leave the decision about whether or not to include them until later.

The references quoted in this section show that scholars have been thinking about the outlining component of writing for some time. There is a vast literature out there. Perhaps the most salient point, for the purposes of this chapter, is that juggling outlining and writing is a difficult process that may itself have to be learned. Moreover, it supports the suggestion that you should be writing regularly during this outlining stage.

Level 3 outlining

Everyone does outlines. Many people actually use them to shape their writing. Some use them most at the start of the writing process as a device for getting a sense of the paper as a whole, and then abandon them as they write. Others create an outline at the start and then modify it as they go along, making outlining part of the iterative process of writing, using the outline to document the changes they make as much as to structure the writing they do. Some develop a brand new outline for each revision and start from scratch with each new version of an article.

Everyone knows what an outline looks like:

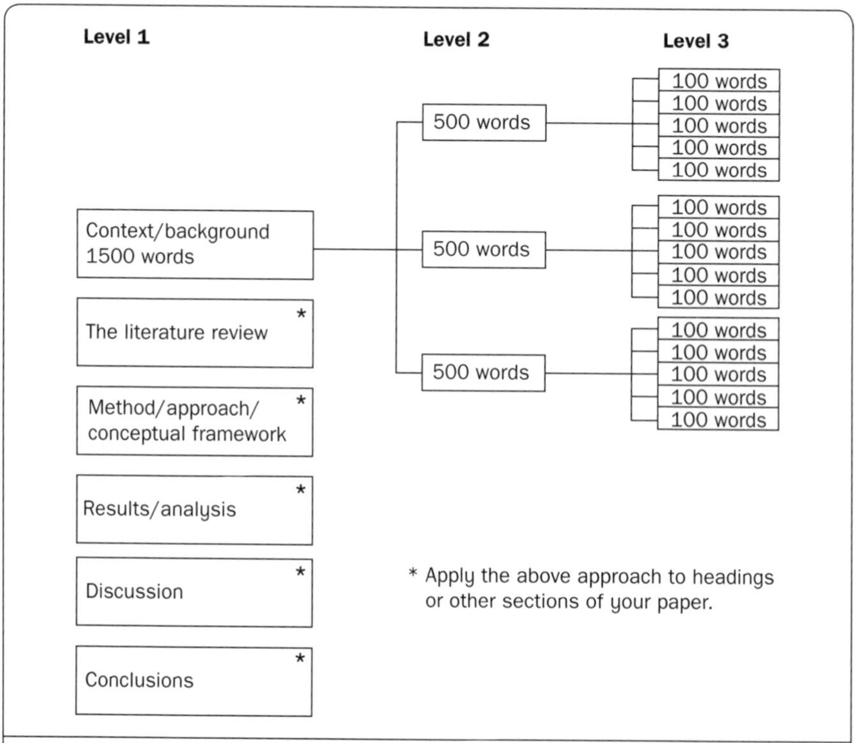

Figure 5.1 Outline

Everyone does a column 1 outline – the first level of outlining – some go into a bit more detail, moving into column 2, but, as far as I can tell, almost no one goes as far as column 3.

There may be good reasons for this. Perhaps people feel that they will be wasting their time by doing so much outlining. Perhaps they have internalized the sub-structures that column 3 requires, although for new writers this may be less likely. Perhaps those who never go as far as column 3 are not aware of the benefits; they are not aware, for example, of how the columns can structure the essential thinking processes that are an important part of writing an academic paper. Producing column 3 may take hours of thinking, cross-checking columns and lists, rethinking and revising the outline.

The word allocations in the graphic should not imply that all your sections will be the same length. Surely some will be longer and others will be shorter? Yes, but why? Why will one section be longer? Because the subject is more complex? Not necessarily, since you can simply state that the subject is complex, perhaps citing references, and then move on to the point you want to make in that section. Thinking about the number of words per section, sub-section and sub-sub-section is, therefore, a way of thinking through the content for your article.

Each level of outlining has a purpose in focusing your thinking. Each level has a role in the writing process. All of them can be used for different purposes, as you design your paper. Specifically, in practice, you may find that while you favour one or other level – or perhaps you have another format – of outlining, each has a distinct effect:

- **Level 1 outlining** is useful for setting out the proportions of your main sections in terms of the number of words you will write for each. It is easy to calibrate this with the target journal, checking that your sections are named in a way that is appropriate for that journal and that the proportions you allocate for each section match what usually happens in such sections in that journal at this time.
- **Level 2 outlining** means making more decisions about content and structure, again in terms of numbers of words per sub-section. You can also do some checks on continuity: are the sub-sections in the right order? Do you really need them all? Can some section topics be compressed into a sentence or two? You can begin to think of the links and transitions you will need to use to make connections or changes of direction in your argument explicit.
- **Level 3 outlining** is a way of developing a detailed 'design' for your paper. You decide exactly what is going into each section in terms of sub-sub-headings and numbers of words for each. You can also check for internal continuity: are content, proportions and connections coherent?

Each level therefore has a purpose. Each helps you make a level of decision. Staging the decisions in this way may be easier for new writers and for busy, experienced writers who can only work on their outlines in short time slots.

Of course, you will adapt your outline – even level 3 – as you write, but you will more quickly and coherently be able to distinguish between what to add and what to cut from your paper if you have level 3 outlining; even with a detailed outline, you may find that you write a section that is not relevant to your paper. You can calibrate your writing with your outline: should you change one or the other? Will that still fit your target journal?

There may, of course, be a level 4 outline, which is even more detailed:

- **Level 4 outlining** is defining the content of your sub-sub-sections, the points to which you have allocated 100 words. For example, if you decide you want to make three points, that could be three short sentences of about 30 words each, or a long one of 60 words plus a short one of 30 words.

This level of outlining raises recurring questions: are your points in the right order? Or should they be the other way round? Your choice of sentence length depends, of course, on how your points relate to each other: which ones will make sense handled in the same sentence, and which ones need separate sentences? Which of your points can be treated quickly, perhaps in general terms only, and which require more detail? How much more detail? And how are these points linked? Which link word will you use to make that link explicit?

This is where you may find that while you set out to write 100 words, you have written 500 words before you know it. Will you then keep all of these words? Do they make the point that you set out to make in that sub-sub-section? Possibly not. You then have to cut out the sentences or part of sentences where you have gone off your point. Or you can change your outline, but you have to then check that your revision to your outline still fits the rest of the section, which still fits the rest of the article. If you lose sight of your main point, this is an ideal time to do freewriting or writing to prompts:

Writing activity to recover focus

What is it I am trying to say in this section?
What is the main point of this part?
The main point of this section is . . .

Outlining is not about word counting for its own sake; it is about you finding a way to prompt yourself to make the numerous decisions about content and order that will construct your argument.

Each stage of outlining involves much more thinking than counting, but counting words as you go is a way of keeping a check on your thinking and writing. It is also a way of setting realistic, achievable goals, sub-goals and sub-sub-goals, and these smaller tasks can be done in smaller increments of time.

It is safe to assume that you will not always write exactly the number of words that you set out to write and that you will not always sit down to write for exactly the same number of minutes. You are likely to write more or less, in unpredictable patterns and in different time slots. In order to keep control and focus, however, it is good to have this way of checking that what you are writing is relevant to your paper. An added benefit – and an important motivational tool – is that as you complete each section you see yourself achieving numerous sub-goals.

What are the implications of these approaches for your writing practice? If you only do level 1 outlining, you create a set of writing tasks that inevitably require large chunks of time. If you only do level 2 outlining, you still have decisions to make about content and continuity, and you will have to make these as you write. If you do level 3 outlining and have writing tasks as small as 100 words, you know that you can do these in short bursts. You can more easily fit them into your schedule. Your writing process is more easily and coherently 'fragmented', in a positive sense. The multiple sub-tasks and sub-routines of writing can be held together by a detailed outline.

Once you have designed writing tasks, get them into your timetable, diary or electronic device. Create a writing slot for each task: how much time will you need for each task? When will you find it? This may involve trial and error: how much time do you need, for example, to write one of those 100-word sub-sub-sections on a specific subject? Does it depend on the subject? You probably have some idea, but can you be sure till you try?

Scheduled short focused writing task

Tuesday, 2 June, 9–9.30am

- Time allocation: 30 minutes
- Start with 5-minute warm-up: 'What I want to write about is . . .'
- Then do 25 minutes of writing to a prompt from your outline: 100 words
- Finally, if you've done that, write another 100 words for another sub-sub-section

---

If you do not define your writing tasks precisely – perhaps even, at least sometimes, as precisely as this – you may struggle to learn how much time you need for each one.

In fact, you may not even see the point of doing so. You may decide not to learn how long you need for each writing task. This is not to say that there is one set pace of writing to which you should aspire, but if you note how long you take to produce each section you can set yourself realistic goals, goals based on your experience of writing, rather than on someone else's output or some notional ideal rate. Setting specific, realistic goals is an important step in the process of becoming a productive writer.

Allocating word lengths

I never approach writing thinking about quantity. I think about what it is I want to say.

(hooks 1999: 16)

Many writers, like bell hooks, approach writing 'without thinking about quantity'; surely what you say matters much more than how many words you use to say it? Yet, just as your time for writing is not unlimited, so too your space – in terms of number of words – for writing it is limited. Clearly, it will depend on context; journals have stated word limits.

This is your starting point: take the total number of words available and divide them up according to what you think needs to be said. If this sounds too simplistic, you will soon find that it is far from simple, since it involves high-level decisions.

Academic writing involves thinking as you write, but you can think through some of the points you want to make – or know you have to make for the context in which you are writing – before you start to generate what you might call your first draft. Writing this way, with limits and limitations quite explicit at an early stage, means that your first draft will be good and may need less revision.

At the same time, regular freewriting – and other activities for generating text covered earlier in the book – will help you work out what you 'want to say' (hooks 1999: 16).

Writing a 275-word abstract – Brown's 8 questions

> Only by introducing formal procedures such as a list of questions to be answered – procedures that effectively disrupted the continuity of production – was it possible to get idea generation to take place apart from text production.
>
> (Bereiter and Scardamalia 1987: 202)

A list of questions is a device to help you structure your ideas and move towards outlining and 'text production'. The many steps in writing – thinking, 'idea generation' and composition – can be progressed using different devices. It may even be that different stages require different frameworks. For many years, scholars and researchers of writing have asked themselves these questions:

> There is a venerable tradition in rhetoric and composition which sees the composing process as a series of decisions and choices. However, it is no longer easy simply to assert this position, unless you are prepared to answer a number of questions, the most pressing of which probably is:
>
> 'What then are the criteria which govern that choice?'
>
> (Flower and Hayes 1981: 365)

Flower and Hayes's (1981) paper is one of the key contributions to the development of cognitive approaches to academic writing, but for those not working in that field, their questions may not be as 'pressing'; you may be more interested in frameworks that help you to make writing 'choices' and less concerned about the criteria on which they are based, but you need criteria for judging them.

You can use frameworks to help you think about writing, think as you write and write as you think. Most academic and professional writers I have met have taken a passing interest in explanations of the thinking processes involved in writing, but they are primarily looking for ways of translating their thinking into writing, although when the discussion focuses on writing, someone usually asks, what about the link between thinking and writing?

One device for structuring your ideas is 'Brown's 8 questions'. This has proved to be a useful tool for prompting those writing for academic journals, particularly new writers, to do some of the important thinking required for writing their papers. It provides a framework for drafting the abstract or summary of a paper, considering such key questions as audience and the paper's purpose for that audience. It lets you create your paper as a whole, a perspective that helps you hold the paper together throughout the writing process.

An abstract is, in some ways, different from other forms of academic writing; you have to make a rhetorical adjustment. For example, while in the full paper it is essential to provide a context for the work you have done, in the abstract you assert a reason why the work needed to be done, perhaps in no more than one sentence. This thinner contextualization liberates you from providing much in the way of definition and explanation. This again means you can focus on the main points of your argument. At later stages in your writing process, you can use your abstract as a tool for maintaining focus; it provides a filter, helping you to decide what to put in and what to leave out as you write.

This has advantages at this stage: writing on such a small scale (most abstracts are between 100 and 250 words), particularly at an early stage, means that it is easier to match up the different elements of your story; there are fewer distractions, fewer definitions and fewer explanations than will appear in your completed paper, so it is easier for the reader and, more importantly, for you as writer, to make explicit connections between, for example, your aims and your methods. Nor do you have to represent the debate that preceded your work in the abstract. If you have to refer to it at all – it depends on the target journal – you might have a sentence at most in your abstract or summary.

You have to write the abstract so well that the so-called 'general reader' can understand it. However, this does not mean that you should write it for someone who is not an expert in your area. When people tell you that a general reader should be able to read your paper or abstract, what they probably mean is that it should be extremely well written, with the connections between sentences crystal clear and the purpose and value of your paper explicitly defined.

For all of these reasons it is useful to write your abstract at an early stage in the paper-writing process. In the past, you may have thought of it as the last writing task; many people do. But if you write it first you can use it as a touchstone as you write. In addition to revising it as you go along, you can revise it after your final revisions of the paper. In other words, write it first and revise it last.

Writing the abstract of your paper, therefore, forces you to capture the 'essence' of the whole: 'The word limits are arbitrary, but important for the discipline of getting down to the essence of what needs to be said' (Brown 1994/95). This means leaving out key details that you will provide in the article (Hartley 2008).

Use Brown's 8 questions to draft your abstract:

How to use Brown's 8 questions

- Answer as many of the questions as you can in 30 minutes.
- If you get bogged down in one question, move on to another.
- Take all the questions literally, including the first one. Do not simply answer 'Those who are interested in my subject', since to assume that readers are inherently 'interested' in your writing is a mistake. People often ask, how am I supposed to know who reads the journal? How indeed? How can I find that out anyway? The best excuse I ever heard was, 'How can I find that out? I live in Fife'. This question makes you focus on a real audience. As soon as you come up with two or three names, you see that your audience is more mixed than perhaps you thought it was – international? – and you explore what they are likely to find 'of benefit' (question 7).
- Adapt your writing about your work to these questions, rather than vice versa.
- Do not be put off by the apparent focus on experimental research, implied by the word 'results'.
- Stick to the word limits. Twenty-five words is one short sentence.

- If you find questions 5 and 6 overlap, think of 5 as asking if your 'findings' should affect how we think about the subject and 6 as asking if your 'findings' should affect how we do something. If you find your answers still overlap, you may not have worked out the difference between the two.
- Answer question 7, as it is the most important. Revise your answer several times, if necessary. Once you have that sentence (25 words) you have the 'destination' of your paper, the answer to the 'so what?' question. It defines your contribution to the field. In academic journals this is often the last sentence of the abstract – check your target journal to see what forms this sentence can take.
- Discuss your answers – and emerging abstract – with someone/others.

Remember that these questions, which might seem to belong to scientific disciplines and empirical work only, have been successfully used across a wide range of disciplines, including many non-scientific areas and non-empirical research. According to those who have used these questions to draft abstracts, one reason why it works is that the form of the questions prompted them to think through their answers more than a checklist would, while the word limits forced them to think their points through and decide on the main point. Checklists can also be useful (Hartley) but Brown's 8 questions is a device for doing your thinking and deciding *through* writing.

Brown's 8 questions (write for 30 minutes)

1 Who are the intended readers? List three to five of them by name.
2 What did you do? (50 words)
3 Why did you do it? (50 words)
4 What happened [when you did that]? (50 words)
5 What do the results mean in theory? (50 words)
6 What do the results mean in practice? (50 words)
7 What is the key benefit for readers? (25 words)
8 What remains unresolved? (no word limit)

(Brown 1994/95: 6)

In practice some writers, perhaps those with experience of reading and/or writing abstracts, get through all the questions in 20 minutes. Whether you take 20 or 30 minutes may also depend on your discipline. Some journals, of course, require very particular forms of abstract. Your next step is to adapt your draft abstract to that form, but the purpose of this activity, at this stage, is to outline your whole paper.

If you want to analyse why Brown's questions work well at this stage in writing a journal article, note the proportion of the whole abstract allocated to each question. Specifically, note how much is allocated to writing that deals with your work – questions 2, 3 and 4 – as opposed to the proportion allocated to contextualizing and providing rationale and explanations – questions 5 to 8. This allows you to concentrate on the main moves in your argument.

If reading an abstract lets you see the paper as a whole, writing an abstract lets you work on it as a whole. The fixed limits for each sentence, moreover, ensure that you keep to appropriate proportions, not allowing any one element of your argument to overshadow any other. This could save you revision time, since many new writers spend the first half of the abstract on context and ratio-nale, often providing no more than a sentence on their research.

Brown's statement that the 'word limits are arbitrary' should not be taken to undermine his strategy. In fact, I am not convinced that they are entirely arbi-trary, since they work so well for so many writers in so many different con-texts, and since they do help you to set appropriate word and content limits. Yet, I do not want to give the impression that number of words is more import-ant than choice of words; in fact, the word limits are so important because they make you choose – what is your main point?

Choosing an article's main point often involves thrashing through a number of other interesting – but not 'main' – points. In some disciplines the process of weeding out all the points that are not the main point is what reveals, for the writer, what the main point is. Working to these specific word limits is very hard work, but it is the type of hard work that produces a focused paper.

Whether or not your paper is ultimately, in its final version, preceded by your answers to these questions is not really the point. This may not, in fact, be the form your abstract will take when you submit your article. The point is that answering these questions will help you to sketch the whole paper and seeing it as a whole lets you check its internal logic. You can, of course, adapt the questions to suit your discipline – and many have been tempted to do so – although in practice they have worked well across a range of subjects. Alternatively, take your target jour-nal's criteria and transform them into prompts for writing if, and only if, you find that this works to generate focused text. If it does not, use Brown's 8 questions.

What is it, in any case, that makes writers want to adapt the Brown frame-work? Is it that they already have a series of questions in mind? Is it that the discipline base, and being steeped in the journal's conventions – even as a reader – has given them an alternative set of questions? Or have they never thought of writing for academic journals in this way? Many new writers have never broken the whole process down into stages like this.

For these reasons, this approach can come as a surprise, if not a challenge. The best response – surprise or no surprise – is to try the approach with your writing. Simply acknowledging that you understand what Brown's 8 questions are doing, or that you can see the sense in such an approach, is not enough; understanding will not necessarily lead to writing. Try this approach and then decide. Once you have spent 30 minutes answering these questions, you will have a basis for your argument. You can then revise it, get feedback, revise some more and use your abstract to construct the sections of your paper.

As you adapt your abstract to your target journal's criteria and conventions, you may want to make use of some of the key words that are dominant in your field at the time of writing. Alternatively, you may deliberately move away from them. Again, as discussed earlier, this may feel like you are cloning yourself to the values of the journal and its select group of editors and reviewers, but being rhetorical is about pitching an argument in a way that is likely to be persuasive to the group who will read it.

Which types of abstract does your target journal publish? Structured abstracts, with headings? The whole story in miniature, or just the background, leading up to the point where the introduction starts? Are the published abstracts mostly background, outlining the problem, problematizing the issue, making the case that it is a problem, that it is where work needs to be done? Do they include no more than general reference to or much more detail on methodology? Do your target journal's abstracts foreground results or outcomes? Or are these only alluded to, not specified? Again, study, as if you were a scholar of your target journal's abstracts.

Then there is the question of the extent to which the sentences – their order, proportion and level of generality or specificity – signal the structure of the papers that follow. To what extent, in other words, can you shape your paper around what you have written in your abstract? This is an important question, as it affects the next step in developing your paper.

In any case, you can use these sentences – your answers to Brown's 8 questions – as prompts for your writing. You can take this suggestion quite literally: copy each sentence of your abstract to the corresponding section of your paper. Repeat these points, with elaboration, at the start of each section:

Building from your abstract

- Take the key words in each sentence of your abstract.
- Write them into section headings.
- Use them in the topic sentence and throughout the section.
- Define and explain the terms, as needed.

In other words, each sentence in your abstract appears, in an expanded or developed form, in your article. Develop your draft article by using your abstract as a key for your paper. Of course, this will not prevent you from changing your mind as you go along, but it may stop you from adding something that requires a complete rewrite, unless, on balance, you decide that a complete rewrite is unavoidable, once you have seen how the paper looks, and then you can begin again by using Brown's 8 questions to do a complete rewrite of your abstract.

However, if you decide to keep your abstract as it is, for the moment, as you make changes in your paper, adjust the abstract to match.

Remember also that you may do too much 'smoothing' in your first paper, and certainly for the purposes of the abstract. Do not worry about this. You can always go back and write problems, glitches and unanswered questions back into your paper. They may, in fact, strengthen your argument. For example, acknowledge limitations in your research. Claim a modest contribution. Include things that did not go well in your study but are not so serious that they undermine your results, outcomes or conclusions – things that you left out of your abstract.

Writing a 375-word abstract – Murray's 10 prompts

. . . word limits for abstracts may restrict the presence of key information to some extent.

(Hartley and Betts 2009: 2010)

Using Brown's 8 questions does not provide enough information on the research or the article for some contexts. Some journals require more detail on methods. If you need to write that type of abstract, use Murray's 10 prompts – a variation of the approach that works well with Brown's 8 questions and an example of 'writing to prompts' (explained in Chapter 4). Use these specific prompts to make decisions about the main points of your article and establish a logical flow to it at an early stage.

Murray's 10 prompts allow more time and space for you to write about what you did, rather than why you did it or what it means. For the purposes of your paper, of course, you will be writing in the past tense, reporting on work done, which is why the 10 prompts are in the past tense.

To do this, take 30 minutes to complete these sentences within the word limits shown. If you find you complete them in less than 30 minutes, go back and revise: for example, is there a logical flow between all of your completed prompts?

Murray's 10 prompts

1	This work needed to be done because . . .	(25 words)
2	Those who will benefit from this include . . .	(25 words)
3	What I did was . . .	(50 words)
4	How I did that was by . . .	(50 words)
5	When I did that what happened was . . .	(50 words)
6	I worked out what that meant by using . . .	(50 words)
7	I did what I set out to do to the extent that . . .	(50 words)
8	The implications for research are . . .	(25 words)
9	The implications for practice are . . .	(25 words)
10	What still needs to be done is . . .	(25 words)

If we compare Brown's 8 questions with Murray's 10 prompts, we can see the main difference in proportions allocated to each element:

		Brown	**Murray**
1	Your work	150 words	250 words
2	Context, rationale, explanations, implications	125 words	125 words

The purpose of this comparison is not to show that one framework is better than the other, since they both have different purposes and work for different contexts; instead, it is to make the point that you need to decide about the proportion of what might be considered writing about your own work and writing to support your writing about your work for the context of your target journal.

How you decide to write your abstract will be shaped by, and be calibrated with, your target journal, but you can also write about your own work first, so as to generate ideas and text based on your work, rather than based on others'. Yes, you are joining an on-going conversation by targeting a journal, but you can use these frameworks to focus on developing your ideas in writing, by writing.

Calibrating your outline

The point was made earlier in this chapter that you have to check that your article is aligned with your target journal. This subject is given a final separate section here for emphasis. It may also work as a reminder. Even when you find that you are, finally, relatively happy with your outline, give it a final check: does it fit or challenge – as you intend – the norms and forms of your target journal at the time of writing?

Go back to your target journal and your initial analysis of it. As with any stage in the writing process, you may have become so engrossed in what you have to say in your paper that you lost sight of what they want to hear.

Remember that the point of this exercise is not to compromise your research – though it can feel like that – but to be persuasive in your writing, fitting it to the rhetorical context you selected: the journal.

What to check

- Cut and save in a new file any section that does not fit.
- Adapt the style of your headings and sub-headings.
- Do you have too many? Can you cut one or two?
- Check the relative length of your sections.

In fact, in the 'outlining' stage described in this chapter, you could and perhaps should be doing several different activities at once – these parallel writing tasks:

> **Parallel writing tasks**
>
> 1 Calibrating your outline with your target journal.
> 2 Copying and pasting your Brown/Murray sentences into your outline.
> 3 Writing sub-headings and sub-sub-headings in the form of sentences – or prompts for every section.
> 4 Setting word limits for all sections of your article.
> 5 Freewriting and generative writing on these headings – or to these prompts.

Simply drawing up a graphical outline, even to level 3 or 4, will not necessarily produce writing. Do at least some of these other activities, some form of regular writing. These parallel activities show how to integrate the various types of writing and thinking to progress your paper.

Checklist

- Do various levels of outlining – they all have their purpose.
- Write in sentences.
- Write headings.
- Write prompts for every section.
- Plan time for parallel tasks.

Further reading

Hartley, J. (1994) Three ways to improve the clarity of journal abstracts, *British Journal of Educational Psychology*, 64(2): 331–43.

Hartley, J. (2004) Current findings from research on structured abstracts, *Journal of the Medical Library Association*, 92(3): 368–71.

Hartley, J. and Betts, L. (2009) Common weaknesses in traditional abstracts in the social sciences, *Journal of the American Society for Information Science and Technology*, 60(10): 2010–18.

Reif-Lehrer, L. (2000) The beauty of outlines (http://sciencemag.org/careers/2000/06/beauty-outlines).

Silvia, P.J. (2018) *How to Write a Lot: A Practical Guide to Productive Academic Writing*, 2nd edn. Washington, DC: American Psychological Association.

Chapter **6**

Drafting

What constitutes good writing in journals? • Shaping sections
• Streamlining • Turning headings into prompts • Internal critique
• Checklist • Further reading

Drafting involves many different activities: writing to develop your idea in paragraphs and sentences, outlining and revising your outline as you go along and producing features of academic writing.

The key point of this chapter, the secret that no one sees fit to tell us during our undergraduate or even postgraduate years – perhaps, to be fair, because it is not widely understood or acknowledged – is that when you do regular 'snack' writing about your paper and you have a detailed outline to guide your writing, then your first draft will be pretty good. You will have less revising, and that saves you time and energy.

However, unless you write regularly, you will not be able to write 'on demand'. You may find that you do not stick to the focus provided by your outline. You may find yourself veering off onto other subjects. You may not actually get any writing done, even though you have a great outline.

The short, sharp 'snacking' writing tasks can change how you write, not just in letting you dribble on about whatever is on your mind, but in helping you to keep your focus. Because such snack writing is low stakes, academics and professionals often get the impression that they are no more than therapeutic, but you can learn to focus immediately on the topic or prompt for your five or ten minutes of writing. If you persevere with this for a few weeks, you will get better at it. Even when you are writing about a subject you do not know very well, where your confidence in what you have to say and how you are going to say it is low, your focusing skills will help you to develop your thinking.

Many projects falter at the drafting stage, as writers fail to use the work they have done so far in structuring the whole paper. They enjoy freewriting, or resist it, or fail to make regular time to write. They fail to keep up their promised writing buddy or writers' group meetings. They allow writing time in the diary to go to other priorities. They lose sight of what they were trying to do – and its value – and to get back on track begins to feel like starting over again.

Just as writing without a detailed outline can leave you feeling that you are starting over every time you sit down to write, not having a sense of your 'time outline' means that you are likely not to progress your paper. Having an image of the paper as a whole – in the form of your outline, your abstract and your analysis of the journal's framework (as explained in previous chapters) – helps you to focus and, therefore, write. Having a sense of the whole timeline for your paper means that you know where you are in the process at any given time. You are more likely to stay on course, resist distractions and defer other 'priorities', even if only for 30 minutes.

There can be deep-seated reasons for not writing. Or, it may be that there are cognitive or behavioural gaps at this point, as there were, arguably, at earlier stages in the writing process. In other words, some writers, particularly new writers, simply do not have a process for progressing from outline to draft.

The structure of your whole paper can be designed using one or all of the range of strategies covered in this book so far: developing your answers to Brown's 8 questions, using Murray's 10 prompts, adapting generic structures or modes, or one of the dominant structures in the target journal. Your key strategy is to produce a detailed design for the whole paper, perhaps more detailed than you usually do, before starting to write paragraphs and sentences.

Otherwise, you may defer setting conceptual and word limits to each part of your paper, and you will still be making structural decisions, still facing options and choices on several levels: structure, content, focus, wording, style and so on. In practice, in order to manage these very different processes, you can continue to do different types of writing activity:

1 Outlining
2 Revising the outline
3 Writing-related tasks.

What constitutes good writing in journals?

Researchers and professionals are familiar with the norms and forms of good academic writing in their disciplines from reading journals in their fields. Where their knowledge may be limited is on rhetorical strategies used in published papers.

When you analyse published papers you see that there are effective – and recurring – strategies that you can use in your papers. This type and level of analysis prompts some to respond, 'Aren't we analysing this too much?' But how else will you increase your understanding of what constitutes good writing at this level in your discipline at this time?

The examples analysed in this section may not be in your field, but they demonstrate the type of analysis you can do on papers in your field.

This is one way of developing your expertise in academic writing. If you do not do this analysis, you will write using your existing knowledge of academic writing, and that might not be enough.

The key strategies of academic writing in journals, it could be argued, are similar across the board: academic writing is highly signalled and signposted, there is often a forecast of the whole paper in an introduction, and there is acknowledgement of other people's work.

Example 1

More has been written on The Duchess of Malfi **than on almost any other** non-Shakespearean tragedy of its time. **Yet the major** thematic **issues** with the play **remain in dispute: the question of** the Duchess' guilt, the motives of Bosola and Ferdinand, and the difficulties posed by the allegedly 'anti-climactic' final act **still invite contention.** While the emotions that the Duchess and her play inspire may be too heated for one more article to cool, **I nevertheless believe that a fresh approach** to the play – **an approach that investigates** the conflict between merit and degree – **can contribute to a resolution of these issues.** Indeed, **an assessment of** Webster's treatment of the tension between merit and degree not only helps **to vindicate** the Duchess' actions, **to explain** the actions of Ferdinand and Bosola, and **to justify** the play's final act, but it also **establishes** Webster's play as an unblinking assertion of the primacy of worth over inherited position.

(Selzer 1981: 70–1)

If you can get past the unfamiliarity of this article's subject and ignore its citation system, you will see many skilful rhetorical features in this argument, which is why the example is included:

- uncontentious opening sentence, identifying the field for this paragraph and the paper;
- identification of the 'issues' that 'remain in dispute' and 'still invite contention';
- statement of the author's proposed contribution, 'I nevertheless believe' (alternative style could be 'It nevertheless could be argued');
- branding of the type of contribution, 'fresh approach' (alternatives could be 'new', 'different', 'innovative' and so on – which ones are used in your target journal?);
- claim that this paper 'can contribute to a resolution of these issues', not out to 'prove' anything, still open to further debate, writing in the language of debate;
- purpose of the paper identified in key verb, 'investigates', purposes of stages in the argument – or sections in the paper – also in verbs, 'assess . . . vindicate . . . explain . . . justify . . . establish'.

Example 2 is from a different discipline, but displays some of the same features of academic writing:

Example 2

A literature review demonstrates that since 1969, many authors have used variances of Verkhoshanski's methodology in an attempt to establish the best stretch-shortening technique and training program (3, 6–8, 11, 32, 36). **There is agreement on** the benefits of basic stretch-shortening principles, **but controversy exists regarding** an optimal training routine (12, 16, 29, 38). Today, the chief proponents of the stretch-shortening approach are still found in the track and field society, since they continue to use Verkhoshanski's 'reactive neuromuscular apparatus' for reproducing and enhancing the reactive properties of the lower extremity musculature (1, 5, 32, 36). **Numerous authors have documented** lower quarter stretch-shortening exercise drills and programs, **but the literature is deficient in** upper extremity stretch-shortening exercise programs (16–18, 42–45).

Adaptations of the stretch-shortening principles can be used to enhance the specificity of training in other sports that require a maximum amount of muscular force in a minimal amount of time. All movements in competitive athletics involve a repeated series of stretch-shortening cycles (5, 13, 15). Specific functional exercise must be performed to prepare the individual for return to activity. **Perhaps in no other single athletic endeavor** is the use of elastic loading to produce a maximal explosive concentric contraction and the rapid decelerative eccentric contraction seen more than in the violent activity of throwing a baseball. To replicate these forces during rehabilitation is beyond the scope of every traditional exercise tool. **For example,** the isokinetic dynamometer that reaches maximal velocities of 450–500°/sec is not specific to the greater than 7,000°/sec of shoulder angular velocity seen during base-ball pitch (20, 34). Consequently, specific exercise should be an intricate part of every upper extremity training program to facilitate a complete return to athletic participation. **The purpose of this paper is to explain** the theoretical basis of stretch-shortening exercise **and to present** a philosophy for utilizing the stretch reflex to produce an explosive reaction in the upper extremity.

(Wilk *et al.* 1993: 225–6)

The comparison of the Selzer (1981) and Wilk *et al.* (1993) papers shows that very different disciplines share common rhetorical features. Separated in time and discipline they clearly are, but there are direct links. The authors set out their arguments in almost identical ways. This is not to say that you can write in one way for all journals – quite the opposite is argued throughout this book – but you can and perhaps should reveal the deep or generic structure underlying much research: context, rationale, problem, method, result, interpretation, implications. Exactly how you do this will depend on your target journal.

Examples of articles published in journals in different fields show not only the generic features of academic writing but also the range of genres that you have to choose from if you are writing in this area. Your choice of target journal may not be an entirely free one; it may depend on the type of research you are doing and the stage that it has reached, for example.

The range of publications within a discipline, in terms of length, depth of treatment and balance of theory and other content, can be demonstrated in the field of organic chemistry. The next example comes from a quick-turnaround journal that does not require details: in the journal *Chemical Communication* the priority is to get the information out quickly, while *Tetrahedron* publishes more detailed papers. These journals, therefore, range from concise to complex, with some combining the two. All may require careful communication of the methods, but in different forms.

Example 3

Optically pure lithium amide bases **have proven to be versatile tools** in modern asymmetric synthesis. *Indeed,* highly enantio-selective deprotonation reactions **have been accomplished** for several sets of substrates, including conformationally locked ketones . . . *In turn,* **many of the more recent advances in this area have been accomplished by** the development of new homochiral ligands and the tuning of reaction conditions to improve the selectivity of *these* lithium-mediated deprotonations. *In contrast* to the Li-based strategies, magnesium reagents **have received relatively little attention** for use in asymmetric synthesis . . .

More recently, **studies** within our laboratory **have shown how** . . . magnesium amides can be employed as alternatives to their more widely used lithium counterparts . . . *Consequently,* **with a view to developing** asymmetric Mg-based protocols **we considered that these observations . . . would allow** good levels of stereoselectivity in organic transformations **to be achieved.** Herein, **we report the first use of** homochiral magnesium amide bases as reagents . . .

(Henderson *et al.* 2000: 479)

Even if the content is difficult, you can track the stages in the argument in the usual way: the words in bold signal the movement from existing work and what it showed, to the area that has received less attention to date, and finally to proposed new work and its specific aim.

Note also the use of link words between and within sentences (in italics), and that many of the link words are positioned at the start of the sentence. Note the popular academic sentence that tells us, in a verb, the purpose of this paper: 'report the first use of'. Not everyone likes this writing style – some find it annoying to have everything spelled out in this way – but it does appear in published papers, and when it is not there, readers in many disciplines, in many discussions, often say that they missed it – they missed the main point on their first quick read. So it serves a useful purpose.

By contrast, the journal *Tetrahedron* requires much more detail. In order to preserve the unity of the more complex paper the authors maintain focus on the aims of the study by pointing out how each successive phase of the experimental work moved them forwards:

Example 4

In an effort to further establish and, moreover, widen the scope of our novel Mg-amide mediated enantioselective depronotation process, our attention was turned to consider the desymmetrisation reactions of alternative prochiral cyclic ketones and, more specifically, 2,6-disubstituted cyclohexanones.

(Henderson *et al.* 2000: 479)

This sentence makes a coherent and explicit link not only between one stage of the work and the next, but between the stage being discussed and the 'big picture' of the research aims. Further links between stages in the work are used throughout the results section at the beginning of each paragraph:

> **Based on these** promising results and to further explore the potential of this reaction system . . .

> **Returning to** our Mg-amide base (R)-**3,** we remained unsatisfied at the length of time required to achieve an acceptable level of conversion of *cis-6* to **7** . . .

> **Moving on to consider** reaction of *trans*-2,6-dimethyl-cyclohexanone . . .

> **Following on from these** encouraging results, we then decided to investigate the behaviour of . . .
>
> (Henderson *et al.* 2000: 479)

A fifth example was published in 1985 and then republished by the editor in 2000 to represent the editor's years in office. It is worth noting the editor's reasons for positioning this one paper in this way, since it gives insights not only into this editor's perspective but into good academic journal writing:

> Val Belton described a project which, as she took great pains to point out, was very simple and did not even solve a problem. It merely helped the decision-makers to understand the problem before taking the decision. I have to take issue with the *'merely'*. It is a well-researched fact that the majority of 'bad' decisions stem not from a poor selection from available options but from the mis-identification of the real problem. Providing a better understanding of problems is generally what I have hoped to achieve.
>
> (Hough 2000: 896)

Belton's (1985) paper demonstrates many of the skills covered in earlier chapters:

- The purpose of the paper is stated in the opening sentence.
- There is little background/context – focusing on the 'project'.
- Analysis criteria are defined and numbered.
- Pros and cons are addressed, showing knowledge of research method.
- There is effective use of mini-arguments.
- A 'model' is constructed from research data.
- There are links at the start of paragraphs.

Example 5

INTRODUCTION

This paper describes the use of a simple multi-criteria model as a decision aid in a large service company, which will be called Financial Information Services Ltd (F.I.S.L.) engaged in the process of choosing a company with which to place a contract for the development of a computer system. The computer system, a financial management aid, was to be provided to clients as a chargeable service. [66 words]

F.I.S.L. did not have expertise in-house to develop a proven and reliable system of the type it wished to market sufficiently quickly to respond to pressure from competitors. By involving an outside organization, it hoped to be able to overcome these difficulties whilst meeting the objective of educating its own staff in this type of system. A further possible objective was to bring the system in-house at some time in the future. The system is a large-scale one involving the extraction and collation of data from worldwide sources and the formatting of the data into reports for use by clients anywhere in the world. [104 words]

Evaluation

. . . **No formal checks were made of** the independence assumptions necessary for an additive model of this type to be valid, **but we were aware of these** in the specification of the model and throughout the analysis. **It is generally accepted that** the additive model is a robust one, 2,3 **and it was felt that greater insight would be gained** in the time available from the use of a simple model than to attempt to construct a more complex representation of the decision. [82 words]

The next stage was to weight the criteria at level–2 in line with their contribution to the overall objective. The weights at this level represent the cumulative weight of all level–3 criteria which are sub-criteria of a particular level–2 criterion. **These** weights can be assessed either by direct comparison of the criteria at level–2 or by selective comparisons of criteria at level–3. **It was decided to adopt** the former, more direct approach and to supplement this by consistency checks using the implied level–3 weight. **Initially** the persons responsible for each section of the analysis were asked to give their personal opinion on the weights to be used at level–2. **This information was used as the basis for** sensitivity analysis before the group came together to discuss this issue. **This approach avoided** the possibility of long discussions about these weights when the disagreements may have been inconsequential. [146 words]

Thus it seemed that the real decision was to be made between Company A and Company B. The overall weighted score emerging from the multiple-criteria analysis indicated a preference for Company B. The scores were 59 and 68 for Company A and B respectively; Company C had scored only 27. **However, too much emphasis should not be placed on these numbers. Further inspection** of Figure 2, the graph of results aggregated to level–2 of the hierarchy, **shows** that there are criteria of greater and lesser importance on which each company is ranked more highly. A thorough sensitivity analysis was carried out to identify those changes in inputs to the model which would significantly affect the outcome – i.e. which would reverse the ordering of companies A and B in the overall evaluation. **The working group was confident about** the evaluation of the companies on the majority of the criteria, **although there were a few areas for which information was lacking** which were considered in detail in the sensitivity analysis. [167 words]

We were aware that such an analysis is necessarily simplistic and that if more than one weight or score were to be changed simultaneously, the outcome may be more marked. . . .

Thus, at this stage of the evaluation, it appeared that Company C was emerging as preferred, with Company A a close second and Company C a distant third. This was in accord with the feelings of the working group [short paragraph] . . .

The decision to recommend Company B was not shaken by further recourse to the negative review of each company. [One-sentence paragraph]

(Belton 1985: 265–274)

This paper makes a clear case not only for the study's contribution, but, perhaps more importantly, for the scale of that contribution; as the editor said, the results of this study did not solve all the problems – in fact, potential weaknesses in the study itself were identified in the work and were addressed in the paper – but provided a means of understanding them.

A key feature of good academic writing is that it tells the reader in advance what it does and why and, sometimes, what it does not do and why not:

The six stages specified by the TM are (a) precontemplation, (b) contemplation, (c) preparation, (d) action, (e) maintenance, and (f) termination (Prochaska & DiClemente, 1983). **Precontemplation is present when** an individual does not intend to change their high-risk behaviours in the foreseeable future . . . **Contemplation is present when** an individual is giving serious consideration to behaviour change . . . **Preparation is present when** . . . **Action is present when** . . . **Maintenance is present when** the new behaviour requires increasingly less effort to maintain.

Finally, **termination is present when** the new behaviour has become rather automatic and requires no conscious effort.

(Guillot et al., 2004: 1091)

This is a good example of an author not only planning a detailed section of the paper well, but also revealing the plan in the opening sentence of the paragraph – that there are 'six stages'.

This paragraph also features the strategy of putting key words at the start of the sentence – the terms (a) to (f). For each element of this sequence, the same sentence structure is used, which makes it easier to read through a lot of information and may make it easier to write.

In some journals, the outline of the argument can be followed in the topic sentences of subsequent paragraphs, where, without the use of linking words, the repetition of key words makes the continuous line of argument clear. Repeated key words become link words. In some cases, many of the paragraphs begin with statements, which are then supported by the contents of the paragraph:

A number of theoretical models have been proposed and used in an attempt to explain physical activity behaviour . . .

A large amount of research supports the use of the transtheoretical model for physical activity behaviour change in the general population . . .

A meta-analysis [19] of 71 published reports in 2001 summarized the findings from applications of the trans-theoretical model to physical activity in the general population by investigating . . .

Variables associated with physical activity behaviour can provide important information for the design of effective physical activity interventions . . .

Low motivation in physical activity is a major factor associated with poor physical activity participation in healthy individuals . . .

Physical activity knowledge has been shown to correlate poorly with physical activity behaviour . . .

Social support for physical activity behaviour change has been consistently correlated with physical activity participation in the general population . . .

(Kirk et al. 2007: 810–12)

None of these examples is presented as a model for your writing; instead, they are models for your analysis of articles in your target journals.

All of these examples of published academic writing show similarities and differences across the disciplines, but even within disciplines there are variations in published papers. This type of analysis reveals rhetorical modes, norms and forms and dominant conventions operating at a particular time in a particular journal. The question for new writers is which ones are operating in your journals at this time and how can you incorporate your work within that format?

Shaping sections

As you do this kind of analysis of articles published in your target journal, as you develop your detailed outline of the article and draft abstract, you can draft of all the sections of the article.

Building on the abstract

- Take each sentence of your abstract (using Brown's 8 questions/Murray's 10 prompts).
- Copy and paste these sentences into your draft article.
- Write for five minutes on each sentence.

Write topic sentences on each step in your argument. Will these be paragraphs? Then develop the point in each topic sentence. In this way, use the writing of topic sentences as a bridge between your outline and your first draft, moving towards paragraphs and sentences step by step.

Look again at your target journal, particularly the type of paper that you are aiming to write. Are there any changes you should make to the shape, such as:

- making mini-arguments;
- including internal critique;
- anticipating refutation;
- writing the debate into your paper?

If someone just published a paper in that journal that is like yours, say so. Cite it. Refer to it in your introduction, literature review and/or discussion. It is part of the debate. It represents part of current knowledge about the subject. Say how your article differs. Say what yours adds.

From this point on, you may think there are endless revisions to be done, when, in fact, you are probably responding to internal prompts, assumptions and understandings of what is expected in writing for a particular journal. However, if your revisions are focused in this way, you will have less uncertainty about the direction of your writing; you will know that revision will fit your plan for the paper. This gives you a perspective that lets you see your revisions are moving in the right direction – the direction you set and fixed, as far as possible, in your outline.

Streamlining

This is for when you realize that you have more than one paper in your paper. Many new writers do. They want to put all their eggs in one basket, thinking that it will make for a stronger paper, when, in reality, it weakens the paper by making it unfocused. Cut out anything that is not part of it, saving it in a new file. At some point you have to acknowledge that you will not include all the points you thought you would because you have run out of time, ideas or energy or, more importantly, because you realize that those points are not relevant. Be prepared to abandon material, notes, ideas that you think are excellent. Save them for another paper.

Turning headings into prompts

It is all very well having a detailed outline of your paper, but it does not guarantee you will write it. Designing an outline is, after all, a very different activity from writing in paragraphs and sentences.

Yet the two are so closely bound together – and both are important for progressing a writing project – that you have to find a way to keep both going.

Perhaps most importantly, you have to persevere with regular writing while still working on the outline, so that you can stay in the writing 'habit'. If you do not write regularly, getting started can be much more laborious, and this can undermine your confidence. This is possibly where those who tried to write and failed lost momentum or motivation; perhaps their writing process would not see them through this stage.

You can bridge the activities of outlining and drafting by using prompts, using your outline as a driver for writing. If you re-write your headings and sub-headings in the form of sentences, you can turn them into prompts for writing, even for writing in short bursts. This is an important way of integrating the strategies covered in this book: combining the 'simply start writing . . . just do it' approaches with the rigorous academic thinking and structured writing needed for a journal article.

In order to use headings as prompts, they have to be written as prompts. The characteristics of good prompts are: simple language, personal pronouns and verbs. There are, of course, other styles of prompts; in fact, you may prefer to use prompts in a more academic style.

For example, instead of headings that are one or two words or a short string of words, write a sentence that describes the writing task for each section in more detail, using a verb:

Comparison of a heading and a sentence

Heading   *Cardiac Rehabilitation*
Prompt   *Define the form of cardiac rehabilitation involving the use of exercise, as developed in the west of Scotland over the past ten years, in 200 words (in 30 minutes).*

The heading defines the subject of the section, while the prompt has its purpose in the verb 'define'. In writing the heading 'Cardiac Rehabilitation' the writer has not yet defined the purpose and scale of this section. By contrast, the prompt does. Prompts include verbs because they show the purpose of each section:

Choosing the verb for your paper

The aim of this paper is to . . . [verb].

You can also select verbs to articulate the stages in your argument:

Choosing verbs for your sections

This paper analyses . . .

It argues that . . .

It also illustrates . . .

It goes on to argue . . .

Using . . . the paper analyses . . .

to illustrate . . .

The paper concludes by suggesting . . .

(Kitson 2001: 86)

Once you have written your string of verbs, you can check that your sequence is coherent, logical and sufficient to add up to the verb you chose to define your main argument. In other words, before/as you start writing paragraphs and sentences you have a checking mechanism, so that you do not waste time and give yourself extra revision work to do. This is how you can develop a progressively more and more detailed design for your paper, and the more detailed it is, in theory, with practice, the less time you will need for revision.

Verbs can help in this way because they make you define the function of your argument – what is your paper trying to *do?* – and the function of the stages in your argument – how is each section moving your argument forward – what is each section *doing?* Even if, in your completed paper, you do not use verbs in exactly this way, it is a useful outlining tool, prompting you to make decisions.

For further examples to add to your repertoire of verbs for academic writing, see Ballenger's (2015) list of 138 'Active Verbs for Discussing Ideas'. The first ten in this wide-ranging list signify different lines of argument and/or types of paper that, for example, the main verb will promise to the reader:

informs

reviews

argues

states

synthesizes

asserts

claims

answers

responds

critiques.

(Ballenger 2015: 210)

These are possible lines of argument, each requiring a particular type of writing. Some will be more relevant to your discipline than others. Analyse the use of verbs in your target journal. There is probably a limited set of verbs, not an infinite list of possibilities, that is acceptable in that journal at this time. Think about what each verb signals in terms of type of argument and structure.

For example, a paper that 'narrates' will move through a set of time stages, with those stages marked out by time words, like 'In the beginning . . . later . . . next . . . after . . . following . . . subsequent' and so on towards 'finally'. If you write a 'narration' paper, or if part of your paper is narration, think about what time period you will cover – and why – and how much detail you will allocate to each stage – and why. Do you really need to write about all the phases? Or will you select some and leave out others – probably, and why. Which will you include, and why; which will you not include, and why not. How many words will you need – according to the journal's style – for these mini-arguments? Are they even there at all in recent issues of your target journal?

If you find yourself writing, firstly . . . secondly . . . thirdly, is that not a process rather than narrative?

Alternatively, if you are writing a 'categorize' paper you have to decide which categories to put items into and why this might constitute a 'contribution' to the literature or to knowledge. Does this bring a new perspective to your subject? That might be sufficient in some disciplines, in some journals.

How would you organize a 'contrast' argument, perhaps contrasting your work or idea with others'? First deal with one subject or approach, then the other? Treating each separately? Describing their pros and cons as you go along? Then dealing with their main similarities and differences in a third main section? Or focusing on the main difference? Or the main similarity? Would that be the main point of such an argument? How would it contribute to knowledge of the subject?

While this discussion of four types of argument, signalled by four different verbs, handles each separately, you can, of course, combine these – and many others – in your paper. With one eye on 'what you want to say' and another on 'how they want to hear it', you decide how to focus and pace your argument. These structural decisions are difficult to make as you go along. It is not impossible to make structural decisions as you write – and you will make changes as you go anyway – but it is a more complex process and much more demanding for new writers.

There will, of course, be other ways of signalling the main line of argument and its articulation, other than using verbs. You may find that your target journal uses a different style. You could focus on the types of article a journal publishes, and consider how each type might be described in verbs or other terms, as you decide whether or not any of them is appropriate for the article you want to write. For examples of types of papers, see Petre and Rugg (2010: 86–93):

'Paper types'

Data-driven papers: meta-study papers, artefact papers, work-in-progress papers.

Methods papers: method introductions, tutorial papers, method-mongering, demonstration of concept.

Theoretical papers: introducing new theory, explaining someone else's theory, refining or extending theory, critiquing existing theory, setting the agenda for needed new theory.

Consciousness-raising papers: pointing to issues often ignored, applying methods that are established in another field.

Perspective papers: showing what it is and how it affects research and knowledge.

Agenda-setting papers

Review papers

Position papers

In the first edition of their book, they suggested other hybrid papers: formal experiment, field experiment, case study, action research, survey (Rugg and Petre 2004: 83).

Even if your target journal uses a different style, using verbs at the outlining stage can help you during the writing process to work out the stages in your argument, even if you finally change the style of writing before you submit it.

If you do not particularly like this style, with its predominance of verbs, personifying the paper and its sections, as if sections – rather than the author – were 'doing' the analysis, as in the Kitson paper quoted above, there are two points to bear in mind as you decide whether or how to use this style: first, Kitson's (2001) paper was published, which means that this style was acceptable for that journal at that time; and, second, our own preferences in style and structure should not limit our stylistic choices. If you were to target that journal, that would be an appropriate style to use. This is not to say that you should plagiarize, but that you should consider the extent to which you observe and (re-) produce features of the style that are implicitly endorsed by your target journal, rather than simply acting on your preferences. While this may seem like common sense, it does not, from discussions with writers, appear to be common practice: they sometimes do resist the idea of writing in a style they 'don't like' or don't currently use.

Here is the whole abstract of the Kitson article with all the verbs highlighted:

> **This paper analyses** the relationship between government and nurse education policy using the current changes in England as a case study. **It argues that** there are times when ideologies of governments and professions coalesce, signifying the most opportune times for advancement. **It also illustrates** times when policy shifts are made because nursing is perceived as relatively insignificant in the order of health policies and politics. **It goes on to argue** that nursing leaders need to be aware of the political and policy context in order to select the most effective methods of moving the agenda forward. Using UK reforms, particularly the English strategy document 'Making a Difference' (Department of Health 1999d) as a case study, **the paper analyses** recent events in nurse education **to illustrate** key points. **The paper concludes by suggesting** that the nursing profession must recognize promoters and barriers for change and commit itself to the transformation of nursing practice through the realization of a new educational agenda that embraces the principles of new democracy. Namely, these are equality, mutual responsibility, autonomy, negotiated decision-making, inclusivity, collaboration and celebrating diversity.
>
> (Kitson 2001: 86)

Another example of an abstract shows similar techniques:

> This article seeks **to explore** the complex underpinnings and dynamics of the act of forgery, compared with instances of copying witnessed in art therapy sessions involving people with learning disabilities. The argument **focuses on** two theoretical frameworks: the first **concerns** the concept of joint attention behaviours; whilst the second **focuses on** psychoanalytic concepts which underlie both the infant's early visual experiences and the nature of the art object for the perceiving individual and its relevance to the broader culture. The central intent is **to establish** an equitable confluence of both developmental and psycho-analytical concepts – the product of which can usefully inform the art therapeutic process.
>
> It is **proposed** that forgery and copying, although separate in essence, share similar factors, insofar as both seek to adopt a false and acceptable image for the spectator. This is traced to, and **given meaning by**, Winnicott's concepts of the mirror-role and the false self.
>
> The text also **concerns itself with** the biographical interpretation of three well-known forgers, whose lives appear to indicate causal reasons for their eventual act of deception. This is **juxtaposed with** the learning disabled client's need to employ the work of 'recognised artists' **to present** an acceptable and valued self-image.
>
> (Damarell 1999: 44)

Further examples of abstracts in different disciplines show other uses of verbs, including nominalization – turning verbs into nouns – such as 'overview' and 'analysis', and the passive voice:

This paper **seeks to identify** whether the slow progress in transition experienced by the countries of the former Soviet Union (FSU) arises from weaknesses in implementing effective corporate governance or from weaknesses in the broader economic environment. **An overview** of progress in transition in the FSU **is presented** followed by **analysis** of developments in enterprise ownership and governance. Problems in measuring the link between governance and performance and alternative mechanisms for enhancing the efficiency of enterprise in the FSU **are discussed.** The paper **concludes that** the problems of transition in the FSU concern delays both in introducing corporate governance mechanisms and in introducing an appropriate competitive market environment.

(Estrin and Wright 1999: 398)

Personalized Web applications automatically adapted for different clients and user preferences gain more importance. Still, there are barely technologies to compensate the additional effort of creating, maintaining and publishing such Web content. **To address this problem,** this paper **introduces** a declarative, component-based approach for adaptive, dynamic Web documents on the basis of XML-technology. Adaptive Web components on different abstraction levels **are defined** in order **to support** effective Web page authoring and generation. . . . Finally, hierarchical document components playing a specific semantic role **are defined.** The hyperlink view for defining typed links **is spanned over** all component layers. Beside the reuse of both implementation artifacts and higher level concepts, the model also **allows to define** [sic] adaptive behavior of components in a fine-granular way. As a further benefit the support for ubiquitous collaboration via component annotations **is introduced.** Finally, the stepwise pipeline-based process of document generation **is introduced** and performance issues **are sketched.**

(Fiala *et al.* 2003: 58)

There are other ways to signal structure, along with verbs, such as combining problem and solution, cause and effect, and verbs that refer to the work done, rather than to sections of the paper:

Optically pure lithium amide bases **have proven to be versatile tools** in modern asymmetric synthesis. Indeed, highly enantio-selective deprotonation reactions **have been accomplished** for several sets of substrates, including conformationally locked ketones . . . In turn, many of the more recent advances in this area **have been accomplished by** the development of new homochiral ligands and the **tuning** of reaction conditions **to improve** the selectivity of these lithium-mediated deprotonations. In contrast to the LI-based strategies, magnesium reagents **have received** relatively little attention for use in asymmetric synthesis . . . .

More recently, studies within our laboratory **have shown how** ... magnesium amides **can be employed** as alternatives to their more **widely used** lithium counterparts ... Consequently, with a view to **developing** asymmetric Mg-based protocols we **considered** that these observations ... would **allow** good levels of stereoselectivity in organic transformations **to be achieved.** Herein, we **report** the first use of homochiral magnesium amide bases as reagents.

(Henderson *et al.* 2000: 479)

You can also use 'Verbs That Help You Integrate Quotations' (Rozakis 1999: 110).

Examples of published papers show us how stylistic variation, or any other form of variation, can challenge our sense of what constitutes 'good academic writing'.

At this point, it might help to refocus on your goal: is it to write what you like as you like, or is it to get published? This may sound cynical, but it is not intended to be; instead, it is about being rhetorical, making writing choices that are appropriate not in terms of your own taste but for your audience and the discourse in which they perceive themselves currently to be engaged.

Your outline is a set of prompts, each an instruction for your writing. In fact, the verb 'write' is too vague; a more precise verb, describing what will go into the text – like 'define' – is more useful, and makes it easier to manage your many writing tasks. In this way, your outline becomes a list of writing tasks. Taking more time over these prompts involves deciding on content. This then makes it easier to see your writing tasks.

This is not a matter of counting words until you have enough; it is about making tough decisions about how much, or how little, to say about each subject or, when you review your set of prompts, to check whether you need to write about a subject at all.

This process requires you to do a lot of hard thinking; in fact, this can be one way of structuring that thinking. It is also a means of stopping yourself from running off after interesting tangents – or finding ways to fit them into your article.

People often ask me where, in all my writing activities for just 'getting on with it', all the thinking that writing requires is going to happen. They imply that I am somehow misrepresenting the labour of academic writing, drawing an idealized process. They point out my apparent assumption that everyone has the material, knowledge and intellectual capacity required to write for academic journals. Not at all. You may find, in the course of doing the writing activities I suggest, that you do not have enough knowledge, that you do need to check references or that you have a limited understanding of what constitutes a publishable argument.

My point is that this is the hard work of writing. The activities I suggest do, I am told repeatedly, make writing seem more 'manageable', but it is still hard work. This is not a reason to stop, but a point at which to persevere. My argument is that these writing activities will expose such limitations, not hide them.

Your task is not to try to fill all your knowledge gaps before you write, but to use writing to develop your understanding. In some fields, this statement will seem plainly absurd, but even in chemistry, writing about an experimental process with all the required precision and accuracy can reveal limitations in the new writer's knowledge. Putting your knowledge down in writing is, literally, a testing – you could even say almost 'experimental' – process in itself. In fact, because the approaches suggested here are new they may seem strange in other fields too, but if you wait until you have 'done all your thinking' before you write, you may find, and I repeat this for emphasis, that you do not write at all, or, at least, you do not publish as much as you want to or as much as you could.

Ultimately, of course, you will find a way to connect up the stages in your writing-thinking process. Clearly, this may be a very individual matter. It may be related to your discipline base, learning style and other factors. Or it may not be. Whatever your starting point, you can use these outlining strategies to keep your thinking focused and keep writing. Remember that people in many disciplines have used them to do so. Of course, you will only realize these benefits if you try these strategies.

You can also use freewriting to produce draft text. How does freewriting progress a paper? How does it progress to draft? If you have practised it enough, you will find that you can write on demand, as if you were simply freewriting, to the headings or sentences in your outline. Again, it is not enough to think about these practices in the abstract; you have to develop practices that produce writing.

Since you will be no less busy at this stage in your writing process than you were when you started writing your paper, it may be important to continue to 'snack and binge' write. The strategies for generating text covered in Chapter 3 will help you to work out what you want to say, to focus on actually writing it and to avoid procrastinating.

As you write, keep checking your word count – easy to do, if you are writing on the laptop – so that you see when you achieve, or exceed, your writing goal. As the words mount up, it helps to keep your motivation going. As you meet one target – for example, mine was to write 100 words for this section – set yourself a new target – such as 100 more words to complete this section (because my outline has two sections of 100 words). Again, when you reach that target, set another one. Checking the total word count will help you to calibrate your writing with your outline and your word limit per section.

Internal critique

Many new writers assume that they have to 'smooth' out weaknesses in their research and ignore potential refutations in their paper, but building critique into your paper, writing the debate into it, will strengthen your argument.

You can do this either early on in your paper, as you review pros and cons of your method or approach to your subject, for example, or at the end of your paper, where you anticipate refutations of your conclusions, or both.

Anticipating refutation

- What are/were the pros and cons of your approach or research design?
- Why did you reject reasons for doing it differently?
- Have you built a strong enough case for your methodology?
- Have you made a strong case for adaptations you made to standard methods?

These are not just prompts for your thinking; you can write about these questions, checking whether or not they appear at all, and if they do in what form(s), in your target journal. How much you should write about them depends on the context, but you could write a sentence or two now, acknowledging that there are other ways of doing what you did and of making sense of it; and also that there are different interpretations others could make. It would not hurt to include this even as a kind of aside. It does not need a whole section, unless, of course, some aspect of your paper is highly contested or controversial, in which case you might write a section on it, perhaps as much as 500 words, perhaps more. Clearly, you have to balance this word allocation with other parts of your paper.

If you really have to write so much justification for this section, perhaps that is a paper in itself, in which you really go into detail on the pros and cons. You could consider more of the complexities of research choices and interpretations, such as pros in certain contexts being cons in another. This paper could make a specific contribution to debates about methods and/or methodology.

As you weigh the pros and cons of internal critique, go back to your outline: where and how does this phase in your argument fit? Revise your outline: add detail and strengthen your argument. Your outline, however detailed, may change as you write, but if it is very detailed, it will not completely change shape. You may find that you want to make sweeping changes in light of a new insight or something you read recently, but it might be a better idea to save that for future papers. You have to weigh it all in the balance. If you have already had good feedback on your discussions, scribblings and outlinings from trusted colleagues, then it might be a mistake to pull your paper into a new shape. Likewise, if you sounded out an editor and he or she showed interest in your paper as you wrote about it then, they might lose interest if you change it too much. Go with what you have.

Checklist

- Use both structuring and generative strategies. Combine both kinds of writing. Write regularly. Use freewriting, generative writing and prompts to develop your outline into a full draft of your article.
- Get feedback on your draft and revised outline.
- Check that your abstract and outline cover the same ground.

Further reading

Ballenger, B. (2015) *The Curious Researcher: A Guide to Writing Research Papers*, 8th edn. New York: Pearson Longman.

Kurcikova, K. and Quinlan, O. (eds) (2017) *The Digitally Agile Researcher*. London: Open University Press.

Petre, M. and Rugg, G. (2010) *The Unwritten Rules of PhD Research*, 2nd edn. Maidenhead: Open University Press McGraw-Hill [on academic writing genres].

Rozakis, L. (1999) *Writing Great Research Papers*. London: McGraw-Hill.

Chapter 7

Revising the draft

Foregrounding generic aspects of academic style • Revising the outline • Revising drafts • Generative writing • Using the writers' group • The critical friend and the 'tame' subject expert • Revision processes • Iterative processes • Developing a concise style • Grammar • Polishing • The final revision • Checklist • Further reading

Even after all your work on structuring, there may still be work to do in revealing the plan of your paper. In reality, what this means is that you probably did not produce, in paragraphs and sentences, an exact replica of your outline. And even if you had, you would still be revising it at this stage. In other words, in revising your draft, you will be looking to make the structure clearer and more explicit, but you will likely be reviewing and perhaps rethinking that structure at the same time.

You used the outlining process – your graphic or drawing of the outline, list of sentences or series of prompts with verbs, and word limits allocated for each – to decide what you were going to write about – and that is crucial for stimulating focused writing – but the revising process still involves discovery of the structure in the course of writing. If this sounds contradictory, it may be because this stage of writing *is* contradictory: writing involves both deciding in advance what to say and discovering what you want to say as you make choices about how to say it. It is not, therefore, a weakness to make changes to your text that are not based on your outline; quite the reverse – this shows that you are thinking about your subject, perhaps refining your ideas. You can, of course, still use your outline as a point of reference, to check whether you should add anything to your draft paper.

Moreover, at this late stage in your paper-writing process, you are not simply looking to complete your outline, you are aiming to invent a form of closure for your paper, whether or not that involves replicating, or even completing, your outline. It may not even mean retaining all of your draft.

At this stage, when you are most acutely aware of your potential audience(s), therefore, focus on the coherence of your text – its internal coherence. Whether or not it will be seen as coherent by those judging your paper is another matter. Their impending judgement can interfere with the essential revision processes, sometimes leading writers to work too hard at buttressing their arguments:

> The specter of . . . judgment . . . has created problems for the woman writer: problems of contact with herself, problems of language and style, problems of energy and survival.
>
> (Rich 2001: 13)

Assuming this to be as true for male writers seeking to enter the select group of published writers for the first time as it is for females, while recognizing that their experiences are likely to be different (Leonard 2001; Ryan-Flood and Gill 2010), this presents a new set of potential barriers to writers. This analysis might also explain why writers' energy for writing threatens to seep away in this last stage, even when they have done so much and have relatively little left to do. Revising is still writing, with all the same decisions and, perhaps, uncertainties of the earlier stages.

There may be more to the revision step, therefore, than simply honing academic writing style. It comes as a shock to many researchers and academics that so much revision is required, but lengthy revision may be the result of inadequate planning and feedback.

Some see the need for multiple revisions as a weakness in their thinking: 'I thought I had finished that bit . . . How did I miss *that?*' You may, therefore, learn something about the strengths and weaknesses of your outlining process during the revision stage. There may be things you did that you would do differently for your next paper. Or you may just realize that no matter how much outlining you do, no matter how detailed you make it, there are still revisions to do – it's just part of the process.

Finally, whether your outline works well or not, revision involves many iterative steps, as you make smaller and smaller changes to your text, and this iteration is reflected in the sections of this chapter: an initial long list of revision steps is gradually whittled down to a smaller list of minor refinements. As the list of revisions reduces, the revisions are themselves scaled down.

As you make changes, you may have to go through certain steps in the revision process again, so that you are working more iteratively on your writing than generatively – making changes to text rather than generating much new text. These are your next writing goals.

Foregrounding generic aspects of academic style

Academic writing is highly signalled and signposted. Readers are generally supplied with a route map for the whole paper at the start, assisted by signposts along the way and signals to take a turn here or make a connection there. This should mean that readers never get lost in your paper. They never have to retrace their steps. They always know where they are, how far they have travelled along the road, and how long they have to go to reach the end of your paper. They know how everything fits and, most importantly, they do not have to read your mind to work out how sections or paragraphs are connected to each other or to the 'big picture' of your on-going argument.

Consequently, the most important revision – and one that new writers often forget or simply do not know – may be signalling your structure explicitly. It is one thing to have a logical structure and another to make it transparent in your writing. This may mean making it more explicit than you think it needs to be. Even if you feel you have done this already, check it. This is not about leading the reader by the hand through your argument but about explaining the rhetorical choices you have made so far – in terms of which structures you choose to use and how you have laid out your argument – and perhaps providing an explanation of them, as required.

Reveal the plan

- Do you have a forecasting paragraph at the start, saying what each section does?
- Do you state how each section develops your argument?
- Do you end each section with a sentence about how it progresses your argument?
- Do you start each section with a reminder of what it is going to do?
- Does your key term appear throughout the paper? If you used different terms – say why?
- Have you built the case that your research makes a contribution throughout your paper, and not just at the end?
- Do you start the conclusion with a summary of the research?
- Do you use the same words in the aim, at the start, and claim to contribution, at the end?
- Have you put link words at the start of paragraphs and, if necessary, at the start of sentences? Scan each page: is the logical flow obvious? If there is a jump in the story line, insert link words at the start of paragraphs.

If this seems too deliberate, do at least a couple of these revisions. It might be a good idea to have one last look at a recent paper from your target journal, just to see how the line of argument is signalled throughout.

Work at getting a few sentences very clear, particularly those that mark key steps or turning points in your paper, as in the following examples from papers published in various disciplines, illustrating concise writing, link words at the start of sentences, sentence length variation and even a one-word sentence (in number 4, 'No').

Ten clear sentences

1 In conclusion, we have been successful in developing a straightforward preparative route to a novel homochiral Mg-bisamide reagent, from a structurally simple, readily available, and relatively inexpensive chiral amine. (Henderson *et al.* 2000: 479)

2 The model was never viewed as prescriptive or normative by the decision-making group; neither was it a descriptive model, nor a requisite model, as described by Phillips[1] – 'a model whose form and content are sufficient to solve a problem'. (Belton 1985: 273)

3 I do not mean to overstate the positive resolution of the conclusion of *The Duchess of Malfi.* (Selzer 1981: 79)

4 Are we arguing that facts are useless, or that the discourses of expository intent, such as the modernist research paper, be abandoned? No. We are suggesting, however, that facts and expository writing have limits; they allow only certain types of inquiry to take place. (Davis and Shadle 2000: 440)

5 Other factors must be considered in order to answer the question as to why the nanomechanical properties of the treated samples (cryosectioned and time-varying etched UHMWPE samples) were higher than the untreated samples. (Ho *et al.* 2003: 364)

6 Furthermore, this short study demonstrates that, depending on the nature and demands of the cyclisation substrates, mild modification of the initially established DSA protocols can lead to further improvements in reaction efficiency. (Caldwell *et al.* 2001: 1429)

7 Although the existence of the slow component has been demonstrated, the putative mechanisms have not been clearly established. (Carra *et al.* 2003: 2448)

8 Prima donnas seldom write great scholarly books. (Pasco 2002: 82)

9 But these survey data have a limitation: They only show what people are willing or able to tell us about themselves in regard to writing; awareness of inhibitions about writing, as teachers or writers, is probably incomplete at best. (Boice 1990b: 14)

10 Thus, this study aimed to extend the study of Bethell *et al.* [6] by defining the grade and involvement of physiotherapists in the United Kingdom in delivery of cardiac rehabilitation. (Thow *et al.* 2004: 99)

What is it that each of these sentences does well? What can we learn from looking at them in isolation, out of context? There are features of good writing in each that you can adopt in your papers. Above all, these examples demonstrate how important steps in academic arguments can be taken in a single sentence. The following commentary on these ten examples explains how they do this.

Key steps in an argument – in one sentence

1 Does not claim too much. Uses the word 'successful'.
   Explicitly defines a contribution.

First words of the sentence make a link.

Patterning: makes three points about what they developed and three about the amine.

2 Clarifies that the contribution is not a solution but a means of understanding the problem.

Three negatives – 'never . . . neither . . . nor' – define what is *not* claimed as contribution.

3 Makes explicit what is *not* claimed in the paper.

4 Rehearses decisions made in analysis or interpretation.

Uses a rhetorical question to focus.

Writes about what they 'are arguing' using these exact words.

Uses a one-word sentence, unusual in academic writing, but very clear.

Uses semi-colon to combine a concise point and elaboration.

5 Makes the transition between one phase of discussion and the next.

Distinguishes stages in the answer to the research question.

Says how stages in the research relate to each other.

Says how these stages, taken together, build up to the answer.

6 Starts sentence with link word.

Clarifies factors/conditions in which interpretation will stand up.

Still claims a result explicitly.

Specifies the scale of the result: 'short study'.

Modulates the claim to contribution: '*can* lead to'.

7 Distinguishes, in one sentence, what has and has not been done: there is evidence of an effect, but not of the mechanism that creates it.

8 Short sentence asserts a view.

Sums up the point to be made, using colourful language.

9 Short opening sentence, linked to elaboration by colon.

Distinguishes what can and cannot be evidenced.

Says explicitly what the data can show, using exactly those words.

10 Links the research to the literature.

Moves from previous research to new work in one short sentence.

Links with a specific, named piece of published work.

Each of these stages in an argument could, of course, be allocated more than one sentence in a paper. The point is to check that you have included such important statements, and if you need to add them, one sentence may be enough.

You have to judge whether these steps can be handled in a long complex sentence, for example, linking the paper to the literature, or in one simple sentence, followed by amplification, or in one sentence divided into two parts. There are, of course, disciplinary differences between these examples, but they display characteristics of good written debate, and these work in different disciplines.

In practice, you may end up with a much longer version of the point you want to make in your article, perhaps a string of sentences, and then have to prune them back to one sentence. Or the reverse may happen; having written one sentence, you then feel that you need to elaborate. You will, surely, choose to do both these types of revision, for different purposes, perhaps at different points in your paper, with the overall 'design' and intended structure of your paper shaping your revision decisions. You may also change your mind later and have to cut the new text you just inserted or add more.

Revising the outline

Your outline can also be a useful part of the iterative process of revision: all along you might have used it as a kind of touchstone for your writing, providing focus at every stage, but it too may still be evolving. There may be a point that requires, on reflection, more words than you had allocated for it in your outline. Go back to your outline and use it to judge whether or not you need to add anything. You will, of course, also have to circle back to your abstract and introduction, whether or not you decide to make the change you are considering.

Probably the best way to make sure that you do not go off on a tangent and lose the coherence you worked so hard to create at the outlining stage is to force yourself to revise your outline before you write the extra section you think you now need:

- What is the subject of the new section?
- Write a one-sentence prompt.
- Set a word limit.
- Insert this into your outline: what is the effect?
- Where will you take the extra words you need from?
- What does that do to the overall balance/sense of your paper?
- Are you sure you *have* to add this to your paper?
- Or can you save it for another paper?

There may, of course, also be sections or sentences that you now see should be cut. Again, check your outline first: will the paper still be coherent if you make that change, and will other changes need to be made in order to smooth over what might now be a 'jump' in your argument?

These questions merely make explicit the decision-making process, creating a pause in your rush to revise. Consider the possibility that your paper may be good enough – although it could always be improved – as it is.

Revising drafts

Topic sentences are important; they clarify what the topics of your paragraphs are, in the first sentence of each paragraph. In a well-written paper it is often possible to scan the topic sentences and follow the whole argument. This can make your argument clear and shows your reader that it has a logical structure. The series of topic sentences can also work like a visual overview of your logical structure. In this way, topic sentences are like headings and sub-headings; in fact, topic sentences, used well, develop the key words you use in your headings.

In practice, it may take several revisions to achieve this effect. Drafts can move some way towards it, but there may be further honing to do, and topic sentences should be close to the top of your routine checklist of revisions.

For example, you may have written two points in a topic sentence, without indicating, through punctuation, which one is the more important point:

Example

It has only been since the early 1960s that isokinetic devices, i.e. devices that allow for movements to be performed at controlled velocities, have been available on the commercial market. These devices such as the Cybex II Isokinetic Dynamometer (Lummex Inc.) measure the torque produced throughout the range of voluntary limb movements held at constant pre-set velocities. It has been suggested that these devices provide an ideal means of measuring an individual's torque generating capacities and that the measures given provide greater information on the expression of strength in maximal voluntary limb movements relative to other methods traditionally used.

You could improve this paragraph – and clarify how it develops the argument – by making three simple changes:

- Put one point in the topic sentence, not two.
- 'It has been suggested' is ambiguous; clarify who 'suggested'.
- Cut the long last sentence; state the main point at the end of the paragraph.

If you decided to keep two points in this topic sentence, you could use parentheses, e.g. two commas, to show which of the two points is more important:

Either

It has only been since the early 1960s that isokinetic devices, **which allow for movements to be performed at controlled velocities,** have been available on the commercial market.

Or

Isokinetic devices, **which have only been available on the commercial market since the early 1960s,** allow for movements to be performed at controlled velocities.

The words in bold mark the main point; the point between the commas is secondary. The first option means that the main point of the paragraph is the commercial availability of the devices; the second option means that the main point is what these devices do.

Once you have made the first change in the topic sentence, it becomes clear what you should do to revise the rest of the paragraph, since the rest of the paragraph should develop the main point – not the secondary one – of your topic sentence:

Revision

Isokinetic devices, which have only been available on the commercial market since the early 1960s, allow for movements to be performed at controlled velocities. These devices, such as the Cybex II Isokinetic Dynamometer (Lummex Inc.), measure the torque produced throughout the range of voluntary limb movements held at constant pre-set velocities. They provide an ideal means of measuring an individual's torque generating capacities (Reference), and thereby greater information on the expression of strength in maximal voluntary limb movements. This is what traditional methods could not do.

For the purposes of illustrating the role and impact of link words, two have been added and emphasized in this revision in bold. When you put a link word at the start of a sentence, it is clear how the reader should connect your sentences. If the link words appear later in the sentence, the reader has to hold some information in his or her head until the link word arrives.

Again, you may be thinking that this is just too much linking, but over the course of several thousand words, and at certain points in your argument, you really have to ask yourself if there is any such thing as 'too much linking' and what could be the potential disadvantages of 'overdosing' the reader on link words? Furthermore, at certain points in your argument, even what you might see as 'over-linking' might, in fact, be essential, if you are to take the reader through every step of your procedure, your justification or your interpretation, for example.

You can also use topic sentences to make it clear what your main theme or key words are, regularly throughout your paper. This will work to unify it.

Your study's aims or paper's purpose can be used as key, unifying words. You may wonder whether this, too, is a repetition too far – many new writers worry about using any repetition at all, when, in fact, it is a useful device. Moreover, if a key word is not repeated, it may not be seen as a key word.

Links within paragraphs and links between paragraphs do not, of course, all tumble out in all the right places in your first draft. These are further items for your revision checklist.

Generative writing

What is the purpose of five-minute bursts of writing when you are doing revisions?

- to write about uncertainties in or about your paper;
- to develop answers to anticipated critiques;
- to continue writing practice – maintaining the writing habit;
- to maintain confidence in your ability to put words on paper/screen;
- to write about part of your paper you are not happy with, to find a better way of saying it;
- if it gets complicated, to start with the prompt, 'what I'm trying to say here is';
- to decide how much or how little you have to do before you can submit your paper;
- to write about your sense of audience for this paper, how they will read it;
- to rehearse ways of including uncertainties or limitations without undermining your argument.

Generative writing is perhaps most useful at this stage for keeping you focused on the task in hand.

Using the writers' group

Writers' groups are discussed in more detail in Chapter 8, but at this late stage in your writing process, you can do some of the work of thinking about and rehearsing revisions in discussion. More specifically, at this stage, a writers' group can serve a number of purposes:

- providing general support;
- doing readings of and giving you feedback on your final draft;
- giving an objective assessment of your paper;
- providing hints and tips on effective targeting and writing;
- acknowledging how much you have achieved – motivating you to keep going;
- affirming the professional/personal purposes of writing for academic journals;
- reminding you of your personal writing goals.

Perhaps the most useful purpose of being in a writers' group at this stage, as you are forcing yourself to complete your paper, is helping you to make time for the many final revisions.

The critical friend and the 'tame' subject expert

Recruiting a critical friend, who knows the aims and plan of your paper, and a 'tame' subject expert, who will not rip your paper to shreds (although that can be useful too), can help at this stage. The former can help you maintain focus within a series of drafts; the latter can provoke the sharpness and accuracy needed for your final draft. Both types of reader can help the writing project along if they are aware of what it involves: realizing the planned structure.

This is when you need 'hard' feedback. Although it might not be comfortable, if this is your first paper, it is likely to have weaknesses, mistakes or omissions in the research or the writing or both, and you can safely assume that some of them will not be apparent to you. The purpose of getting hard feedback at this stage is to make sure that you correct errors before submitting your paper. Do not look to journal editors to provide that feedback – they will not appreciate you using them in this way.

Acknowledge that no matter how much time you put into revising, there will be more to do. It might help if you can also acknowledge that you are still, even at this late stage in the writing process, learning about writing for academic journals.

If you feel some of the feedback your subject expert gives you is more savage than 'tame', then you can, of course, go back and discuss this with them. But first check that there is not some purpose to their apparently over-critical comment.

Tell your critical friend what your deadline is – when you want to submit your paper – and, if you can, give him or her a deadline for getting feedback to you.

Finally, remember to acknowledge them – if you and they think that is appropriate – when you submit your article and/or when you resubmit.

Revision processes

Instead of thinking that everything must be revised, to infinity, focus on key points in your text:

- Forecasting: have you written a short summary of your whole argument at the start of your paper, including the paper's purpose and stating how each section moves towards achieving it?
- Signposting: do you refer to your main line of argument throughout your paper, stating, possibly at the end of each section, how that section advances your argument?
- Have you explicitly linked your analysis to your conclusions?
- Signalling: do you have links and transitions – when you change direction – at each stage in your argument?

If this seems like overkill, remember that if you do not provide these signs, readers have to work out how your paper holds together as they go along.

In many cases, of course, they will do this; but if you are asking them to think along the lines that you do, this is likely to raise questions. They will find points to challenge. They will do so anyway, of course, but there is no need to provide further opportunities for critique.

Assume that however well argued your paper is, it is still subject to debate; it is still contested. It will be contested as part of the peer review process (see Chapter 9). This is why you need to make the logic of your argument explicit, anticipate critique and refutation and respond to them in your paper.

Iterative processes

Move from abstract to draft and back to abstract again, as you verify that what you said you would say is, in fact, what you do say in your paper.

Notice how you circle back and forth, making smaller and smaller changes. See this as a process of refining, and spare yourself the misconception that you should have spotted a required revision earlier. Recast what you might previously have seen as errors or lapses in concentration as necessary steps in a thorough academic writing process.

You can take this a step further and establish a systematic iterative sequence:

1 **Abstract**: which words are used to describe the aims/purpose of your paper?
2 **Introduction**: are these same words used here? If you have used different words, should you revise them to match?
3 **Abstract**: does your revision match the terms you use in your abstract? Are you making the same point?

This may seem a bit tortuous – more irritation than iteration – as if you are simply making more work for yourself: one change surely leads to another. There may be some truth in this: you may be adding rather than matching, and, if this is your first journal article, watch out for that, or get your readers to watch out for it. Expect it. Look for it.

This is iteration with a purpose. You will make smaller and smaller changes, as you consolidate and reveal your outline. This is not to say that major changes are forbidden, but to acknowledge that they might not always be as important as you think they are.

Any continuing uncertainty about how your paper will be received by reviewers may lead you, at this late stage as at earlier stages, to feel that you have to add 'extra-strength' arguments, as if that would, in any case, forestall further debate. Be careful with this. Get feedback. Assume there will be debate – say so explicitly in your paper (as appropriate).

Developing a concise style

The first principle of developing a concise style must surely be accepting that you can cut words, sentences and even whole sections of your hard-earned writing.

What to cut

- Some words you know you use have no particular effect and are sometimes just vague, like 'some' and 'sometimes' in this sentence.
- Instead of saying 'some', why not give a number?
- Make it one of your revision tasks to check for these words from now on.
- Make a list of words you know you will regularly have to cut.
- Adjectives and adverbs – are they really making your point or your emphasis clear? Sometimes a sentence is stronger and clearer when an adjective or adverb is cut, like the adverb 'really' in that first sentence – cut it – and do I really need both 'stronger' and 'clearer' in this sentence? And there's another redundant 'really' – cut that too.
- Bullet points? Use one-liners. Use verbs to start them. Prune them so they fit on one line.
- If your word count is over the journal's limit, cut all of these – it is amazing how much is non-essential when you have to cut 1000 words.

You can cut whole sentences, where there is elaboration – is it needed? – or repetition, even if for emphasis. Consider cutting whole paragraphs, particularly in the conceptual/theoretical sections – is there too much of that? Are there too many definitions? Too much going back to first principles? Do you need them all?

Finally, re-read your conclusions – are there too many? Could you sharpen the focus by cutting one or more? However, think carefully before you cut citations of key people in the field, for reasons discussed in an earlier chapter.

Grammar

This is not the place to provide an introduction to grammar, a task that has been performed so well by so many others (Sinclair 2010), but in the context of this chapter, what I referred to earlier as 'the quality question' now takes precedence.

When it comes to grammar, writers appear to take one of two approaches: they either learn the rules of grammar (if they do not already know them) or they ask someone else to correct the grammar for them. To dispel a minority misconception, it should be added that articles should not be sent to journals to be corrected in this way. Journals provide editing and proofreading, but writers should submit correct grammar.

Definitions of parts of speech – noun, verb, preposition, conjunction, transition, adverb, adjective, etc. – are provided in numerous texts, along with the rules of sentence structure (clauses, etc.) and paragraph structure (topic sentences, etc.). Find a text that makes sense to you. Texts that provide examples of the rules of grammar in practice are probably the most useful (e.g. Strunk and White 2000). For definitions of these terms – adjective, adverb, etc. – see the glossary in Sinclair (2010).

Knowing the basics of grammar not only helps you to get it right, it also helps you understand feedback you get from readers. It can be frustrating if you don't, and it will annoy them if you continue to make the same mistakes they pointed out in your previous draft.

In other words, in order to be a productive writer you should at least know the basics of sentence and paragraph structure, comma, quotation marks and apostrophe rules and conjunctions and transitions. At best, you should know how the semi-colon can be used to indicate links within your text – thus demonstrating and/or creating coherence in your writing – and know how to use it correctly.

Understanding the rules of grammar may have an impact on your ability to develop a range of rhetorical choices, and this in turn will affect your ability to make coherent choices from the options. Finally, even if you know the rules, use the software to check grammar.

Polishing

The word 'polishing' implies minor, surface revisions.

- Check the format against the journal's instructions for authors.
- Remove unnecessary words: adverbs and adjectives?
- Check your references, including punctuation marks.
- Check them against references in your paper.
- Check the word count. Note it at the end of your paper.
- Check you have the current editor's contact details.
- Check that you created an account on the journal's website, and that it is still active.
- When submitting electronically, tell the editor which word processing package you used.
- Check to see if they have any other requirements at the point of submission.

These are far from superficial in the sense that editors report, informally, that they will not read papers that have not been submitted in the required format or where references are not in the correct style. With the quantity and quality of submissions arriving on journal websites at this time, they can afford to do so.

This final 'polishing' is not superficial in the sense that it requires your close attention to detail, and that may be difficult if you are approaching your deadline, desperate to send your paper off, or just tired and demoralized:

I am having such trouble this week – it is a sloppy slippery week. My work does not coagulate. It is as unmanageable as a raw egg on the kitchen floor. It makes me crazy. I am really going to try now and I'm afraid that the very force of the trying will take all the life out of the work.
(Steinbeck 1970: 130)

Sometimes you just lose sight of what still needs to be done, of whether any polishing is needed, of whether it is good enough yet for the polishing stage. Ask someone to read your paper and to answer the question, 'Is this ready to submit?'

You may feel that by doing any more revision at all you will be squeezing the life out of your writing – or out of yourself. You may not recognize when you have done enough. Or your paper may cease to make sense or to have value. You are too close to it.

There is no definitive answer to the question of when you know that it is time to stop revising. Feedback is crucial at this point. Do not just let it go and send it off if you have not had feedback on the version you are about to submit.

At this stage, an agreed deadline is useful. It helps the people you ask for final feedback to organize their time to read your final version, and it forces you to submit your paper in spite of a potential array of dissatisfactions. At some point the iterative process, going back and forth between text, outline and abstract until you get them to match, has to stop. The list of polishing steps may help you move on to that point.

The final revision

No more, the text is foolish

King Lear, IV, ii, 37

Read the whole paper, from start to finish, one more time, going through all the sections in order.

Check that it is crystal clear what you are – and are not – claiming to contribute in your paper.

Checklist

- Reveal the outline. Make rhetorical decisions explicit. See if/how your target journal does this.
- See your article as a draft – there are still changes to make.
- Decide when 'enough is enough', so you can submit it to the journal.
- Get people to read your complete draft. Ask someone to comment on content. Ask someone else to comment on coherence. Ask someone else to anticipate critiques. Then make these revisions, if they fit. Don't forget to thank these people for their time and effort. Perhaps offer to give them feedback on their drafts? Have deadlines – when do you need their feedback?
- Revise key points in your paper – abstract, introduction, forecast of the whole argument, summary of the work. Make sure they match up. This 'matching' is the focus for final revisions.

- Before you submit, get feedback on the version you are about to submit.
- Keep up the regular writing.

Further reading

Leonard, D. (2001) *A Woman's Guide to Doctoral Studies*. Buckingham: Open University Press.

Ryan-Flood, R. and Gill, R. (2010) *Secrecy and Silence in the Research Process: Feminist Reflections*. London: Routledge.

Sinclair, C. (2010) *Grammar: A Friendly Approach*, 2nd edn. Maidenhead: Open University Press/McGraw-Hill.

Strunk, W. Jr. and White, E.B. (2000) *The Elements of Style*, 4th edn. New York: Longman.

Sword, H. (2012) *Stylish Academic Writing*. Cambridge, MA: Harvard University Press.

Chapter 8

Dialogue and feedback

A writers' group • Writing retreat • Dialogue • More freewriting and
generative writing • Checklist • Further reading

This chapter argues that writers can use or build a network of contacts – people
engaged in writing or who want to write – meeting regularly to write and for
support and feedback, online, face to face, or both. Evidence of their benefits
is provided in the further reading at the end of this chapter.

New writers can benefit from having access to different audiences at different stages in the writing process. The value of writers' groups and retreats is in
providing a space where you can rehearse your arguments orally among others
who are active in writing and research. The key point is to get as much feedback as you can, but also to engage in dialogue about your work. There is also
value in talking about the writing process, and hearing how others manage it,
and writers' groups and retreats are the only spaces available for this, for many
researchers, academics and professionals.

Such networks of writers may exist already in your institution or in your
department, but if not, you can set one up yourself (Aitchison and Guerin
2014). In what is often a competitive culture, you can build collegiality. In the
midst of fragmented days, it is possible to meet to write. It may seem paradoxical to suggest that writers take individual responsibility for creating collegiality, but for many it is the only option. Otherwise, you have to go it alone, and
that can take much longer. Moreover, changes in writing behaviours suggested
throughout this book will be difficult to sustain without the support of other
writers.

Choose your writing colleagues carefully. If this sounds overly cautious and
perhaps paranoid, then count yourself lucky that you have not yet encountered
colleagues who undermine each other. Just when writing becomes the first
thing you want to do – rather than the last thing you want to do – other people
may start to put up new barriers for you.

Of course, if your department is already collegial, and you are surrounded by mentors and positive peers, then this is not an issue, as long as you are able to get the type of feedback on your writing that actually moves your paper towards publication and helps you develop your understanding of what writing for academic journals involves. In that setting, there may be writing groups already, or people are more likely to be receptive to the idea.

A writers' group

There is no point in waiting for the culture around you to change; you can, instead, create a micro-culture that supports you as a writer. This micro-culture need not only include people in your own area. There may be someone in your institution who can set up and/or run a writers' group of people across the institution but, if not, do it yourself.

While the idea of a writers' group will seem new to some, it is similar to other activities routinely used to support research in some disciplines, such as reading or journal groups. The difference is that in a writers' group you focus on writing for journals (and/or writing a thesis) rather than reading them.

Clearly, there are many ways of using such interactions, but having a source of positive – yet critical – responses to writing-in-progress can help you to keep writing. The knowledge that someone values your writing and sees you as a writer can be motivating. Writers – even new writers – can facilitate each other's writing. 'Buddy' relationships often spring up in this context, and two writers working together can share the load of researching target journals, pool information on editors and combine this knowledge to develop journal-specific writing.

This book draws on writers' experiences, and in this chapter they illustrate how writers' group discussions of writing can normalize barriers to writing and neutralize some of the guilt and 'baggage' that often comes with writing.

Why set up a writers' group? Why not just get on with your writing? Think through the potential purposes of a group, particularly if you are going to be the one to set it up. This need not be a huge task; a 'writers' group' can be as little as two or three people, as long as you all want to write. With such a small number, it should be easier to focus on one main purpose that suits everyone. Frequently, the most motivating purpose is simply making time for writing. Making even a small amount of time for writing – such as two or three hours per month – can be an effective starting point, since it is a small, achievable goal. Trying to make more time, on your own, without support, is more likely to fail.

Define and agree the purpose of your writers' group – virtual and/ or face to face

- Making time for writing
- Getting feedback on writing
- Sharing drafts

- 'Road-testing' ideas
- Building networks
- Developing your research profile
- Discussing writing practices
- Having research dialogues
- Developing productive writing practices
- Sharing information about journals, editors and reviewers

This is not a hierarchy of tasks; nor is any one of these exclusive of the others. It is up to your group to establish its primary purpose. In fact, there is no need to fix one purpose and then try and limit the group's discussions and activities to that; there probably has to be flexibility. Each member of the group may well be looking for something different, and while no group can accommodate everyone's needs, there has to be agreement on the broad purpose, so that it can become a collective purpose. Since the problem of making time for writing – and protecting it once you have made it – seems to be so prevalent for academics and professionals, and not just new ones, this should probably be a kind of 'bottom line': whatever the level of productivity, and it might be slow at first, at least the group will have made real time to write. This is why it is so important that meeting time is not taken up entirely with talking about writing – interesting as that is – a writers' group involves participants doing writing at every meeting.

For some, this will be the only time they have for writing, at least initially. It may be that they have no control over the allocation of their workload, but if they can secure agreement that they can attend a writers' group, they have started to make professional time for writing. Once they are in the group and discussing ways to write, they will find other strategies for making other time slots available for writing. If this leads to outputs, then the case is made that a writers' group has benefit for the institution and the department, not just for the individual.

Some new writers have felt the need to 'cloak' their writing time as 'meetings', because they find time for meetings is easier to justify than time for writing. It is easier to decline another meeting if you already have one in your diary. It is already established practice to have meetings; it is not, therefore, a practice the writer has to 'invent'. This demonstrates how difficult it is to establish time to write and to legitimize it in that person's workplace. It may seem dishonest, since it involves deception. An alternative is to arrange a real meeting with other writers in the writers' group and to establish that this is a regular and legitimate use of your time – your professional time, not just your personal time.

Once you have started writing, every group has an important choice to make: are you going to read, and comment on, each other's writing, or not? It is legitimate and useful to discuss writing practices, including writing goals and progress towards them, and that may be enough for your group – talking about your writing. Or, you could agree to review each other's work:

To improve your writing you don't need advice about what changes to make; you don't need theories of what is good and bad writing. You need movies of people's minds while they read your words. But you need this for a sustained period of time – at least two or three months. And you need to get the experience of not just a couple of people but of at least six or seven. And you need to keep getting it from the same people so that they get better at transmitting their experience and you get better at hearing them.

(Elbow 1998: 77)

'You don't need advice about what changes you need to make' – this is an interesting statement, since it does not represent new writers as novices. New writers already have knowledge of what does and does not work in academic writing. More importantly, Elbow defines the learning that is needed: developing a sense of audience. This important lesson, in Elbow's view, can occur in writers' groups.

Elbow's representation is of a sustained development period, more sustained than a one-day workshop or a couple of discussions with your head of department at review or appraisal time. An initial commitment to meeting to write for two or three months is helpful, since it provides a framework for the first stage of a writers' group. In fact, some people make such speedy progress, in terms of acquiring skills, strategies and confidence, that two or three months may be all that they need.

Elbow's advice is novel, given the reticence that often surrounds academic writing. It makes sense to develop such reading knowledge, so as to be able to provide informed help, informed in the sense of someone else becoming familiar with the developing argument of your paper and aware of what you are trying to achieve in it. There is also the frequently neglected and underdeveloped skill of listening to feedback. This too might take two or three months, if you meet once or twice a month.

As the purpose and membership of your group are established, discuss and agree on specific aims.

Aims of your writers' group participants

- To progress writing projects
- To make real time for writing at work
- To provide a forum for discussing writing
- To provide a framework for the writing process
- To provide support for writing and writers
- To develop and exchange effective strategies
- To complete and submit a paper to a journal/chapter for a book, etc.

Each member of the group should have a specific writing project, and a specific aim to achieve within the first three months. Aims will change over time, and you can review them regularly, briefly. Everyone in the group should know each other's writing goals.

As each group meets for the first time, there may be all sorts of potential talking points on the agenda. At first, some people will want to sound off about how hard writing is, about how unfair it is that there is no support and about the absurdity of writing for or in academic journals. This is an important discussion, but it can only go on for so long. The first development phase for your group may be moving past this point. If you have one or more of these voices in your group, you, or someone, are going to have to facilitate a 'moving on' discussion. Simply talking about these problems is not the only way to resolve them; you can also write about writing problems and solutions. However, you can also write about potential topics for articles at this stage, in ways described in Chapter 4.

The very plurality of the group can, of course, be a strength, even if it takes some getting used to. Naturally, as an academic or professional, you want to develop the area you are interested in, but your development can be accelerated by interactions. Their unpredictability can be both refreshing and frustrating.

There may be dominant characters in your group. That can be a strength or a weakness, depending on how you all manage each other. There may be too many agendas running. There may be uncertainty about the writers' group as a mechanism to increase productivity. There may be resistance to the idea of increasing 'productivity'. There may be confusion about what you are actually meeting for or about what useful purpose the group is likely to serve. You may lose sight of what you set out to do and you may not realize that you are already beginning to achieve your appropriately modest goals. The answer is always to focus on the goal: the group meets to write. Individuals set their specific goals.

Shared goals in the group

- We all want to publish in academic journals.
- We can give each other feedback on writing practices.
- Our writers' group will make time for writing during the working week.
- We can support each other in our writing.
- We can develop more productive writing habits in this group.

It is easy to over-complicate the writers' group. Focus on its main function of prioritizing writing. Many say that it is the group process that helped them to hold on to the time slots they arranged for writing. You therefore all have to bring group work skills to this initiative and you have to be comfortable with others in your group fairly early on. If you have hand-picked your own group – not a bad idea – you should be off to a strong start in this respect. However, remember that you are all in this for yourselves, and participants – not the groups – are responsible for their progress.

If the group does not work, for any reason, or if there is not enough writing going on, change. Start again. Find people you can write with. Write with people from other departments. You may worry that you cannot give each other feedback on writing, but perhaps you can. You can also share your experiences of writing and provide support to keep each other going. Try both types of group. Set up or join more than one group. Set up a group with students. Prompt them to set up a group. There is plenty of advice on how they can do this and evidence that it is useful (Aitchison and Guerin 2014). When I researched what people did in writers' groups, asking about when and where they met, how they ran them, etc., I found that it did not matter where or when they met, or which disciplines members of the group worked in; what mattered most to them was writing with people who bought into this model (Murray 2014).

Activities at writers' group meetings

- Setting goals for writing
- Discussing writing goals
- Doing writing: writing about writing or writing your paper
- Monitoring each other's progress towards the goals

For the structure of your group's meetings, you can opt for a loose or tight set-up, but the key elements are (brief) discussion and (mostly) writing, and for these you can use activities described in earlier chapters.

'Presenteeism' – the pressure to simply be present and visible in your department – can be a deterrent to participating in writers' groups, but as long as your head of department has not actually said you must be in the department at all times you have the option of writing elsewhere.

You cannot allow others' reactions to shape your writing. There have even been situations where the head of department has agreed to writing time away from the department, as long as no one else knows about it. This is, by design or otherwise, likely to create division between you and your colleagues – which may, of course, be the intention – but if it is your only option, and if it gives you what you want – time to write – then you might want to jump at it. You are never going to be able to keep everyone happy, nor are you responsible if everyone is unhappy because you are writing. As long as you achieve the necessary outputs, this is good for the institution and the department. This may be yet another motivation for working with writers in other departments.

There are pros and cons to working across disciplinary boundaries. Some of the pros are: (1) you are less likely to get bogged down in discussing the content of a paper; (2) you can concentrate on the flow of each other's argument, spotting gaps or inconsistencies; and (3) you leave behind the 'baggage' of the department. Some of the cons are: (1) you will not get expert feedback on the content of your paper; (2) this may create uncertainty that you feel you cannot resolve and that, in turn, may inhibit your writing; and (3) you may not be able to 'road-test' your idea sufficiently at an early stage.

For new writers, the pros should outweigh the cons for one main reason: the group will help you get started and keep going. It is, of course, important to have input from people who have published in your field and you will, of course, be hugely grateful if you can find someone who is prepared to give up their time to give you feedback on your paper. But it is equally important to get feedback along the way, as you draft your paper, that is not too critical and focuses on developing your paper's argument. If that sounds too 'soft' – or even unwise – combine the two.

You may not be looking for 'profound insights about' yourself, and since the learning that people do in writers' groups has not been evaluated, you may not be persuaded that it actually occurs as claimed. However, there is more to writing well, at the top of your profession, than grammar and punctuation. It is difficult to disentangle thinking and writing abilities; they may develop in tandem. For example, as you improve your skills of articulating your ideas to others, you may find that this improves your ability to articulate your ideas to yourself, that is, your thinking.

Finally, perhaps the greatest reported benefit of attending writers' group meetings is the shift from arriving at the meeting 'in a frenzy', but leaving 'on a high'. Some people turn up feeling very negative about their writing, and sometimes about academic or professional life in general. Yet they leave writing meetings with a sense of satisfaction at having, in spite of everything, progressed their writing projects. This facility for turning around what can be very negative feelings is perhaps one of the healthiest rationales for writers' groups.

Writing retreat

One way to kick-start a writers' group is to have a writing retreat, taking writers away from their workplaces. Of course, there may be permissions to seek in order to do this, and even when you do have permission, there will be those who think you are mowing the lawn, putting up shelves, going to the gym, watching daytime TV or whatever it is that these people think when they cannot actually see you in the workplace, while they are slaving away on the treadmill.

A writing retreat is an effective way of creating time for writing. While you might think that getting completely away to do nothing but write is a luxury that you simply cannot afford, you can adapt the retreat mode to your environment. The idea is to protect some time – however short – for nothing but writing – and talking about your writing with others who are prepared to do so too.

One of the potential benefits is that in a retreat environment you can make swift changes to your writing behaviours. A vast literature tells us that changing behaviour takes a long time, that there are numerous 'steps' to follow to achieve long-term change and that we need social support to make it stick. Clearly, there is so much evidence across such a wide range of human behaviour that we would not want to challenge this. Yet, when you take people out of their work environments and make writing the only task, change comes quickly.

The difficulty is when you go back to your work environment: if there is no protected time there for writing, the momentum can run into the sand. In this instance, you can adapt features of the away-from-work retreat to your workplace, with short 'meetings' to write, ideally with a colleague or two. If it is not possible to bringing the retreat strategy into your office, for example, find another place where you can. In other words, create mini-retreats in a variety of places and at different times.

There are several modes of retreat, each suited to different goals and each making different demands on your resources: the week-long retreat, the two-day mini-retreat, the 'day away' and the one-hour retreat meeting. They all share the same key features:

- Get away from your workplace and, if you have more than a day, make it residential.
- Unplug from distractions, email, phone, other responsibilities.
- Focus on your writing and actually write.
- Set a specific goal for the time slot you actually have.

The key is to get away from the workplace, since many find that they can do no writing whatsoever there. A few people do find it possible to write in their offices, as long as they can quit email, turn on the answering machine and have an office where they can shut the door, put up a notice saying 'Meeting in progress – do not disturb' and know that they will not be interrupted.

Some people find that they can 'retreat' to write at home; but others find it impossible, as they are distracted by tasks that need to be done there, or there are potential interruptions there too. Where you go to retreat to write is a personal choice, and if you go with someone else, or several others, you have to find a space that suits you all or, more realistically, that suits most of you most of the time.

The longest of these modes, the complete retreat, involves a week off campus. This can be organized with a self-selecting group from work, and/or from other workplaces, perhaps by those who do staff development or training at your institution. One of the best examples of this mode has been run for several years at the University of Limerick (Ireland) (Moore 2003). In that model, briefing sessions before the retreat established the retreat concept, prompted participants to prepare and focus and firmed up commitment to the full week.

The programme for the week's retreat starts with an orientation session on the first night, followed by social time over dinner. Every morning participants attend 'springboard' sessions for the first hour each morning, if they wish, and then have the rest of the day, from 10.30 am until 8 pm, to write. These sessions help participants to get started, set goals for the day's writing and, after the first day, take stock of their progress since the previous day. Private writing, freewriting and pair-share discussions seem to work well to trigger focused writing during these sessions. Some of the strategies for regular writing are new to many participants, and therefore time is allocated for discussions of the strategies themselves, their immediate impact and their long-term use. Other subjects covered in brief presentations include finding your voice, responding to reviewers' feedback and behaviour change. The writers can also have discussions with each other in the course of the day, and one-to-one discussions with a reader in residence, who reads and comments on drafts.

A strength of this model is that participants have plenty of time and space to write. The downside is that they have to be ready to write right away. You might be thinking that having so much time and space would take the pressure off, and that does seem to happen to begin with. By the middle of the week, however, participants begin to feel that they should have achieved much more than they have, and often feel under even more pressure to produce precisely because they have so much uninterrupted time. Even though there is no 'account' taken of people's written output at the end of the retreat, departments who contribute to the cost of participation will no doubt want to see a 'return' for their money in terms of publications or other outputs. This is yet another reason to set explicit goals and let others know what they are. Almost all participants are highly productive during this week, achieving their goals and, often, making progress towards other goals and defining new goals for future outputs.

There are additional challenges for writers with families, particularly if they have young children. Some single parents find it a struggle to get childcare. Anyone with a caring role might simply find that this is not a model that works for them, in spite of its benefits, but there have been participants with these responsibilities on previous retreats.

Participants' evaluations show that this form of writing retreat is not only a productive but also a very positive experience, but there is always the 'return to reality' factor: will they be able to continue to do any writing at all when they return to their departments, where their first task will be to catch up with everything they left behind in order to attend the retreat? This is such an important question that it is directly addressed as part of the retreat experience, on the last day. This is where the writers' group comes in, since it is one way of sustaining the impact of a retreat over the longer term and transferring some of its features to work environments.

Another approach is the Writing Meeting, developed for precisely this moment: to support the transition from writing retreat back to work (Murray and Thow 2015).

A retreat of this type obviously comes with a cost; in fact, it can be quite expensive to run, although the argument can be made that the return to your institution – in terms of research culture and outputs – and benefits to users is worth the investment. It is possible to include external participants and to use their fees to subsidize internal participants. This might be beyond your remit, but you might suggest this strategy to someone who can make it happen. You may have to push for this, or find someone who is prepared to do so, since even when funding has been secured, it is not always possible to find someone who is prepared to take on this new and substantial task.

You might also need support, at least initially: the person who does the 'springboard' sessions probably has to be someone who is an enabler, who knows a bit about writing and is not too focused on any one discipline to the exclusion of others. This is someone who can look across the disciplines and stimulate discussion of writing across disciplinary boundaries. They can use activities described in this book for the important 'getting started' and 'warm-up' writing sessions.

If a week-long retreat is not feasible, there are other shorter modes of retreat: the two-day mini-retreat, the 'day away' or, at the very least, the one-hour retreat meeting.

The two-day retreat, whether residential or not, allows you to focus on your writing without worrying about the work you left behind. Unlike the week-long retreat, which is ideally held far enough away from campus that participants are not able to get home, the two-day retreat allows participants to meet domestic responsibilities. It is also cheaper. Because time is short, it is probably as well to include only those who have specific papers or other projects in mind.

The programme should be more structured than the week-long model. The writing day is timetabled with a series of writing timeslots.

If your aim is to build, or build on, long-term writing relationships and on-going research discussions, or if participants are all working on the same funding proposal or all writing chapters for an edited book, for example, you can intersperse writing time with discussion. The proportion of writing time to other activities can be as much as one third; that is, 20 minutes in any one hour can be spent writing. Using or developing a detailed outline is a key task for the second half of the first day, since that drives focused writing on day two.

Some participants may respond that they have not yet chosen their topic, but this should be the work of the first half of the first day; until the topic has been fixed, it is difficult to make progress in writing. Of course, the topic can be selected and focused through writing, and writing tasks that do this could therefore feature in the first half of day one.

The retreat programme brings together all the strategies described in this book:

Two-day retreat

Day 1	Morning	Programme	Writing prompt and 'sandwich'
		Choosing topic	Freewriting
		Developing topic	Generative writing
		Discussion	
		Focusing topic	
		Discussion	
	Afternoon	Developing abstract	Brown's 8 questions

		Detailed outline	'Level 3' outlining
		Discussion	
		Writing	
Day 2	**Morning**	Targeting a journal	Discussing extracts from published papers
		Reasons for rejection	
		Writing prompts	Using the outline
		Writing	
		Discussion	
	Afternoon	Writing	Writers' group
		Discussion	
		Planning	
		Goal setting	

You can vary the order of these activities. For example, it might make more sense, in some groups, to start a retreat with 'targeting a journal', rather than leaving it until day two. It depends on the group: what stage are they at? Will they find the analysis of published examples intimidating if it comes first? Do they already have topics to write about, such as conference presentations to convert into publications? Are some of them writing a thesis, with publications a secondary goal? As long as both text-generating and structuring strategies are in the programme, as long as there is time for both writing and discussion, and as long as the participants are willing to write there and then, it will work.

A further alternative is the quick retreat: a day away. There is more of a tradition of departmental away days at some institutions, but the one-day retreat for writing might be a new format, and a new case might have to be made for it. It may be that only some members of the department want to participate, and it is probably as well to establish who wants to and to work with them. Others will find their own ways to write.

Keeping it in the department is not the only way to run a one-day retreat. Mixed groups can work just as well, sometimes better. It could be more difficult to organize, you might think, but if all the writers are self-selecting, and you start with the people you already know, and if they are all keen to write, it is easier than you think.

The value of the one-day retreat is that you do not have to drop everything else for more than a day. The value of the departmental retreat is that you establish a culture of writing in the department; the department has acknowledged that writing is sufficiently important to attract dedicated time.

The format alternates writing and discussion: writing for different periods of time – 5, 20, 30 and 60 minutes at a time – discussing in pairs and in the whole group. Discussion provides peer review, support and encouragement, as required. The specific writing activities maintain focus while prompting structured development of the paper. All of these techniques are described in this book.

One-day retreat

Programme			
Morning	Decide on topic & type of writing	*Write to prompt*	10 mins
		Writing sandwich	10 mins
	Set goals for the day in pairs		20 mins
	Introduce Brown's 8 questions		
	Draft abstract/summary	*Brown's 8 questions*	20 mins
	Break		15 mins
	Discussion in pairs		15 mins
	Writing		30 mins
Afternoon	Outlining/writing to outline		30 mins
		Whole group	
	Peer review discussion		30 mins
	Break		15 mins
		In pairs	
	Writing		60 mins
	Long & short term goals		20 mins

If the day has been even partially successful, you can consider when you want to repeat it: could there be regular writing days? Could there be one per month? Or one per year, always in the same month? Could it be held in the department? As with other interventions described in this chapter, such days might constitute some people's only writing time.

Alternatively, you can dedicate almost all the time at retreat to writing. The model of retreat described above – combining workshops and solitary writing time in separate rooms – relies mainly on individual motivation, and this 'solitary confinement' model does have benefits on motivation and outputs (Moore 2003). However, there are other models: the 'typing pool' model – brief discussions and mostly writing, all in the same room – also has benefits in terms of improving writing practices and increasing outputs (Murray and Newton 2009; MacLeod *et al.* 2012).

Structured writing retreat programme

Day 1	5–5.30	Introductions
		Writing warm-up
	5.30–6.30	**Writing**
Day 2	9.15–9.30	Goal-setting
	9.30–11.00	**Writing**
	11.00–11.30	Break
	11.30–12.30	**Writing**
	12.30–2.00	Lunch
	2–3.30	**Writing**
	3.30–4.00	Break
	4.00–5.30	**Writing**
Day 3	9.15–9.30	Goal-setting
	9.30–11.00	**Writing**
	11.00–11.30	Break
	11.30–12.30	**Writing**
	12.30–2.00	Lunch
	2.00–3.30	**Writing**
	3.30–4.00	Break
	4.00–5.00	Taking stock, setting new goals

Writing retreats and writers' groups create new structures that support writing, establish collegial relationships and bring writing – and discussion of writing – into the working day. Because becoming a regular writer, to the standard required, takes considerable time and effort, it makes sense to have developmental – rather than remedial – activities in place, but many find that they continue with these approaches, in different combinations, for many years because they are so productive in these groupings.

This programme has changed since I first created it: there is now a longer lunch break, with time to be active, for those who want to be, and time to eat lunch. This new structure follows guidelines on the proven risks of sitting for extended periods. As already stated, if you read one piece of research on this, make it Dunstan *et al.* (2010). Since 2010, there has been abundant research not only into the risks of sedentary behaviours – as when we are writing – but also explaining the mechanisms for the life-limiting side-effects (Thow 2015). This is why there is no longer a two-hour session of writing in this programme. In addition, writing retreats can, and should, attend to all health and wellbeing factors (Thow *et al.* 2013). It's not just about 'productivity'; because writing retreats involve intensive periods of concentration and writing, while sitting, it is also about finding healthy ways to write.

How much time you put into making the case for such interventions, or getting someone else to take up the case, is up to you. But you do not need a full-blown institutionally funded system to initiate some of the more small-scale versions of them. How exactly you begin to set it all up is simply to get together a few colleagues and run the first and all subsequent sessions with a fairly loose agenda. The following starter prompt can be used to start numerous meetings, not just the first one:

Writing 'warm-up'

1 Warm-up for writing (five minutes, in sentences, private writing) on the subject:
   What writing have you done for your writing project, and what do you want to do?
   or
   What part of your paper/outline are you going to write today?
2 Writing on your chosen topic (20–30 minutes, private or for peer review)
3 Discussion of writing done, progress made and/or exchange of papers for review

---

The structured writing retreat helps participants take stock and look forward, using their goal-setting skills. While stopping a discussion and immediately starting to write is unusual – it's not how we normally work – it does create writing time.

Defer the 'quality question' for the moment. If you are writing to your outline, which you should be as soon as possible, the goal is not to produce 'quality' academic writing right away, but to generate a draft. It can be useful to keep telling each other that.

I am not sure that every writers' group has to spend time and energy thrashing out its aims or objectives before participants start writing. I am not even convinced that you really need an agenda, in the normal sense of the word. It seems to me that you can focus the whole session – 60 or 90 minutes – on writing and talking about the writing you have done, are about to do and have just done. If this seems simplistic, I should add that this structure seems to work quite well with diverse groups, and on that basis it is worth trying. In the course of trying, you will quickly learn what works and what does not: going round the group asking, 'Have we completed the tasks we set ourselves at our previous meeting?', may not be conducive to sharing and collegial discussion. Instead, taking stock may work better in pairs, and it will save time. But we all learn from our mistakes. If you find something does not work, or seems to work against writing and sharing, then you can all agree not to do that again.

Dialogue

Dialogue – meaning genuine, engaged, two-way discussion of writing, in which you discuss the content of your article with someone who has read your writing and doing the same for them – has real value.

Online or face to face, it can help you to clarify a point in your argument; in fact, it can persuade you to clarify a point that you thought you had already stated sufficiently clearly. Thanks to the response of a real reader you see your writing in a new light. You can even begin to write in a more positively dialogic way, taking more account of the different perspectives in current debates in your area. You may end up worrying less about what your intended readers might think and more immediately getting on with the task of addressing their needs and interests.

You can use dialogue with peers to grow your sense of audience: by addressing real audiences' responses to your writing. In a writers' group you can develop a sense of where your writing needs revision. If you do this regularly and if your discussion goes into some depth, you can develop your skills of written argument and, sometimes, be prompted to develop alternative lines of argument. You can also become much more sensitized to the value – rather than feeling that you are going through the motions – of making a strong case for your work, perhaps stronger than you thought you needed to. You can become much more confident and skilled in addressing refutations and including them in your writing. This helps you with the important task of writing debates into your paper.

The nature of such discussions, the potential for instant feedback and the opportunity immediately to engage with feedback mean that you cannot just note the feedback, thank your reader and head off to mull it over on your own. Although that is an option, you have an opportunity to go into more depth and to rehearse one or two options for revising what you have written. If the writing your reader was looking at was, in any case, a rough draft, then this is extremely valuable revision time: you can get some revision done, or at least started, immediately. Leaving it until later may mean that the clarity, purpose and usefulness of your reader's comments may be less clear or may have evaporated altogether. It also wastes time and energy if you have to take time to recall what your readers said, try to place their comments in your draft and reconnect with them to rehearse your revisions. In virtual or face-to-face writers' groups and retreats, these activities occur regularly, although you should be careful to privilege writing time, some of the time – or, arguably most of the time in your group. This is what seems to make them so valuable – privileging writing over everything else.

Dialogue is, therefore, a part of writing. But for this to occur, there has to be both talking and writing time, so that you can capture some of the revisions you know you have to make, some that your reader suggests and other points that occur to you in the course of the discussion.

More freewriting and generative writing

The stakes are higher at this stage in the writing process, as you are now committed to delivering a certain line of argument, having moved well beyond the exploratory stage, the planning stage and even the research stage. The stakes are also higher because you have contacted journal editors, and one of them is now, if not exactly 'waiting' for your paper, at least expecting it to arrive some time soon.

Yet there is still value and purpose in low-stakes writing. The original uses of these activities, such as using freewriting as a warm-up for academic writing, are still there, but they may have different purposes at this time, or you may use them in different ways. This is not to say that you should move on from the earlier uses; quite the reverse. The writing habit is always supported by low-stakes writing. Both high- and low-stakes writing can run in tandem from now on.

Continuing uses of freewriting and generative writing

- To work out your responses to your readers' feedback
- To work out a step in your argument that is still not clear
- To clarify a complex section in your argument that is not yet clear
- To fill a gap in your argument that has just been pointed out
- To begin to articulate why you disagree with some of the feedback

---

As with the uses of freewriting suggested in previous chapters, deferring the 'quality question' can help you to focus on developing your point. The aim is to work through your writing problem *in writing*. The result may be that you clarify your thinking or that you produce writing you can insert – as it is or with some revision – into your paper, with one eye on the total word length, in relation to your target journal's maximum.

A missing step between you choosing one of the purposes in the above box and generating text might be that you do not yet have a prompt. You could, for example, use a question posed by your reader as a prompt for your writing. Or you could use the prompt, 'What I am trying to say here is' to start your writing. You can then compare it with the text that you have already written to see if there are any major or minor differences, any sentences or fragments that will clarify your point in your paper.

Freewriting, generative writing and writing to prompts can, therefore, still be useful at this late stage in the writing process. This is when you can see the range of writing strategies covered in this book combining to make up your productive academic writing practice.

Checklist

- Working with a writing 'buddy' or writers' group can help you make time to write.
- Don't worry if your writing group is only two or three people – as long as you are writing, it works.
- Get to a writing retreat to see for yourself how productive it can be.
- Never sit for more than an hour.
- Try different types of retreat: 'solitary confinement', 'typing pool' or hybrid.
- If you can't go to a writing retreat, bring features of retreat into your workplace.
- Use the structured retreat programme to schedule writing slots in any place.
- Keep up the regular scribbling, using it to solve writing problems, as required.

Further reading

Aitchison, C. and Guerin, C. (eds) (2014) *Writing Groups for Doctoral Students and Beyond: Innovations in Practice and Theory.* London: Routledge.

Elbow, P. and Sorcinelli, M.D. (2006) The faculty writing place: a room of our own, *Change*, November/December: 17–22.

Grant, B. (2006) Writing in the company of other women: exceeding the boundaries, *Studies in Higher Education*, 31(4): 483–95.

MacLeod, I., Steckley, L. and Murray, R. (2012) Time is not enough: promoting strategic engagement with writing for publication, *Studies in Higher Education*, 37(5): 641–54. DOI: 10.1080/03075079.2010.527934.

Moore, S. (2003) Writers' retreats for academics: exploring and increasing the motivation to write, *Journal of Further and Higher Education*, 27(3): 333–42.

Moore, S., Murphy, M. and Murray, R. (2010) Increasing academic output and supporting equality of career opportunity in universities: can writers' retreats play a role?, *Journal of Faculty Development*, 24(3): 21–30.

Murray, R. (2012) Developing a community of research practice, *British Educational Research Journal*, 38(5): 783–800. DOI: 10.1080/01411926.2011.583635.

Murray, R. (2013) It's not a hobby: reconceptualizing the place of writing in academic work, *Higher Education*, 66(1): 79–91. DOI: 10:1007/s10734–012–9591–7.

Murray, R. and Cunningham, E. (2011) Managing researcher development: 'Drastic transition'?, *Studies in Higher Education*, 36(7): 831–45. DOI: 10.1080/03075079.2010. 482204.

Murray, R. and Newton, M. (2009) Writing retreat as structured intervention: margin or mainstream?, *Higher Education Research and Development*, 28(5): 527–39.

Murray, R., Steckley, L. and MacLeod, I. (2012) Research leadership in writing for publication: a theoretical framework, *British Educational Research Journal*, 38(5): 765–81. DOI: 10.1080/01411926.2011.580049.

Chapter  9

Responding to reviewers' feedback

The 'grim reader' • Examples of reviewers' comments • Destructive feedback • What to do with hostile reviews • Contradictory comments • Rejection • Resubmission • Responding to feedback from editors and reviewers • Acceptance • Proofs • Offprints • Checklist • Further reading

It would be easier for them to reject your paper outright.

(Day 1996: 120)

Start by assuming that you're fully entitled to applause if you have: . . .

• Gotten bad reviews with good lines in them.

(Appelbaum 1998: 241)

Even famous novelists have had their share of bad reviews: '*Catch-22* has much passion, comic and fervent', said *The New York Times*, 'but it gasps for want of craft and sensibility' (Appelbaum 1998: 241). You should expect to get some bad reviews, and there is no reason, when you think about it, that you should not learn something from some of them.

This chapter covers the critical final step in writing a paper: what to do when your paper is returned for revision. Reasons for rejection are covered first: anecdotally, we are told that the most common reason given is that the paper was sent to the wrong journal, although this may just be the editor's way of saying your paper has not met the journal's standard in some way, without taking the time to tell you why.

Insights into why papers are rejected are provided by Greenhalgh (2019); and the argument is made that inadequate targeting might be a more common problem than you might think. Targeting a journal is not, it seems, simply a matter of common sense. It seems that people frequently get it wrong, which is why targeting was covered early in this book (Chapter 2).

However, it may be that your paper has not been rejected, and that you have revisions to do – celebrate! A non-rejection is, these days, a cause for celebration. A process for working through your reviewers' comments is described in this chapter, along with discussion of examples of reviewers' feedback. A strategy for focusing on what revision actions to take is provided, along with guidance on how to write your report on how you responded to reviewers' feedback.

If your paper was rejected, and if you received feedback, keep working on it, since it is much worse when a paper goes missing for months or more, or when there is rejection without feedback.

This chapter should help you not only to address reviewers' comments in a systematic way but also to anticipate such comments before you submit your article to a journal, and this will help you strengthen your article.

The 'grim reader'

Be courteous throughout. There is no need to be superior, sarcastic or to show off. Remember the paper that you are refereeing might have been written by a postgraduate, and it could be a first attempt at publication.

Avoid criticizing the paper because it does not do what you might have done. Judge it on its own merits.

Explain any criticisms that you make. There must always be a reason for them. This will help the author(s) to respond to any criticisms (or not) when they are resubmitting.

(Hartley 2008: 154–5)

This selection from a list of pointers for journal article reviewers shows sympathy for both writer, especially new writer, and reviewer. This type of material may be provided by journals to reviewers, but in some cases there is no such guidance. It is often assumed that reviewers will be 'courteous', professional, fair and specific in their criticisms of papers.

When you were writing your paper you naturally had a sense of your reader in mind. In practice, that imagined reader may be quite different from the actual readers – the reviewers. Reviewers do generally give papers a thorough critique. This may well be the toughest critique you will ever receive on your writing (until you submit your next paper for publication).

Sometimes one or more reviewers appear to be unnecessarily 'grim'; they seem to take too hard a line, to miss points you felt you had made thoroughly in your paper or to want you to write a completely different paper. After all the work that you have put in to get to this point, you feel that you simply cannot be bothered to revise it again. This is a mistake. If the editor invites you to resubmit, get on with the revisions right away, as you have a good chance of being published if you can respond positively to the reviewers' comments. There are no guarantees of publication even at this stage, but you have a good chance if you can make the revisions they are looking for.

Reading reviewers' feedback on your writing is not always fun. Sometimes the feedback seems plain wrong. But you can always learn from it – perhaps an overstatement to say 'always', but when you look at the paper in its published form, you will probably, from that secure position, be more able to admit that, yes, the reviewers' comments did improve your paper. If you never got any negative feedback, or if you never had to do any revisions, how would you learn? – is one way of looking at it. It can almost be said that you should expect to have revisions to do. For whatever reason, it's the norm.

Expect there to be differences of opinion among or between reviewers; this is not that unusual in many disciplines. Expect reviewers to write as if they did not see the coherence of your argument, the clarity of your conceptual framework or the contribution your evidence makes.

Expect them to take issue with your literature review and, particularly, with your definition of the 'problem' you set out to solve in your work. This can be a sensitive area: in your work, you were by definition critiquing a situation, perhaps even people who worked in that context, perhaps also people who had researched it before you, including, perhaps, established authorities in the field. The statement of the research problem at the start of your paper, however carefully you crafted it, is itself open to debate and may draw fire.

Sometimes it is just one word that presses a reviewer's button. You may have been just too challenging or raised a challenge that the reviewer was not comfortable with, or in terms that he or she would not use. Modulating an assertion by beginning with the words 'It could be argued that' may dampen the dramatic effect that such statements can have on reviewers. You can also align yourself with an authority in the field or, even better, quote an established figure in the field whose critique of the way things are is even stronger than yours. This will make yours seem moderate by comparison.

This is not to say that you have to comb through every single word of your paper looking for triggers that have set the reviewer off, but bear in mind that reviewers will bring not only a different perspective, but also, potentially, a different vocabulary and a different sense of what constitutes publishable work than you have, particularly if this is your first paper. Their feedback will tell you a lot about where they are coming from, much of which you cannot anticipate.

Examples of reviewers' comments

The purpose of this section is to show how bad reviews can be. My intention is to take the shock – though perhaps not the sting – out of negative, verging on hostile, reviews you might receive. While you may never receive hostile reviews, the aim is to walk you through a process for dealing with them, so that they don't stop you writing or revising and resubmitting.

The following two reviews of an article are reproduced here, word for word as I received them, including Reviewer 1's emphasis in underlining. This was a co-authored paper, although I was singled out by Reviewer 1 by name. Reviewer 2 wrote in French, but even if you don't know French, you can see the positive words, which I have underlined. The paper has since been published, with revisions.

Reviewers' comments

Reviewer 1

My impression on the paper by Dr R. Murray entitled [title] is _very negative_. A short, 2-printed-pages statement would be useful as an invitation for discussion. The authors make many superficial statements, often clearly not based on any direct experience of curricular developments.

I am convinced that our Journal of [title] would not benefit from such a lengthy manuscript whose content is very limited.

Reviewer 2 [with key words underlined]

Cet article aborde la question de l'interactivité dans l'enseignement. C'est un problème important et l'exposé est très intéressant.

Même si on n'y trouve pas d'éléments nouveaux ni de recette miracle, il me semble que le problème est bien posé et les considerations énumerées me semblent constituer un bon point de la situation.

Ainsi par exemple, je trouve que pour organiser un débat sur la question, la lecture préalable de ce texte constituerait un excéllent point de départ et éviterait de recommencer une analyse classique des avantages, inconvenients et difficultés de l'enseignement interactif.

J'ai toutefois quelques interrogations (concernant plutôt la forme): . . .

Moyennant ces quelques remarques, je crois que, par sa bonne synthèse d'une importante problèmatique, cet article mériterait une publication dans l'[title of journal]

The key message we take from reviewer 1 has to be those two words 'very negative'. By contrast, while Reviewer 1 has rejected the paper, Reviewer 2 says it should be published.

When I show these two reviews to new writers, their first reaction is shock at the first review – 'that must have hurt' – well, yes, it did – and surprise at the many differences between the two reviews, particularly in their opposing judgements of the suitability of this article in that journal.

New writers make a number of interesting observations:

1 The reviews are contradictory.
2 The first one doesn't really say what is wrong with the paper and what you can do about it.
3 This is unprofessional. It's just too destructive. Unnecessarily so.

My co-author and I made similar observations, when these reviews arrived, but we were reassured by the editor's letter, which helped us to put the reviews in perspective. Above all, the editor decided this was not a rejection.

Editor's letter

Two experts on the Editorial Board of [*journal title*] examined your paper . . .
One is very opposed to the publication of your paper in its present form.
Another considers your paper interesting but suggests a re-writing of the document. You will find, attached, their comments. . . . Here are the most important points to take into account:

- Introduce the problem of interactivity within the title of the paper;
- Avoid superficial statements not consolidated by results;
- Reduce the length of the paper, limiting your text to the main points;
- Avoid, in the body of the text, the use of dialogue;
- Avoid also the use of 'I' if the paper is written by more than one author.

You will understand the need of such rewriting of your paper and I am pleased to invite you to submit your new document as soon as possible.

Yet, this letter comes as a surprise to new writers: how can the editor have decided to go ahead with the paper after even one hostile review? This example is included here because, in many fields, reviews are often as contradictory as this.

How should the authors reply to the editor? We began with the words 'thank you'. We kept the email short, in order to save the editor time and effort, and because we were not going to say much at this time, apart from signalling the crucial point that we intended to resubmit:

Authors' reply to the editor

Thank you for your feedback on our paper [title] which we found very useful. As suggested, we will change the title.
We are revising the paper now and will resubmit later this month, or, at the latest, early next month. If there is a particular deadline you would like us to meet, can you let me know now?

'Thank you' is a positive start to our letter/email. What else were we saying in this reply? We signalled that we intended to be responsive to the critique by our immediate action on one of the reviewers' suggestions, changing the title.

We tell the editor our deadline, in order to motivate us to get the revisions done by then. Without a deadline, or if we were the only ones who knew when it was, revisions would likely fall to the end of a long list of priorities. By inviting the editor to give us a deadline, we were trying to be accommodating and prompting the editor to think about which issue of the journal we will be published in. We then did the revisions and resubmitted.

What we learned from this experience and, it must be said, from these reviewers' comments, is that we had overstated our critique of the research problem. While we provided evidence of our contribution, we had not evidenced our critique. We realized that this problem was located in one section, so we cut it. This was another important lesson: do not keep every word, or even every section.

There are, therefore, potential lessons for writers in reviewers' feedback. The challenge is to work your way through what can seem harsh, even overstated, critiques, from reviewers who seem to be implying – and sometimes stating – that the author does not know what he or she is writing about. Some reviewers appear to want to undermine – rather than assist – writers, while others take a more 'instructional' approach, though sometimes in a dogmatic tone:

Reviewer 1

Problem Number 8
Location – Page/Para: 21, last paragraph
The focus of the paper is on the quality assessment of research. The final paragraph makes no reference to research. It reflects an issue of the paper warranting attention: this initial focus is on quality, but as one moves through the paper the focus increasingly moves toward assessment and evaluation. They are similar; quality is achieved through assessment and evaluation. But the paper is on research quality. **Keep to that topic.**

Reviewer 2

The general case made in this paper is clearly stated and given quite good general support both from the literature cited and from arguments within the paper. However, I have several serious reservations, which can be summarised as follows:

1 I think that the paper reveals **a lack of comprehension** about TQM and furthermore it **merely asserts** its central influence in UK Higher Education **without citing evidence**. The result is that some of its criticisms are not necessarily aimed at the most appropriate target.
2 A number of assertions are made, especially in the central part of the paper, **without adequate referencing or supporting evidence.**
3 The recommendations in the final part of the paper are **rather sketchy** and **lacking in both detail and justification.**

The reference to 'several serious reservations' rings alarm bells, but, again, as long as the paper was not actually rejected, this meant that there was work to be done and a chance of publication.

We could critique the critiques: there are, of course, certain principles in any field that we can legitimately 'merely assert', since they are not open to question, or, you may have judged, not as open to debate as other statements in your paper. Yet, clearly, the resubmission would distinguish more carefully and perhaps explicitly between what can and cannot be merely asserted. Comment number 2 makes this point again, locating the flaw more precisely in the paper. Comment number 3 may be making the point a third time, though it would be worth thinking about this carefully.

As for the comment about recommendations: is it not the nature of recommendations to be 'sketchy'? Yet, further development was required in this case. This comment is a reminder that even conclusions should be mini-arguments, with the case made for them, and the link between evidence and conclusions made clear: what is it that you can – and cannot – evidence?

By contrast, some reviewers can be positive, even encouraging:

The encouraging review

Thank you for asking me to review this paper. This a **comprehensive and well-written** paper about the use of medical humanities in occupational therapy. While **I enjoyed reading it**, I am not sure it is ready for publication as yet. Essentially it describes 3 courses in which medical humanities are used. Although the courses do have outcomes, there are assumptions made within the article that the outcomes have been met without any evidence or data to support this.

It is difficult to predict what kind of feedback you are going to get. The point is to be prepared for the worst, to try to treat any feedback analytically – to dampen the emotional impact – and to work out the extent to which you can deliver what they have asked for and how you are going to do it. If there are issues raised by the reviewers with which you disagree, go back to the editor for further discussion.

Destructive feedback

It does sometimes seem that there are reviewers out there who like nothing better than to tear a paper – and its author – to shreds. New writers sometimes feel that they are being held back for no good reason, that the reviewers are simply protecting their power base and the narrow concerns of a small group.

Reviewers, given the chance, might reply to that accusation by asserting that they are responsible for upholding the standards of the journal specifically and the discipline generally. They might complain that this is an arduous job, when they are already very busy people, for which they receive no reward. In fact, many reviewers report that they are frustrated by the falling standard of papers they receive to review and are impatient when they feel that authors have simply not done enough work, have not bothered to present their papers in the appropriate format, or use peer review as a development process.

All of this speculation does nothing to take the sting out of destructive feedback. Neither is it entirely acceptable to be destructive when we all know reviewers can write their comments in a different way. You have to wonder, if reviews were not anonymized, would reviewers be so destructive?

However, there is another way of reading destructive reviews: what seems 'destructive', when you first set eyes on it, may not, in fact, be as serious as you think. Comments may be 'very negative', yet the editor may only request 'minor revisions'. Even comments that seem to destroy your structure and style – carefully considered and targeted though they were – can be translated into revision actions, as long as the editor has not used the word 'rejected'. Editors are not out to undermine or contradict reviewers, but they do often soften the blow. For example, the following reviewers' comments did not stop the editor from using the word 'positive' in his or her cover letter, inviting the authors to resubmit:

> The title is a bit **weak, long-winded, and descriptive.** A more direct title is suggested.

> The text uses a **plodding and subject-indeterminate passive form,** and some **awkward construction,** such as, 'The results identified . . . to be . . .'. Sentences tend to be **long and over-structured,** '. . . the epidemiology of . . . on . . . may be influenced by . . . of . . . and . . . at . . . during'. . . . Results and Discussion: The authors proceed to analyze different factors and conclude that some are more important and others not. They proceed to discuss in great length various factors, explaining why some intuitive ones, such as water temperature, did not turn up as significant, while others did . . .

> Overall, I found the paper meritorious, but **difficult to read.** The study is of practical value and consequence in the industry, and may be applicable in other organizations. I do not have specific scientific changes (the authors appear to be careful researchers), but it would help the authors' case if they **tightened up their writing style a bit,** especially in the Discussion, which is **much too long.**

What can we learn from this example of reviewers' feedback? That reviewers have idiosyncratic views of what constitutes good academic writing? That there are no general rules in writing for publication at all? Or that the authors of the paper can still improve their style and, more importantly, targeting?

- Some comments seem to go against good practice: for example, the reviewer is not a fan of descriptive titles, although for many of us, keeping titles descriptive is a goal.

- The passive voice seems to be so heavily endorsed in some disciplines that some writers will be surprised to see this critique of its use; but is it a problem with specifically how these authors used it, rather than with passive voice in general?
- Is there an implied negative in 'at great length' – and does it matter? As long as the editor has requested 'minor revisions', all the authors have to do is work out how these comments translate into revisions and how much to cut from the Discussion.

What to do with hostile reviews

Once we lose our sense of grievance everything, including physical pain, becomes easier to bear.

(Greer 1991: 428)

Taking the subject of negative or destructive reviews one step further brings us to what seem to be openly hostile reviews. Any of the above reviews could be seen as hostile, at least in parts, by new writers. (See Murray and Moore, 2006, for further examples of reviews that writers perceived as hostile.) The point is that you have to learn from all the reviews, even if your paper is rejected.

Having a sense of grievance is very different from taking out a 'grievance', formalizing your complaint. A sense of personal grievance about a hostile review can inhibit revision and resubmission. Yet, if your paper has not been rejected, and if you have a good chance of getting published, why not just follow the reviewers' suggestions? Will they really change it all that much?

If your paper is rejected, you can revise it for submission to another journal. There is no point in a hostile response to a hostile review. What, after all, is your goal: to get your paper published or to improve the standard of reviewing in academic journals?

Remember the recurring weaknesses, reasons for rejection and common problems covered in this book – have you committed one or more of these errors? Even if you worked hard to avoid them, you may have made a minor slip that has irritated the reviewer. For example, remember how easy it is to overstate a critique of others' work. There may be one part of the paper that has triggered the hostility, and if you can work out which part it is, cut it. As a first step, take a good look at your contextualizing section(s), where new writers are at most risk of overstating a criticism of someone else's work, or of education in a certain field or professional practice, giving the impression that nothing is right. That may be where you have drawn fire. Sometimes all you need is a 'perhaps' or a 'potential' to modulate your argument where it is overstated. The key point is not to take it personally.

You also have to own up and admit that you can still improve your paper. Even though when you sent it in it was in a form you thought was as close to 'perfect' as you could get it, others will not see it that way. Some of this you can anticipate; some of it will take you by surprise.

You can, of course, object to the hostility. You can complain to the editor and draw his or her attention to the specifics of the review. If enough people do this – or perhaps just one – it might be enough to prompt the editor to communicate with the reviewer. It is difficult to know, as there is no data set on this, but if no one objects, nothing changes.

Contradictory comments

It seemed that reviewers did not overtly disagree on particular points; instead, they wrote about different topics, each making points that were appropriate and accurate. As a consequence, their recommendations about editorial decisions showed hardly any agreement.

(Fiske and Fogg 1990: 591)

It is not unusual for reviewers to disagree – not that they see this themselves, unless the journal has open reviewing – in their comments on a paper. This can be disconcerting, but, once again, if the editor has not used the word 'rejection', then you still have a chance to do some revisions.

There is no need, therefore, to be thrown by such disagreements. Perhaps they merely reflect on-going debates in your field. Perhaps there are shades in this debate of which you were not aware, and this is what has come out in your reviewers' responses.

Whatever the cause – and it might be more interesting than productive to ponder this at any great length – your task is still to work out what the responses mean, not how they came to be so divergent. There may, of course, be lessons to be learned from this, but you should not be surprised by it.

Rejection

. . . perseverance and the ability not to get downcast by rejection, which is certain and ongoing, is just part of the game – even when you're published.

(Messud, quoted in Roberts *et al.* 2002: 50)

You need to be able to transform rejection – and what feels like rejection, but is only a request for changes – into learning and further writing.

There is a useful and thought-provoking list of reasons why papers are rejected in Greenhalgh (2019). Some would argue that papers are rejected because the work is simply not good enough, but the number of contradictory reviews – even in scientific disciplines – suggests that it is not as simple as that.

Your paper may be rejected if there are weaknesses in your work; but there may also be weaknesses in how you have explained your work or, more importantly, in the case you have made for doing the work in the way that you did. The following adaptation of Greenhalgh (2019) is designed to show what you might be able to learn from common reasons for rejection about the skills of written argument:

Common reasons why papers are rejected for publication . . . and what to do about them

- *Your study did not examine an issue considered important by the journal's editor/reviewers.* Spell out why it might be important to the journal's readers. Make a stronger case for its importance.
- *Your study was not original,* or you did not make a strong enough case for its originality. If you cannot make the case for 'originality', try another term, one that suits your work better.
- *Your study did not test your hypothesis,* or you did not make the connection between the two sufficiently clear, strong or explicit.
- *You should have conducted your study in a different way,* or your argument for your method in the context in which you were working is weak. Were your research procedures sufficiently defined and argued for? Were you careful to make the case against logical and widely accepted alternatives that you did not use?
- *You compromised on your research design.* Can you make a stronger case for this? Even if this was the result of practical difficulties or resource deficiencies, can you still learn lessons from this? Is a smaller scale report in order?
- *If your sample was judged too small,* should you be presenting and analysing your data in different terms: as a pilot study or a case study? Are there limited lessons you can learn? Can you make the limits to generalizability more explicit? Did you acknowledge the potential limitations of a small sample?
- *If your study is judged to be 'uncontrolled',* then perhaps you have submitted your paper to the wrong journal. Or perhaps you have to be more selective in what you are calling 'data'.
- *If your statistical analysis is found to be incorrect,* then you have some work to do before you submit your paper elsewhere, if it was found to be inappropriate here.
- *The conclusions you drew from your data were not justified.* Is this, again, a case for strengthening your argument for your conclusions, perhaps even going through them one by one?
- *The reviewers judged that you had a conflict of interest,* for example financial gain from publication. Did you make a sufficient case for your safeguards against bias?
- *If the reviewers tell you that your paper was so badly written that it was difficult or impossible to understand,* then you may have some work to do to improve your writing style – but you probably knew that anyway. Alternatively, you may be a very good writer, but might have to make more of a stylistic compromise between your preferred style of writing and the dominant style in the journal at this time.

When new writers see this list they are either incredulous that authors would submit papers with such serious weaknesses or unclear as to the relevance of these criteria: 'What does this have to do with our writing?'. Presumably, authors who were rejected for these reasons had worked hard to avoid these weaknesses and knew full well how high reviewers' standards would be. Surely these are all common sense? Or perhaps the authors still had work to do, not necessarily on their research, but on their writing.

Of course, this list only provides insight into one set of academic disciplines – medicine and the health professions – but it also shows the range of reasons for rejection, and we should remember that this list is offered as 'common' reasons. There are other such lists and perhaps the best use of them is to consider how you can strengthen your arguments so as to avoid these weaknesses. Some writers who address common weaknesses take the more positive line of suggesting how you might avoid them:

Solving common problems in journal article writing

1 Follow publication guidelines.
2 Use appropriate terminology.
3 Inform the reader of sources of information.
4 Provide sufficient background literature.
5 Analyse and synthesize the literature adequately.
6 Provide continuity of content; use explicit links in your writing.

(Hayes 1996: 25–7)

These suggestions seem to be about solving problems in the text, rather than the methodology. Each reason for rejection may have its origins in insufficient argument for, to take point number 4, the literature that was referenced in the article. In other words, you could argue that the literature you referenced is sufficient, and that to reference other literature would be to lose focus on your topic and, potentially, in your argument. Yet, some reviewers want you to acknowledge a wide range of research. Whether that is because you left their work out of your review, or because adding more references will strengthen your review – and thereby the impact of your argument – is for you to judge, but remember that they will still be judging too.

What revision actions could you take: could you simply add one sentence on all the other sources, or one on each, without doing too much damage to the continuity and focus of your paper? Or could you add a sentence that makes a more explicit case for the literature you have referenced as sufficient for the purpose of this paper? Or should you really have stated, explicitly, why you have not dealt with certain literature that some will think does belong in any discussion of your topic; since you have a sound reason for doing so, should you perhaps go ahead and say what it is? You may be putting your head above the parapet unnecessarily – and for no particular benefit to your paper – since what you most want your reader to notice and think about is, surely, other aspects of your paper.

The point is you will probably have to have this mini-debate with yourself about how to respond to reviewers' comments. This debate may be easier or quicker if conducted with someone else, particularly if this is the first paper you have submitted to an academic journal.

As with the previous list, the context was the health professions, but there are points here that could be helpful to new writers in other disciplines. On the previous list, you may think that these are pretty basic errors for authors to make. You wonder if that is because the discipline context – occupational therapy – is not as mature, in terms of published research, as, say, medicine. Yet the previous list was taken from the medical context, suggesting that such errors are not just oversights on the part of inexperienced authors, since even experienced authors have had such 'basic' feedback from time to time. Remember how 'basic' some of the reviews quoted earlier in this chapter were, commenting on the authors' writing skills, accusing them of not knowing about the subject and of not writing a paper about what they said they would. These critiques may still seem overstated, but they may be valid.

At the end of the day, whatever the reason for the reviewer's comment, be it bias or genuine sense of weakness in your paper, you just have to get on with revising it, unless, of course, you feel that the comment is inappropriate or takes you beyond the scope of your paper. One thing is sure: you will learn about your target journal from reviewers' comments on your article.

Resubmission

If your paper has not been rejected, get on with the revisions and resubmit as quickly as you can. Acknowledge that you may have overstated a point here or lacked clarity in a point there.

For example, if a reviewer says that your critique of the literature, policy or some other dimension of context is 'well worn', you do not necessarily have to dig up the original and intervening critiques and reference them all; nor do you have to invent a new type of critique, since that might not work well with the rest of your paper, nor do you have to delete it, if you think it provides an important foundation for your argument. Perhaps all that you need to do is to follow the reviewer's lead by acknowledging that it is a well-worn critique – i.e. by saying so in your paper – but add that it is an important one that is still current and, therefore, all the more serious for not being new and, worse, for not being 'fixed'. Your revised text might therefore read: 'Although it is now well established that there are weaknesses in the current method of XXX, it seems that, as yet, no action had been taken to address these weaknesses', or 'The argument that XXX is a weak method of YYY has been much rehearsed/discussed in the literature; however . . .' or 'It has been argued convincingly elsewhere (references) that . . .'.

If you are accused by a reviewer of being over-critical or even 'vituperative', you could, again, acknowledge that your criticism is harsh, but well founded or strongly stated for a purpose, such as to draw attention to the seriousness of the issue or the severity of a problem that has been allowed to persist. Of course, if you are going to say that, you will have to be sure that it is true, accurate and/or defensible. You can always take the moral high ground and say that you have to do this difficult harsh critique because there are those who are suffering in some way, or that research itself is weakened in some way. You can modulate such assertions, so as to avoid drawing a new form of critique from the editor when you resubmit, by adding the odd 'perhaps' and 'potentially'. These words will not only show that you understand that what you are saying is open to debate but also that you are making a propositional – rather than definitive – statement.

Check with someone who has been published in your target journal recently, but start thinking about changes you can make and, as you go through the reviewers' comments, note the types of change they are suggesting:

- One section seems to have drawn a lot of fire – consider cutting it.
- You strongly disagree with a reviewer's comment – discuss it with the editor.
- A couple of reviewers' comments are 'beyond the scope of this paper' – say so.
- Offer to discuss your revisions further, if you think/know this particular editor does this.

Once you have had six or seven papers published, you will have your own list of the types of changes to make to your writing and can anticipate some of these comments before you submit future articles.

Responding to feedback from editors and reviewers

Reply immediately:

1 Be positive; thank the editor for the 'useful feedback'.
2 Say that you will revise your paper.
3 Ask for a deadline – or suggest one – for your resubmission.
4 Check and act on the editor's interpretation of reviewers' comments.
5 'Translate' each reviewer's comment into a revision action.

	For example:	Page 2	Cut . . .
		Page 6	Explain . . .
		Page 11	Add . . .

6 Discuss your proposed revision actions with someone who publishes.
7 Do revisions immediately; return the revised paper as soon as you can.

When you submit your revisions:

1 Give a point-by-point account of how you acted on the editor's/reviewers' suggestions, using your revision action list, with verbs in the past tense. Keep these brief, easy to scan.

For example:	Page 2	Cut . . .
	Page 6	Explained . . .
	Page 11	Added . . .

2 Do this in bullet points or a numbered list, in separate lists for each reviewer.

Acceptance

The article's acceptance for publication is the crucial proof of its value.
(Rossen 1993: 161)

What does acceptance of your article signify to you? That you have finally reached the high standard required? That you have packaged your work in such a way that it can be easily assimilated into the academic or research community? Or that you have, with the help of the reviewers, learned how to make your writing persuasive to that community?

What will it signify to others? It may indeed signal to others that your work should be taken more seriously, since someone with power – the editor – has accepted it. It may be time, therefore, for you to acknowledge, if you have not already done so, that your work is important and that your writing can persuade others that it is important. This may be all the more important if, as you go on to write more and more, colleagues challenge not only your publications but also, oddly, the processes by which you produced them, as if you were practising some dark art of writing, when all you were doing was putting into practice the tried and tested methods for productive academic writing:

> As long as I had only written and published one or two books no one ever inquired or commented on my writing process, on how long it took me to complete the writing of a book. Once I began to write books regularly, sometimes publishing two at the same time, more and more comments were made to me about how much I was writing. Many of these comments conveyed the sense that I was either doing something wrong by writing so much, or at least engaged in writing acts that needed to be viewed with suspicion.
>
> (hooks 1999: 14)

In this context, as you write and publish more and more, it may be useful to assume that there will always be people who excel at 'damning with faint praise' and that publication will not give you immunity from that type of assault; in fact, it may increase it.

Do not expect that the new status accorded to your work will be 'accepted' within your department. Colleagues or heads of department may actively undermine your work, perhaps questioning the status of the journal in which you have just been published. You already know who is and is not likely to behave in this way. Welcome, therefore, those who 'damn with faint praise', since that is a relatively mild attack. Above all, do not expect them to change simply because you have. Your goal was to get published; it was not to convert your peers to congenial collegiality.

To complicate matters – and motivations – further, you may have a sense of anti-climax: it is so long since you started your paper, and you are so aware of the modesty of its contribution and are now certain that it will make no more than a gentle ripple in the sea of published work. You may find yourself agreeing with your colleagues' critiques. Remember that their criticisms are probably not based on reading your paper; they will criticize freely whether or not they have even read the sentence or two on your website about this paper.

If their criticisms seem to be marginalizing you – and not just your work – remind them of the relevance and value of your work for the university and the department at opportune moments, such as appraisals, reviews and even staff meetings. Don't wait to be asked; just tell them. If this does not work, persist. Do not expect to see or hear any marked change in their attitudes. They are not going to say 'Oh, yes, I see it now – your work is indeed very important. I'm sorry I missed that before.'

If you feel you are genuinely being marginalized or even bullied, it may be time to take a different course of action, rather than trying to sort it all out yourself. You could start with an informal discussion, seeking advice from your head of department, or manager, or personnel or human resources. If need be, you have a right to take formal action. Some people tirelessly undermine colleagues; be ready to look for ways to make sure that does not happen to you or to stop it if it does.

Once your paper has been accepted, you may feel a bit cynical – now you *know* it's all just a game, and it has to be played by their rules. You knew this would happen. You have had to compromise your work and hedge your statements so much that you feel your voice will not be heard and the value of your work is diminished. You still feel that you should be allowed to write what you think; even if people do not want to know, they should be made to listen.

In some ways, you may still feel exactly as you did when you started. Although you are about to be published, you may be even more convinced that power is wielded by a very select group, that they are not out to share their power and that you will never be able to develop the kind of authority they enjoy when they write. Your writing will always be coming from a more contested place.

In some disciplines, of course, these issues have no relevance; it is the quality of the work that matters. If your work is good enough, the argument goes, you will be published in chemistry, for example. No question. Perhaps this is truer for other disciplines than new writers realize or are prepared to admit.

Proofs

Once you are at this stage, when you know that the next stage is checking proofs, ask the editor when that will be. This is a courtesy that may save you all some grief later. If you are going to be offline for even a day or two, this will cause problems for a journal that has a three-day turnaround time. Some journals allow longer for authors to check the proofs. You need to know exactly what to expect. The editor or the online system will tell you when proofs will be sent out and expected back.

The proofs of your paper show you exactly what it will look like in the journal. This is editors' and authors' last chance to make final corrections. This is not the time for you to make final revisions. Make essential corrections only, since any changes could be costly. Editors will tell you what they want you to do and, more importantly, what they do not want you to do, so check their instructions carefully and follow them to the letter. Check every word of your paper against your original file. Check all your references.

If you really have to make a change that adds even as little as one line, try to 'catch up' by cutting a line elsewhere on the same page. You should have a really good reason for doing this, probably drawn to your attention by the proof reader, such as including a reference in your list at the end of the paper that you have not referred to in the paper. Either insert the reference in your text, if you can find somewhere that it will fit on an existing line, or cut the reference. It may be a reference left over from an earlier draft that can be cut easily.

The key motivation here is not to use this as an opportunity to 'polish' or 'perfect' your paper, but to make no changes at all, if at all possible.

Offprints

Offprints are quality prints of your paper, sometimes with a paper cover, sometimes just stapled together like a high-quality photocopy on good paper. They look a lot better than photocopies. Whether or not that means that it is worth paying for extra copies is up to you. Many journals no longer provide them, and many researchers no longer use them.

If you have some money in a special fund, or if your department has, then this might be a good use of what is bound to be a small proportion of the total fund. It is good for the department and the university, not just for you, to publicize your work by distributing offprints. If even part of the fund is designated for support of research, then you can make the case that this is one way of doing that.

Some journals offer you a set of offprints – perhaps 20 or 50 – at no charge. Others will send you a note of their rate for additional copies, sometimes charging for orders of 50 or 100. Some will give you a complete copy of the issue of the journal in which your paper appears.

The key use of offprints is to send them to people whom you know have an interest in your work, either because they have supported you or because they are working in the area themselves. Send them offprints as soon as they come in. Send them to the people you want to know about your publication, even if you think they are not interested in your area and are unlikely even to read it. Give one to your boss. If your department has one of those glass cases on the wall for publications, get one in there now. If it does not, suggest it. At the very least, you can make your publication more visible in your department by sticking an offprint on your wall, leaving your door open, so that everyone sees it. Or you could stick it on the outside of your door, though it may 'walk'.

Take your offprints to conferences and distribute them to those interested people who come up to talk to you after your session. It may seem a bit arrogant to buy copies of your paper with the express purpose of sending them out to people whom you think will want to read them, but this is just another means of continuing the dialogue with your peers. They will probably read your abstract and then flick to your references to see if there is anything new there, anything they have missed in the literature, any new connections you make or any citations of their own publications.

If you were worried about sending your paper to your peers, you may be even more reticent about sending offprints to people you do not know, but, as with any other aspect of research, you can find out who is likely to be receptive and who is likely to be insulted, if that is what you are worried about. If you have not done so already, research the peers – those writing in your area – whom you do not know and ask around: who knows who? Finally, if there are people with whom you would like to collaborate on research or writing, this is a good way to introduce yourself to them.

Checklist

- First, whatever the reviews say, check whether your article was rejected or not.
- Check the editor's comments carefully. He or she may have a particular interpretation of reviewers' comments, and this should shape your revisions.
- Translate each reviewer's comment into a revision action. Type these up and include them – written in the past tense, e.g. 'Added paragraph on . . .' – in your report to the editor on how you acted on reviewers' comments.
- Discuss reviewers' comments, and your intended revisions, with other people.
- Learn from reviewers' feedback, where possible.
- Anticipate critiques in your future writing.
- Don't take reviews personally – even if they seem to be about you rather than your writing.
- If your paper is rejected, find another journal to send it to. Set yourself a deadline: revise it to suit that journal . . . by when? Don't waste a word – keep going till you find a 'home' for it.

Further reading

Kumashiro, K.K., Pinar, W.F., Graue, E., Grant, C.A., Benham, M.K.P., Heck, R.H. *et al.* (2005) Thinking collaboratively about the peer review process for journal article publication, *Harvard Educational Review*, 75: 257–85.

Peter, D.P. and Ceci, S.J. (1982) Peer-review practices of psychological journals: the fate of published articles, submitted again, *The Behavioural and Brain Sciences*, 5: 187–255.

Valentine, G. (1998) 'Sticks and stones may break my bones': a personal geography of harassment, *Antipode*, 30: 305–32.

Wager, E., Godlee, F. and Jefferson, T. (2002) *How to Survive Peer Review*. London: British Medical Journal Books.

Chapter **10**

After publication

Marketing your writing • Social media • What now? • What next?
• Recycling and 'salami slicing' • Writing a book • Developing a
programme for writing • Checklist • Further reading

Marketing your writing

Given that a small number of people may read your article once it is published in a journal, there is a case for marketing published articles. No one will do this for you; it's up to you.

Since getting people to read, or at least making sure that they know about, your writing is crucial for getting further responses and feedback, and possibly invitations to write, this is an important step in your writing process. Yet, with a few exceptions (Thyer 1994), it gets surprisingly little consideration in descriptions of the process of writing for academic journals.

Some will tell you that if your work is good enough it does not need 'marketing'. Even when you successfully promote your publications, some people will come out with veiled or quite openly snide remarks such as, 'I'll say this for you, you certainly know how to *promote* your work.' Some people will make that a compliment; others will always make it sound like an insult.

You can even try to get your work featured in the newspapers, magazines or educational press. Most newspapers have an education day, often with a higher education section. If you can interest the relevant editor, providing him or her with an 'angle' on your work – make it topical, find something in your work that will be of interest to people outside your field – you will reach a much larger audience. Can you relate your work to recent events, trends or crises? Is there anything contentious about your work? This is a chance to have a say about some of the issues or information you left out of your paper.

There are also professional journals and magazines, for which you might be able to write a short piece. This will not, of course, 'count' in research league tables, but it could come under 'impact' work. It may also develop your profile and network. Again, this may be your chance to bring in some of the issues, perhaps concerning practice or implementation, ethics or costs, policy or production that you had to leave out of your academic paper.

Finally, remember that you can and should still be talking about your subject at conferences and other meetings. Just because you published a paper does not mean that you have to move on to a new topic; your published paper, itself possibly the development of a conference paper, can be the subject of your next presentation. If this seems like just so much recycling, think again: writing about the same subject more than once, in more than one way and for more than one outlet, is the way to develop your expertise and understanding. It is not just a matter of getting the maximum number of 'hits' from your material; it is about getting the maximum amount of learning out of your publishing and reaching as many people as possible.

Publishers, and perhaps others, have certain likes and dislikes (Baverstock 2001: 47–8), which may be instructive to writers for academic journals:

Publishers' likes and dislikes

Dislikes	Rudeness: not thanking them
	Failure to give information on request or help with promotion
	Unrealistic expectations of advertising
Likes	Focus: think about what you want to discuss before you call/email
	Efficiency: ask for things in plenty of time
	Contact: Send your contacts the occasional note of forthcoming key events and what might happen (for example, meetings at which you are speaking and at which information on your book [or paper] could be handed out) and a note of thanks if things have gone well! This is not just good nature – you will be remembered, and if any additional opportunities come up (for example, 'filler' advertisements available at last-minute prices), maybe it will be your book that gets included

(Baverstock 2001: 48)

While this may not all seem relevant to your paper, remember that some journals do feature papers in their leaflets and websites. One of my papers was featured in a publisher's leaflet about the journal, and it was the one most people requested, for a couple of years, which led to new contacts and, more importantly, contact with people who were interested in my work.

Social media

What if the future of scholarship is not in papers and books, but in new forms of dialogue-based exploration of ideals? Could professors in 2035 use some descendent of Weblogs as their site of developing ideas *and* as the main form of dissemination?

(Bruns and Jacobs 2006: 136)

Social media ain't always very beneficial to your social life, ironically, so three cheers for this new events calendar program [LockItDown], which allows you to schedule meetings and parties with your friends, family and colleagues away from the digital white noise of Facebook and Twitter

(*Independent*, 9 December 2012: 7)

Communicative capitalism designates the strange convergence of democracy and capitalism in networked communications and entertainment media. On the one hand, networked communications technologies materialize the values heralded as central to democracy . . . On the other hand, the speed, simultaneity, and interconnectivity of electronic communications produce massive distortions and concentrations of wealth.

(Dean 2010: 4)

The computer has become vital to almost any and every kind of work but it remains a technology that is very difficult to keep focused entirely on the job in hand.

(Miller 2011: 195)

By the time you read this – given the pace of change – everything may be different. The internet, or at least your institution's regulations about your use of it in relation to your work, may be more regulated. Or it may not. There may be new ways of constructing networks of colleagues in your field. There may be more differentiation between how we use social media for work and for play. Or there may not: it has been argued that Facebook changes the relationship between work and leisure (Miller 2011: 195). Whilst it is likely that work and play will continue to intersect on popular social platforms such as Facebook and Twitter, it is also clear that a number of social sites have emerged solely for professional purposes, the most notable of which is LinkedIn (https://gb.linkedin.com), which allows anyone to create a professional profile highlighting career achievements and publications. Social networks have also sprung up to serve the specific needs of researchers, such as ResearchGate (https://www.researchgate.net/), a social platform which also allows users to build a profile to make their research more visible. There are also platforms available to measure the impact and reach of research papers, such as Altmetric (https://www.altmetric.com/) which tracks data on where journal articles have been cited. This landscape evolves rapidly, so the key is to check how journals, universities and research centres use social media, and, more importantly, how they expect you to use them.

Whether you see social media as digital white noise or communicative capitalism, you have to admit that they offer opportunities for promoting your work and your writing. However, this may not only be about marketing your article; it can also be a medium for developing your ideas further. Social media are used to disseminate ideas informally, but there are opportunities to use these media, forums and channels in the research process. Whatever the pros and cons of social media, therefore, they let you go very public with your published and unpublished ideas.

For new researchers, social media can provide a sense of identity and/or agency, as they establish conversations with others in their fields. Some are attracted to the participatory ethos of social media – so different from what might be seen as the exclusive ethos of publishing in academic journals. Others take the view that the absence of peer review makes it risky. Even if Twitter, Facebook and blogs – and/or whatever comes next – do build communities of researchers, these communities are constructed and maintained by people. These virtual communities may be supportive, or they may be as contested as other communities. This construction and maintenance takes time, and it is a cliché to say that some people find they invest too much time maintaining social media identities or profiles. This time and all these activities also have to be managed.

Defining social media communications as part of your research role could improve your writing by providing regular writing practice, as long as you can avoid getting 'blogged down' in writing for social media, and as long as that does not distract you from all the other forms of writing that you do.

As you publish more, and as you develop a research profile, you will proba-bly change your strategy. There may not be a formal process for doing this – apart from disciplinary procedures, if you get it wrong – so it is up to you to find and check appropriate formal guidelines and keep up to date with local and professional codes of practice and/or handbooks. For example, see the following:

- the VITAE *Handbook of Social Media for Researchers and Supervisors: Digital Technologies for Research Dialogues* (Minocha and Petres 2012);
- the London School of Economics' *Maximising the Impacts of Your Research: A Handbook for Social Scientists* (LSE Public Policy Group no date);
- *Using Twitter in University Research, Teaching and Impact Activities* (Mollett *et al.* 2011);
- *The Digitally Agile Researcher* (Kurcikova and Quinlan 2017).

In developing your social media strategy, take account of formal requirements with regard to research, its dissemination and communication:

- Intellectual Property Rights
- Your institution's/employer's guidance/code of practice
- The funding body's guidance/requirements.

Above all, develop ground rules for yourself. For example, what will you say and not say on social media? How will you respond to criticism – i.e. precisely which words will you use and which will you not use? Similarly, how will you articulate criticism? Will you use humour?

While you mull over these questions, use social media to simply let people know about your paper:

- Tweet the title of and link to your paper.
- For Facebook you can say more about it – rewrite the Abstract in Plain English.
- Write a paragraph about it for future career review meetings and other formal processes.
- Put it on your website – link to university and department strategy and priorities.

Look for opportunities to disseminate your paper and its message more widely, for example in mainstream press or journalism that targets academic research as a news source (for example, The Conversation, http://theconversation.com/uk).

The first section of this chapter was about promoting your publications, and clearly social media can be part of your marketing strategy, if that is the appropriate term. This can be a way of developing your research profile and researcher identity. It could also be a way of flagging up and talking through the initial stages of your next writing project(s).

What now?

While as a new writer you were perhaps right to focus on getting one paper into print, in reality, and perhaps from now on – perhaps already – you have to have more than one piece of writing on the go at any one time. If you feel up to it, you can put in place a more complex programme of writing, particularly if your institution has set a target of two publications per year. This type of target might seem like an enormous burden, but it can also provide a rationale to fling in the face of those who do not value your writing efforts.

> Nobody hates writers more than writers do. . . . Nobody loves them more, either.
>
> (Atwood 2002: 97)

Are other people happy with your successful publication of an article? Does it matter? Margaret Atwood's description of the love–hate relationship between writers may apply less to you in the context of your writers' group, if you have one, but it rings true for some of the more competitive and even actively undermining reactions of some colleagues.

Do not be shocked if some colleagues ignore your success while others belittle it by, for example, remarking that the journal in which you have just been published does not have much standing. Even when you write a best-selling book, there will be some senior colleague who is keen to tell you that he or she had a book published that did not sell well because it was 'not that kind of book'. In other words, the put-downs may come thick and fast, and you may find this heartily disappointing if you were expecting collegial mutual respect, but it is not just you – it's them. Some people cannot stand others' success. They are not going to change, and they need not change your attitude to your work. You did what you set out to do. Time to set a new writing goal and get on with that.

Focus on your writing: once you have had a paper accepted, take time to take stock. What, if anything, did you learn in the course of becoming a published writer? Did you find that there were things you still had to learn? As you look to your next paper, can you gather some informal 'intelligence' about other journals from other writers? Other newly published writers may be willing to trade information with you.

On a lighter note, some say that changing your first name to 'Professor' will open doors, but not for long. Another option is to make some effort to join another élite conversation, perhaps by working with a professor. The top journals represent perhaps an even more select group. There may be even more nepotism at that level – a highly contentious statement, clearly, but people do tell me that there is evidence of this. Since much of it is anecdotal, you will have to make up your own mind, perhaps not being swayed by any one person's anecdotes. Yet it has been said to me on numerous occasions, in many institutions and in several countries, that there is discrimination on the basis of gender, race and class in all aspects of academic and professional life, and we only have to do a quick scan of posts, publications and senior appointments to see that they are not representative of the general academic or professional populations. Nevertheless, if you are to be a publishing writer, you have to find a way to join the debate that the senior people are effectively running. This is a discussion that was covered in an earlier chapter, but these issues may raise their ugly heads again as you start to sketch your next paper(s), particularly if you are thinking of targeting one of the 'élite' journals.

What next?

One of the aims of this chapter is to prompt you to think strategically, tactically and creatively about the potential subjects and stories of your papers:

- Which journals should you be writing for next or soon?
- Which ones do you think you have little or no chance of getting into?
- Why exactly is that?
- Can you convert that barrier into an opportunity?
- How could your topic complement their papers?
- What would it take to make them consider your topics/ideas/work?
- Can you make explicit connections with the contents or aims of their publication?

If you are doubtful about these suggestions, remember how doubtful you felt about your first paper – possibly at every stage of writing – and recognize that having it accepted means that your work is worth something. Talk yourself into thinking this way – or get someone to help you to do so – about some other aspect of your work. Be creative. What would it take for one of the top journals in your field to give serious consideration to a paper from you, particularly if you have limited research data, profile or experience?

For your next article, don't think that just because you went through the process once you can dodge the systematic process of targeting a journal. In fact, if you are planning to target a different journal for your next publication, go through the same process of analysing it in detail. This may take you less time, but it should be no less thorough. As before, you can learn a lot about writing from working out how published articles in your target journal are put together.

Consider collaborating with colleagues or students. There may be others, in your writers' group, for example, who are keen to publish in different areas. You can also write about your teaching and supervision roles. Other aspects of academic or professional practice are open to debate. You may want to join current debates on such matters as research training. In some systems these types of publication will not have high scores in research assessment, but they can demonstrate your willingness to develop in these roles and you might also learn something about academic writing.

In some disciplines this will seem nonsensical: surely you can only learn about writing for journals in your field by writing for journals in your field? Surely those who have research to write about do so, and those who do not, write about their teaching and supervision instead? Again, as teacher accreditation becomes more established in higher education, it is a mistake to discount altogether the practice of learning and writing about your teaching, at the very least. That is one way of demonstrating your knowledge in this area, as in any other.

If you are thinking of writing in another area, you might want to co-author with a colleague who is already established in that area, or whose home discipline it is. They will have more background than you; you will have a new perspective to offer them. It can be an interesting combination, and some journals want that.

Many outputs that do not 'count' can be useful stepping stones to publication and regular academic writing. They also get your name noticed in the journals: book reviews, letters about published papers or current debates. There is no need to wait until you are asked to review a book; write to the reviews editor and offer to do so.

As before, you should start looking for your next paper in all the obvious places: your conference presentations, workshops, consultancies and briefing papers can all work as starters for further papers, for disseminating your work and 'marketing your writing' (Thyer 1994; Baverstock 2001). While, in some fields, none of these would be considered as 'research', they can be the starting point for a piece of academic writing that might at some stage become a paper, if you find a journal to publish it in.

The key step at this stage is therefore balancing three factors in your writing decisions:

- Which journal do you want to target now?
- Which topic do you want to write about now?
- What work have you done that is potentially publishable?

In some fields researchers know exactly where their next paper is coming from, since it follows on immediately from the one before. But in others the process is a matter of juggling answers to these three questions; it is unlikely that you will be able to answer all three questions right away and come up with an instant topic. Your answer to one question may not match the others. For example, your preferred topic may be the least likely one for your preferred journal, and you will have to decide whether or not to persevere with it.

Whatever field you are in, there are almost always things you left out of the paper you just published. There are things that occurred to you as you wrote. There are questions you did not answer and possibly new questions generated by your work. There were matters – worth discussing in another forum – that were beyond the scope of that paper. In your conclusion you referred to other questions that merit further study or simply consideration. These can, in some disciplines, be starting points for your next few papers, your future research or for future collaborations.

Recycling and 'salami slicing'

> A variant on duplicate publication is 'salami publishing', in which each bit of research is divided into the thinnest possible slices (sometimes referred to as 'LPUs', for 'least publishable units'), with each slice submitted as a separate article. This is marginally more ethical than duplicate submission, but it is equally wasteful.
>
> (Luey 2011: 16)

Yet, if you are to develop a profile in a certain area, you will have to write about it several times. It may be a mistake, in any case, to look around for a new topic, once your paper is published. Therefore, the term 'salami slicing' – which some see as a cynical or 'wasteful' strategy – can be redefined as a strategy of planning a series of papers from any piece of work or project. It is also a useful reminder to new writers not to make the common first-time writers' mistake of putting the whole salami into one paper.

Similarly, 'recycling' can be a useful term for describing the process of covering the same ground in a series of papers, not in the sense that you are repeating yourself, but in the sense that you are taking up in a new paper where your previous paper left off or drilling down for more detail, for example. This is a prompt to go back to all that material that you cut from your first paper and kept in a separate file. Can that now be the subject of your next paper?

Writing a book

... the so-called research assessment exercise, a crazy Soviet-style set of production targets for goods that nobody wants. It coerces even those who have the decency not to want to publish much into fulfilling their production norms.

(Allison 2004: 14)

Since books can easily be surpassed by events, they appear particularly ill chosen as a medium through which to present a critical media theory. . . . [Yet as] an object whose form installs delays in sampling and syndication and whose content demands postponed gratification, the book mobilizes the gap of mediacy so as to stimulate thought. E-books and articles as well as blog posts on theoretical topics are convenient ways to store and share ideas. But these benefits come at a cost: we pay with attention.

(Dean 2010: 1, 3)

Thinking of writing a book because you want to? Or because you think it is expected of you? Or because a publisher has asked you to? Or some combination of the three? Writing a book can be one way of bringing all your papers together – in a new form – to establish a synthesis, a coherent body of work or to develop new theory. The book form can give you more freedom of expression than is possible in journals. In terms of time, it can take just as long to get a paper from inception to publication, sometimes as much as two years, as it does to write a book.

See publishers' websites for guidance on how to put together a proposal, but, as for journals, contact the appropriate editor first with an initial enquiry to see if they are interested in your topic. For a book proposal writing template, with notes on what to write in each section, see Murray (2006).

Developing a programme for writing

There are several ways in which you could draw up a programme of writing for yourself for the next five years or so.

Year 1   First paper submitted/published (plus ideas for others)

Year 2   Draw up list of other possible papers, convert conference papers into publications, write several papers at the same time, target several journals at the same time, target new journals plus book reviews, small grant proposals, collaborative bids, etc.

Year 3   Targeting higher level of journal
Year 4   Writing for journals and other outlets for dissemination
Year 5   Pulling papers together for a book (depending on the discipline), major research proposals and collaborations

Use the 'Page 98 paper' (Murray 2017a: 118) to develop your ideas in writing, beyond simply being 'ideas', and to contextualize them in the literature. This is an activity that postgraduates and emerging researchers have found useful – to the extent of referring to it as a 'type of paper' – in helping them to map out the context and focus for their work. It might also work for sketching a paper.

What can I write about? (20–30 minutes' writing)

The context/background

- My research question is . . . (50 words)
- Researchers who have looked at this subject are . . . (50 words)
- They argue that . . . (25 words)
- Smith argues that . . . (25 words)
- Brown argues that . . . (25 words)
- Debate centres on the issue of . . . (25 words)
- There is still work to be done on . . . (25 words)
- My research is closest to that of X in that . . . (50 words)
- My contribution will be . . . (50 words)

Once your paper has been accepted, you may find that you have a slightly different view of the publishing game. You may have learned a lot from the reviewers' feedback, and you may have picked up a few dos and don'ts from how they played their role. Whatever you got out of the experience, it is time to move on.

If you do not yet feel that you have a set of productive academic writing practices, it will not necessarily be because you are slow on the uptake; these skills take time to learn. In time, you will also develop your own strategies. In the meantime, writing to prompts, freewriting, generative writing and the outlining strategies in this book will serve as a reminder of the range of writing activities that lie behind many published papers, even if their authors would not all use these terms.

Writing for academic journals is always instructive. It makes us test our ideas and forces us to submit to others' testing. Publication can give you a qualified confidence in your writing, qualified by the knowledge that your future work and writing will have to be tested in these ways if they are genuinely to amount to anything. Ultimately, this is where the genuine rewards of academic writing lie – it's about both the acknowledgement you get and the on-going learning you do.

Checklist

- As a first step in letting people know that your article was accepted for publication, put the reference in your email signature. When it is published, put the full publication details there.
- Send the abstract and/or digital file to key colleagues in the field.
- If there is an institutional repository, send your article in.
- Tell your head of department/manager.
- Report to and/or thank whoever funded your data collection or conference trip.
- Create a social media strategy – what is your purpose in using social media? What do you want to achieve? How will you use social media to achieve that? When will you review this strategy?
- Keep setting new writing goals. Keep reviewing them. Keep writing.

Further reading

Bruns, A. and Jacobs, J. (eds) (2006) *Uses of Blogs.* New York: Peter Lang.

Carrigan, M. (2016) *Social Media for Academics.* London: Sage.

Dean, J. (2010) *Blog Theory: Feedback and Capture in the Circuits of the Drive.* Cambridge: Polity.

LSE (London School of Economics) Public Policy Group (n.d.) *Maximizing the Impacts of Your Research: A Handbook for Social Scientists,* Consultation Draft 3. London: LSE PPG.

Lupton, D., Mewburn, I. and Thomson, P. (eds) (2018) *The Digital Academic: Critical Perspectives on Digital Technologies in Higher Education.* London: Routledge.

Miller, D. (2011) *Tales from Facebook.* Cambridge: Polity.

Minocha, S. and Petres, M. (2012) *Handbook of Social Media for Researchers and Supervisors: Digital Technologies for Research Dialogues.* Milton Keynes: Open University and VITAE.

Mollett, A., Moran, D. and Dunleavy, P. (2011) *Using Twitter in University Research, Teaching and Impact Activities.* London: London School of Economics Public Policy Group.

Rheingold, H. (2014) *Net Smart: How to Thrive Online.* Cambridge, MA: MIT Press.

Conclusion

This book has laid out a structured approach to writing for academic journals. For each step in the process, it provides activities to actually get the writing done. These steps can be combined in a linear process – linear in the sense that it occurs over time – and the activities can be planned in real time increments.

The aim was to provide not just an explanation of 'how to write an article', but to expose the processes for writing it. Some of these are individual; some are 'social'; some are for individual writing that you can do in groups – not co-authoring but communal writing.

The key to productive writing, as far as I can tell from my research and from listening to writers, is to combine two very different types of writing technique: on the one hand, using generative writing strategies – the regular scribbling of what is probably pre-draft or even non-draft text – and, on the other, using structuring strategies – creating outlines (of papers, arguments and paragraphs).

Generative strategies serve three purposes: getting you into the writing habit, getting your ideas down on paper – so you can develop them – and as a way to address writing problems, including overcoming writing blocks. The structuring strategies serve other purposes: producing the kind of text that is appropriate for journals, focusing your thinking on content and determining the proportions of parts of the paper. In combination, these two contrasting strategies are likely to lead to productive, successful writing for academic journals.

This range of writing techniques means that 'writing' is now too vague a term – so many sub-tasks are involved in this complex process. It's much easier when we name them, define them and have specific practices for doing them. Yes, all these tasks and practices must hold together in a complex whole or coherent practice, but the practices may not be identical for every article you write. You can vary the writing techniques you use to suit the timeslot, level of energy, amount of reading you've done or type of article you are writing.

This means that, from now on, when you sit down to 'write', you should define what it is it that you are doing. Are you working out what you want to say, in writing? Are you developing part of the argument, in writing? Are you building the whole structure in miniature by sketching the summary, in writing? For each of these and the many, many other different tasks involved in writing an article, this definition clarifies what you are trying to do, what the purpose of your writing task is, how long it might take and which technique you might use to do it.

Finally, what this book argues from start to finish is that just sitting down 'to write' is sufficiently undefined – which may have a pleasing freedom about it – that it will be impossible to gauge whether or not you achieved what you set out to do. This reminds us of the importance of goal setting and monitoring.

With your writing goals and monitoring the extent to which you achieve them, you maintain your motivation to do all of these tasks and make sure that, in the context of your many other roles and responsibilities, there is less tension between your writing and all the other things you have or want to do in your life, including 'having a life'.

Further reading

For more established writers who want to improve further, and for those who want to learn more about how to write well:

Fish, S. (2011) *How to Write a Sentence and How to Read One*. New York: HarperCollins.

Graff, G. and Birkenstein, C. (2010) *They Say, I Say: The Moves That Matter in Academic Writing*, 2nd edn. New York: Norton.

Lanham, R.A. (2007) *Revising Prose*, 5th edn. New York: Pearson Longman.

Schostak, J. and Schostak, J. (2013) *Writing Critically: Developing the Power to Make a Difference*. London: Routledge.

Sword, H. (2012) *Stylish Academic Writing*. Cambridge, MA: Harvard University Press.

Trimble, J.R. (2011) *Writing with Style: Conversations on the Art of Writing*, 3rd edn. New York: Prentice Hall.

Williams, J.M. (2004) *Style: Ten Lessons in Clarity and Grace*, 8th edn. Glenview, IL: Scott, Foresman and Company.

Bibliography

Acker, A. and Armenti, C. (2004) Sleepless in academia, *Gender and Education*, 16(1): 3–24.

Agenda (2012) App watch: LockItDown, *Independent*, 9 December: 7.

Albert, T. (2000) *Winning the Publications Game: How To Write a Scientific Paper Without Neglecting Your Patients*, 2nd edn. Abingdon: Radcliffe.

Aitchison, C. and Guerin, C. (eds) (2014) *Writing Groups for Doctoral Students and Beyond: Innovations in Practice and Theory*. London: Routledge.

Allison, L. (2004) Why I . . . think we have too many books, *Times Higher Education*, 9 April: 14.

Anglin, J. (1999) The uniqueness of child and youth care: a personal perspective, *Child and Youth Care Forum*, 28(2): 143–50.

Appelbaum, J. (1998) *How to Get Happily Published: A Complete and Candid Guide*, 5th edn. New York: HarperCollins.

Atwood, M. (2002) *Negotiating with the Dead*. Cambridge: Cambridge University Press.

Babel, M. (2010) Dialect divergence and convergence in New Zealand English, *Language in Society*, 39: 437–56.

Ball, S.J. (2003) The teacher's soul and the terrors of performativity, *Journal of Education Policy*, 18(2): 215–28.

Ballenger, B. (2015) *The Curious Researcher: A Guide to Writing Research Papers*, 8th edn. New York: Pearson Longman.

Barrass, R. (2002) *Scientists Must Write: A Guide to Better Writing for Scientists, Engineers and Students*, 2nd edn. London: Routledge.

Baverstock, A. (2001) *Marketing Your Book: An Author's Guide*. London: A. and C. Black.

Beard, M. (2012) *All in a Don's Day*. London: Profile Books.

Belcher, W.L. (2019) *Writing your Journal Article in Twelve Weeks: A Guide to Academic Publishing Success*, 2nd edn. London: Sage Publications.

Belton, V. (1985) The use of a simple multiple-criteria model to assist in selection from a shortlist, *Journal of the Occupational Research Society*, 36(4): 265–74.

Bennett, J.B. (2003) *Academic Life: Hospitality, Ethics and Spirituality*. Bolton, MA: Anker.

Bensimon, E.M. (1995) Total quality management in the academy: a rebellious reading, *Harvard Educational Review*, 65(4): 593–611.

Bereiter, C. and Scardamalia, M. (1987) *The Psychology of Written Composition*. London: Lawrence Erlbaum.

Black, D., Brown, S., Day, A. and Race, P. (1998) *500 Tips for Getting Published: A Guide for Educators, Researchers and Professionals*. London: Kogan Page.

Blaxter, L., Hughes, C. and Tight, M. (1998a) *The Academic Career Handbook*. Buckingham: Open University Press.

Blaxter, L., Hughes, C. and Tight, M. (1998b) Writing on academic careers, *Studies in Higher Education*, 23(3): 281–95.

Boice, R. (1987) Is released time an effective component of faculty development programs?, *Research in Higher Education*, 26(3): 311–26.

Boice, R. (1990a) *Professors as Writers: A Self-help Guide to Productive Writing*. Stillwater, OK: New Forums.

Boice, R. (1990b) Faculty resistance to writing-intensive courses, *Teaching of Psychology*, 17(1): 13–17.

Bolker, J. (1998) *Writing your Dissertation in Fifteen Minutes a Day: A Guide to Starting, Revising and Finishing your Doctoral Thesis*. New York: Henry Holt.

Boud, D. (1999) Situating development in professional work: using peer learning, *International Journal for Academic Development*, 4(1): 3–10.

Boud, D. and Walker, D. (1998) Promoting reflection in professional courses: the challenge of context, *Studies in Higher Education*, 23(2): 191–206.

Bradbury, R. (1994) *Zen in the Art of Writing*. Santa Barbara, CA: Joshua Bell.

Brew, A. (2001) *The Nature of Research: Inquiry in Academic Contexts*. London: Routledge.

Brew, A. (2004) Conceptions of research: a phenomenographic study, in M. Tight (ed.) *The RoutledgeFalmer Reader in Higher Education*. London: RoutledgeFalmer.

Brown, R. (1994/95) Write right first time, *Literati Newsline*, Special Issue, 1–8 (http:#dRwww.literaticlub.co.uk/writing/articles/write.html).

Bruns, A. and Jacobs, J. (eds) (2006) *Uses of Blogs*. New York: Peter Lang.

Burton, S. and Steane, P. (eds) (2004) *Surviving Your Thesis*. London: Routledge.

Bykofsky, S. and Sander, J.B. (2000) *The Complete Idiot's Guide to Getting Published*, 2nd edn. Indianapolis, IN: Alpha Books.

Caffarella, R.S. and Barnett, B.G. (2000) Teaching doctoral students to become scholarly writers: the importance of giving and receiving critiques, *Studies in Higher Education*, 25(1): 39–51.

Caldwell, J.J., Colman, R., Kerr, W.J. and Magennis, E.J. (2001) Novel use of a selenoalkyne within untraditionally mild Dötz benzannulation processes; total synthesis of a *Calceolaria andica L.* natural hydroxylated naphthoquinone, *Synlett*, 9: 1428–30.

Cameron, J. (1998) *The Right to Write: An Invitation and Initiation into the Writing Life*. London: Macmillan.

Carlson, R. (1997) *Don't Sweat the Small Stuff . . . and It's All Small Stuff*. London: Hodder and Stoughton.

Carnell, E., MacDonald, J., McCallum, B. and Scott, M. (2008) *Passion and Politics: Academics Reflect on Writing for Publication*. London: Institute of Education, University of London.

Carra, J., Candau, R., Keslacy, S., Giolbas, F., Borrani, J., Millet, G.P. *et al.* (2003) Addition of inspiratory resistance increases the amplitude of the slow component of O2 uptake kinetics, *Journal of Applied Physiology*, 94: 2448–55.

Carrigan, M. (2016) *Social Media for Academics*. London: Sage.

Cummings, L.L. and Frost, P.J. (1995) *Publishing in the Organizational Sciences*, 2nd edn. London: Sage Publications.

Damarell, B. (1999) Just forging, or seeking love and approval: an investigation into the phenomenon of the forged art object and the copied picture in art therapy involving people with learning disabilities, *Inscape*, 4(2): 44–50.

Darrer, M., Jacquemet-Papilloud, J. and Délemont, O. (2008) Gasoline on hands: preliminary study on collection and persistence, *Forensic Science International*, 175: 171–8.

Davis, M.S. (1971) That's interesting!: towards a phenomenology of sociology and a sociology of phenomenology, *Philosophy of Social Science*, 1: 309–44.

Davis, R. and Shadle, M. (2000) 'Building a mystery': alternative research writing and the academic act of seeking, *College Composition and Communication*, 51(3): 417–46.

Day, A. (1996) *How to Get Research Published in Journals*. Aldershot: Gower.

Dean, J. (2010) *Blog Theory: Feedback and Capture in the Circuits of the Drive*. Cambridge: Polity.

Drake, S. and Jones, G.A. (1997) *Finding Your Own Voice in Academic Publishing: Writing Your Way to Success.* Stillwater, OK: New Forums.

Dunstan, D.W., Barr, E.L.M., Healy, G.N., Salmon, J., Shaw, J.E., Balkau, B. *et al.* (2010) Television viewing time and mortality: the Australian diabetes, obesity and lifestyle study (AusDiab), *Circulation*, 121: 384–91.

Elbow, P. (1998) *Writing without Teachers*, 2nd edn. New York: Oxford University Press.

Elbow, P. (1998) *Writing with Power*, 2nd edn. New York: Oxford University Press.

Elbow, P. (2012) *Vernacular Eloquence: What Speech Can Bring to Writing.* Oxford: Oxford University Press.

Elbow, P. and Sorcinelli, M.D. (2006) The faculty writing place: a room of our own, *Change*, November/December: 17–22.

Ely, M., Vinz, R., Downing, M. and Anzul, M. (1997) *On Writing Qualitative Research: Living by Words.* London: Falmer.

Emerson, C. (1996) *The 30-Minute Writer.* Cincinnati, OH: Writers' Digest.

Estrin, S. and Wright, M. (1999) Corporate governance in the former Soviet Union: an overview, *Journal of Comparative Economics*, 27: 398–421.

Fahnestock, J. and Secor, M. (1990) *A Rhetoric of Argument*, 2nd edn. New York: McGraw-Hill.

Fanghangel, J. (2012) *Being an Academic.* London: Routledge.

Fiala, Z., Hinz, M., Meissner, K. and Wehner, F. (2003) A component-based approach for adaptive dynamic web documents, *Journal of Web Engineering*, 2(1 & 2): 58–73.

Fish, S. (2011) *How to Write a Sentence and How to Read One.* New York: HarperCollins.

Fiske, D.W. and Fogg, L. (1990) But the reviewers are making different criticisms of my paper!: diversity and uniqueness in reviewer comments, *American Psychologist*, 45(5): 591–8.

Flower, L. and Hayes, J.R. (1981) A cognitive process theory of writing, *College Composition and Communication*, 32: 365–87.

Ford, N. and Chen, S.Y. (2001) Matching/mismatching revisited: an empirical study of learning and teaching styles, *British Journal of Educational Technology*, 32(1): 5–22.

Frost, P.J. and Taylor, M.S. (1996) *Rhythms of Academic Life: Personal Accounts of Careers in Academia.* London: Sage Publications.

Gavin, J. and Lister, S. (2001) The strategic use of sports and fitness activities for promoting psycho-social skill development in childhood and adolescence, *Journal of Child and Youth Care Work*, 16: 325–39.

Gere, A.R. (1987) *Writing Groups: History, Theory, and Implications.* Carbondale, IL: Southern Illinois University.

Germano, W. (2001) *Getting it Published: A Guide for Scholars and Anyone Else Serious About Serious Books.* London: University of Chicago Press.

Gill, R. (2010) Breaking the silence: the hidden injuries of the neoliberal university, in R. Ryan-Flood and R. Gill (eds) *Secrecy and Silence in the Research Process: Feminist Reflections.* London: Routledge.

Gilroy, P. and McNamara, O. (2009) A critical history of research assessment in the United Kingdom and its post-1992 effect on education, *Journal of Education for Teaching*, 35: 321–35.

Graff, G. and Birkenstein, C. (2010) *They Say, I Say: The Moves that Matter in Academic Writing*, 2nd edn. New York: Norton.

Grant, B. (2006) Writing in the company of other women: exceeding the boundaries, *Studies in Higher Education*, 31(4): 483–95.

Grant, B. and Knowles, S. (2000) Flights of imagination: academic writers be(com)ing writers, *International Journal for Academic Development*, 5(1): 6–19.

Greenhalgh, T. (2019) *How to Read a Paper: The Basics of Evidence-based Medicine*, 6th edn. London: Wiley-Blackwell/British Medical Journal Books.

Greer, G. (1991) *The Change: Women, Ageing and the Menopause*. London: Penguin.

Griffiths, M. (1993) Productive writing, *The New Academic*, Autumn: 29–30.

Guillot, J., Kilpatrick, M., Hebert, E. and Hollander, D.B. (2004) Applying the transtheoretical model to exercise adherence in clinical settings, *American Journal of Health Studies*, 19(1): 1–10.

Haines, D.D., Newcomer, S. and Raphael, J. (1997) *Writing Together: How to Transform Your Writing in a Writing Group*. New York: Perigree.

Hall, G.M. (ed.) (1998) *How to Write a Paper*, 2nd edn. London: British Medical Journal Books.

Halliday, M.A.K. and Martin, J.R. (1993) *Writing Science: Literacy and Discursive Power*. London: Falmer.

Hamilton, M.T., Healy, G., Dunstan, D.W., Zderic, T.W. and Owen, N. (2008) Too little exercise and too much sitting: inactivity physiology and the need for new recommendations on sedentary behaviour, *Current Cardiovascular Risk Reports*, 2(4): 292–8.

Hanks, R. (2003) Let them eat cake, *The Independent Magazine*, 25 January: 20.

Hartley, J. (1994) Three ways to improve the clarity of journal abstracts, *British Journal of Educational Psychology*, 64(2): 331–43.

Hartley, J. (2004) Current findings from research on structured abstracts, *Journal of the Medical Library Association*, 92(3): 368–71.

Hartley, J. (2008) *Academic Writing and Publishing: A Practical Handbook*. London: Routledge.

Hartley, J. and Betts, L. (2009) Common weaknesses in traditional abstracts in the social sciences, *Journal of the American Society for Information Science and Technology*, 60(10): 2010–18.

Hartley, J. and Branthwaite, A. (1989) The psychologist as wordsmith: a questionnaire study of the writing strategies of productive British psychologists, *Higher Education*, 18: 423–52.

Hartley, J., Sotto, E. and Pennebaker, J. (2002) Style and substance in psychology: are influential articles more readable than less influential ones?, *Social Studies of Science*, 32(2): 321–34.

Hayes, R.L. (1996) Writing for publication: solutions to common problems, *Australian Occupational Therapy Journal*, 43: 24–9.

Henderson, K.W., Kerr, W.J. and Moir, J.H. (2000) Enantioselective depronotation reactions using a novel homochiral magnesium amide base, *Chemical Communications*, 6: 479–80.

Hey, V. (2001) The construction of academic time: sub/contracting academic labour in research, *Journal of Education Policy*, 16(1): 67–84.

Hicks, W. (1999) *Writing for Journalists*. London: Routledge.

Hislop, J., Murray, R. and Newton, M. (2008) Writing for publication: a case study, *Practice Development in Health Care*, 7(3): 143–55.

Hjortshoj, K. (2010) *Understanding Writing Blocks*. Oxford: Oxford University Press.

Ho, S.P., Riester, L., Drews, M., Boland, T. and LaBerge, M. (2003) Nanoindentation properties of compression-moulded ultra-high molecular weight polyethylene, *Proceedings of the Institution of Mechanical Engineers, H, Journal of Engineering in Medicine*, 217: 357–66.

Holsbrink-Engels, G.A. (2001) Using a computer learning environment for initial training in dealing with social-communicative problems, *British Journal of Educational Technology*, 32(1): 53–67.

hooks, b [sic] (1999) *remembered rapture: the writer at work.* New York: Henry Holt.

Hough, J. (2000) Commentary on Belton (1985): the use of a simple multi-criteria model to assist in selection from a shortlist, *Journal of the Occupational Research Society,* 51: 895–6.

Huff, A.S. (1999) *Writing for Scholarly Publication.* London: Sage Publications.

Jenson, J. (2017) *Write No Matter What: Advice for Academics.* Chicago, IL: University of Chicago Press.

Kamler, B. and Thomson, P. (2014) *Helping Doctoral Students Write: Pedagogies for Supervision,* 2nd edn. London: Routledge.

Kaye, S. (1989) *Writing under Pressure: The Quick Writing Process.* Oxford: Oxford University Press.

Kurcikova, K. and Quinlan, O. (eds) (2017) *The Digitally Agile Researcher.* London: Open University Press.

Kirk, A., Barnett, J. and Mutrie, N. (2007) Physical activity consultation for people with Type 2 diabetes. Evidence and guidelines, *Diabetic Medicine,* 24: 809–16.

Kitson, A.L. (2001) Does nursing education have a future?, *Nurse Education Today,* 21: 86–96.

Kumashiro, K.K., Pinar, W.F., Graue, E., Grant, C.A., Benham, M.K.P., Heck, R.H. *et al.* (2005) Thinking collaboratively about the peer review process for journal article publication, *Harvard Educational Review,* 75: 257–85.

Lamont, M. (2009) *How Professors Think: Inside the Curious World of Academic Judgment.* Cambridge, MA: Harvard University Press.

Lanham, R.A. (2007) *Revising Prose,* 5th edn. New York: Pearson Longman.

Lea, M.R. and Street, B.V. (1998) Student writing in higher education: an academic literacies approach, *Studies in Higher Education,* 23(2): 157–72.

Lee, A. and Boud, D. (2003) Writing groups, change and academic identity: research development as local practice, *Studies in Higher Education,* 28(2): 187–200.

Leonard, D. (2001) *A Woman's Guide to Doctoral Studies.* Buckingham: Open University Press.

Lillis, T. and Curry, M.J. (2010) *Academic Writing in a Global Context: The Politics and Practices of Publishing in English.* London: Routledge.

Lodge, D. (1996) *The Practice of Writing: Essays, Lectures, Reviews and a Diary.* London: Penguin.

LSE (London School of Economics) Public Policy Group (n.d.) *Maximizing the Impacts of Your Research: A Handbook for Social Scientists,* Consultation Draft 3. London: LSE PPG.

Luey, B. (2011) *Handbook for Academic Authors,* 5th edn. Cambridge: Cambridge University Press.

Lupton, D., Mewburn, I. and Thomson, P. (eds) (2018) *The Digital Academic: Critical Perspectives on Digital Technologies in Higher Education.* London: Routledge.

MacArthur, C.A., Graham, S. and Fitzgerald, J. (eds) (2006) *The Handbook of Writing Research.* London: Guilford Press.

MacDonald, S.P. (1994) *Professional Academic Writing in the Humanities and Social Sciences.* Carbondale, IL: Southern Illinois University.

MacLeod, I., Steckley, L. and Murray, R. (2012) Time is not enough: promoting strategic engagement with writing for publication, *Studies in Higher Education,* 37(5): 641–54.

Mailer, N. (2003) *The Spooky Art: Some Thoughts on Writing.* London: Little, Brown.

Matejka, K. (1990) Unpublished? Perish the thought, *Management Decision,* 28(6): 9–11.

Mayrath, M.C. (2008) Attributions of productive authors in educational psychology journals, *Educational Psychology Review,* 20: 41–56.

McCall Smith, A. (2003) *Portuguese Irregular Verbs*. Edinburgh: Polygon.

McGrail, R.M., Rickard, C.M. and Jones, R. (2006) Publish or perish: a systematic review of interventions to increase academic publication rates, *Higher Education Research and Development*, 25(1): 19–35.

Miller, D. (2011) *Tales from Facebook*. Cambridge: Polity Press.

Minocha, S. and Petres, M. (2012) *Handbook of Social Media for Researchers and Supervisors: Digital Technologies for Research Dialogues*. Milton Keynes: Open University and VITAE.

Mollett, A., Moran, D. and Dunleavy, P. (2011) *Using Twitter in University Research, Teaching and Impact Activities*. London: London School of Economics Public Policy Group.

Montgomery, S.L. (2003) *The Chicago Guide to Communicating Science*. Chicago, IL: University of Chicago Press.

Moore, S. (2003) Writers' retreats for academics: exploring and increasing the motivation to write, *Journal of Further and Higher Education*, 27(3): 333–42.

Moore, S., Murphy, M. and Murray, R. (2010) Increasing academic output and supporting equality of career opportunity: can writers' retreats play a role?, *Journal of Faculty Development*, 24(3): 21–30.

Morris, E. (2001) The design and evaluation of Link: a computer-based learning system for correlation, *British Journal of Educational Technology*, 32(1): 39–52.

Morss, K. and Murray, R. (2001) Researching academic writing within a structured programme: insights and outcomes, *Studies in Higher Education*, 26(1): 35–51.

Moxley, J.M. and Taylor, T. (1997) *Writing and Publishing for Academic Authors*, 2nd edn. London: Rowman & Littlefield.

Mullen, C.A. (2001) The need for a curricular writing model for graduate students, *Journal of Further and Higher Education*, 25(1): 117–26.

Murakami, H. (2009) *What I Talk About When I Talk About Running: A Memoir*. London: Vintage Books.

Murray, R. (2000) *Writing for Publication* (video and notes). Glasgow: University of Strathclyde.

Murray, R. (2001) Integrating teaching and research through writing development for students and staff, *Active Learning in Higher Education*, 2(1): 31–45.

Murray, R. (2006) Writing articles, books and presentations, in N. Gilbert (ed.) *From Postgraduate to Social Scientist: A Guide to Key Skills*. London: Sage Publications.

Murray, R. (2007) Getting started with writing, in G. Hall and J. Longman (eds) *The Postgraduate's Companion*. London: Sage Publications.

Murray, R. (2008) Innovations, activities and principles for supporting academics' writing, in S. Moore (ed.) *Supporting Academic Writing among Students and Academics*. London: Staff and Educational Development Association.

Murray, R. (2010) Becoming rhetorical, in C. Aitchison, B. Kamler and A. Lee (eds) *Publishing Pedagogies for the Doctorate and Beyond*. London: Routledge.

Murray, R. (2012) Developing a community of research practice, *British Educational Research Journal*, 35(5): 783–800.

Murray, R. (2013) It's not a hobby: reconceptualizing the place of writing in academic work, *Higher Education*, 66(1): 79-91. DOI: 10:1007/s10734–012–9591–7.

Murray, R. (2014) Doctoral students create new spaces to write, in C. Aitchison and C. Guerin (eds) *Writing Groups for Doctoral Education and Beyond: Innovations in Theory and Practice*. London: Routledge.

Murray, R. (2015) *Writing in Social Spaces: A Social Processes Approach to Academic Writing*. London: Routledge/Society for Research into Higher Education.

Murray, R. (2017a) *How to Write a Thesis*, 4th edn. Maidenhead: Open University Press/ McGraw-Hill.

Murray, R. (2017b) Writing prolifically, in S. Carter and D. Laurs (eds) *Developing Research Writing: A Handbook for Supervisors and Advisors*. London: Routledge.

Murray, R. and Cunningham, A. (2011) Managing researcher development: 'drastic transition'?, *Studies in Higher Education*, 36(7): 831–45.

Murray, R. and MacKay, G. (1998a) Supporting academic development in public output: reflections and propositions, *International Journal for Academic Development*, 3(1): 54–63.

Murray, R. and MacKay, G. (1998b) Writers' groups for researchers and how to run them, Universities' and Colleges' Staff Development Agency, Sheffield.

Murray, R. and Moore, S. (2006) *The Handbook of Academic Writing: A Fresh Approach*. Maidenhead: Open University Press/McGraw-Hill.

Murray, R. and Newton, M. (2008) Facilitating writing for publication, *Physiotherapy*, 94: 29–34.

Murray, R. and Newton, M. (2009) Writing retreat as structured intervention: margin or mainstream?, *Higher Education Research and Development*, 28(5): 527–39.

Murray, R., Steckley, L. and MacLeod, I. (2012) Research leadership in writing for publication: a theoretical framework, *British Educational Research Journal*, 38(5): 765–81.

Murray, R. and Thow, M. (2015) Peer-formativity: a framework for academic writing, *Higher Education Research and Development*, 33(6): 1166–79.

Murray, R., Thow, M., Moore, S. and Murphy, M. (2008) The writing consultation: developing academic writing practices, *Journal of Further and Higher Education*, 32(2): 119–28.

Navarra, T. (1998) *Toward Painless Writing: A Guide for Health Professionals*. Thorofare, NJ: SLACK.

Palumbo, D. (2000) *Writing from the Inside Out: Transforming Your Psychological Blocks to Release the Writer Within*. New York: John Wiley.

Pasco, A.H. (2002) Basic advice for novice authors, *Journal of Scholarly Publishing*, January: 75–89.

Pazaratz, D. (2001) Defining and describing the child and youth care worker's role in residential treatment, *Journal of Child and Youth Care*, 14(3): 76–7.

Peat, J., Elliott, E., Baur, L. and Keena, V. (2002) *Scientific Writing: Easy When You Know How*. London: British Medical Journal Books.

Pedler, J. (2001) Computer spellcheckers and dyslexics – a performance survey, *British Journal of Educational Technology*, 32(1): 23–37.

Peter, D.P. and Ceci, S.J. (1982) Peer-review practices of psychological journals: the fate of published articles, submitted again, *The Behavioural and Brain Sciences*, 5: 187–255.

Petre, M. and Rugg, G. (2010) *The Unwritten Rules of PhD Research*, 2nd edn. Maidenhead: Open University Press/McGraw-Hill.

Powell, W.W. (1985) *Getting into Print: The Decision Making Process in Scholarly Publishing*. London: University of Chicago Press.

Rachlin, H. (2000) *The Science of Self-Control*. Cambridge, MA: Harvard University Press.

Reif-Lehrer, L. (2000) The beauty of outlines (http:#dRnextwave-uk.sciencemag.org/cgi/content/full/2000/06/07/2).

Rheingold, H. (2014) *Net Smart: How to Thrive Online*. Cambridge, MA: MIT Press.

Rich, A. (1986) *Blood, Bread and Poetry, Selected Prose 1979–1985*. London: Virago.

Rich, A. (2001) *Arts of the Possible*. New York: Norton.

Roberts, J., Mitchell, B. and Zubrinich, R. (eds) (2002) *Writers on Writing*. London: Penguin.

Rodrigues, D. (1997) *The Research Paper and the World Wide Web.* Upper Saddle River, NJ: Prentice Hall.

Rossen, J. (1993) *The University in Modern Fiction: When Power is Academic.* New York: St Martin's Press.

Rozakis, L. (1999) *Writing Great Research Papers.* London: McGraw-Hill.

Rugg, G. and Petre, M. (2004) *The Unwritten Rules of PhD Research.* Maidenhead: Open University Press.

Ryan-Flood, R. and Gill, R. (2010) *Secrecy and Silence in the Research Process: Feminist Reflections.* London: Routledge.

Rymer, J. (1988) Scientific composing processes: how eminent scientists write journal articles, in D.A. Jolliffe (ed.) *Advances in Writing Research: Volume 2 – Writing in Academic Disciplines.* Norwood, NJ: Ablex.

Sadler, D.R. (1990) *Up the Publication Road: A Guide to Publishing in Scholarly Journals for Academics, Researchers and Graduate Students,* 2nd edn, Green Guide No. 2. Campbelltown, New South Wales: Higher Education Research and Development Society of Australasia.

Salmon, G. (2001) The Business Café Project: Viewing to browsing?, *British Journal of Educational Technology,* 32(1): 91–104.

Sandberg, J., Christoph, N. and Emans, B. (2001) Tutor training: a systematic investigation of tutor requirements and an evaluation of a training, *British Journal of Educational Technology,* 32(1): 69–90.

Sanders, S.R. (1995) *Writing from the Centre.* Bloomington, IN: Indiana University Press.

Schostak, J. and Schostak, J. (2013) *Writing Research Critically: Developing the Power to Make a Difference.* London: Routledge.

Selzer, J.L. (1981) Merit and degree in Webster's *The Duchess of Malfi, English Literary Renaissance,* 11(1): 70–80.

Silvia, P.J. (2007) *How to Write a Lot: A Practical Guide to Productive Academic Writing.* Washington, DC: American Psychological Association.

Silvia, P.J. (2014) *Write it Up: Practical Strategies for Writing and Publishing Journal Articles.* Washington, DC: American Psychological Association.

Sinclair, C. (2010) *Grammar: A Friendly Approach,* 2nd edn. Maidenhead: Open University Press/McGraw-Hill.

Smith, A. and Eysenck, M. (2002) Letter, *Times Higher Education Supplement,* 1 March: 15.

Steinbeck, J. (1962) *Travels with Charley: In Search of America.* London: Pan.

Steinbeck, J. (1970) *Journal of a Novel: The East of Eden Letters.* London: Pan.

Sternberg, R.J. (ed.) (2000) *Guide to Publishing in Psychology Journals.* Cambridge: Cambridge University Press.

Street, B.V. (1984) *Literacy in Theory and Practice.* Cambridge: Cambridge University Press.

Strunk, W. Jr and White, E.B. (2000) *The Elements of Style,* 4th edn. New York: Longman.

Swales, J.M. (2004) *Research Genres: Explorations and Applications.* Cambridge: Cambridge University Press.

Swales, J.M. and Feak, C.B. (2000) *English in Today's Research World: A Writing Guide.* Ann Arbor, MI: University of Michigan Press.

Sword, H. (2012) *Stylish Academic Writing.* Cambridge, MA: Harvard University Press.

Sword, H. (2017) *Air and Light and Time and Space: How Successful Academics Write.* Cambridge, MA: Harvard University Press.

Thomson, P. and Kamler, B. (2012) *Writing for Peer Reviewed Journals: Strategies for Getting Published.* London: Routledge.

Thow, M. (2015) *How to Be Healthy at Work: For People Doing PhDs and Other Higher Degrees, Academics, Teachers and Office Workers Who Sit a Lot.* Kindle.

Thow, M., Graham, K. and Lee, C. (2013) *The Healthy Heart Book*. Champaign, IL: Human Kinetics.

Thow, M., Rafferty, D. and Armstrong, G. (2004) A United Kingdom survey of physiotherapists' involvement in cardiac rehabilitation and their perceived skills and attributes, *Physiotherapy*, 90(2): 97–102.

Thyer, B.A. (1994) *Successful Publishing in Scholarly Journals*. London: Sage Publications.

Tight, M. (ed.) (2000) *Academic Work and Life: What It Is to Be an Academic and How This is Changing*. London: Elsevier.

Torrance, M., Thomas, G. and Robinson, E.J. (1991) Strategies for answering examination essay questions: is it helpful to write a plan?, *British Journal of Educational Psychology*, 61: 46–54.

Torrance, M., Thomas, M. and Robinson, E.J. (1993) Training in thesis writing: an evaluation of three conceptual orientations, *British Journal of Educational Psychology*, 63: 170–84.

Trimble, J.R. (2011) *Writing with Style: Conversations on the Art of Writing*, 3rd edn. New York: Prentice Hall.

Truss, L. (2003) *Eats, Shoots and Leaves*. London: Profile Books.

Valentine, G. (1998) 'Sticks and stones may break my bones': a personal geography of harassment, *Antipode*, 30: 305–32.

Van der Geest, T. (1996) Professional writing studied: authors' accounts of planning in document production processes, in M. Sharples and T. Van der Geest (eds) *The New Writing Environment: Writers at Work in a World of Technology*. Berlin: Springer.

Wager, E., Godlee, F. and Jefferson, T. (2002) *How to Survive Peer Review*. London: British Medical Journal Books.

Wellington, J. (2003) *Getting Published: A Guide for Lecturers and Researchers*. London: RoutledgeFalmer.

Wheatley, M.J. (2002) *Turning to One Another: Simple Conversations to Restore Hope to the Future*. San Francisco, CA: Berrett-Koehler.

Whitman, W. (1855, 1986) *Song of Myself*. Harmondsworth: Penguin.

Wilk, K.E., Voight, M.L., Keirns, M.A., Gambetta, V., Dillman, C.J. and Andrews, J.R. (1993) Stretch-shortening drills for the upper extremities: theory and clinical application, *Journal of Sports Physical Therapy*, 17(5): 225–39.

Williams, J. (1996) Writing in concert, in H.A. Veeser (ed.) *Confessions of the Critics*. London: Routledge.

Williams, J. and Coldron, J. (eds) (1996) *Writing for Publication: An Introductory Guide for People Working in Education*. Sheffield: PAVIC.

Williams, J.M. (2004) *Style: Ten Lessons in Clarity and Grace*, 8th edn. Glenview, IL: Scott, Foresman and Company.

Zerubavel, E. (1999) *The Clockwork Muse: A Practical Guide to Writing Theses, Dissertations and Books*. Cambridge, MA: Harvard University Press.

Ziegler, D. (2001) To hold, or not to hold . . . Is that the right question?, *Residential Treatment for Children and Youth*, 18(4): 33–45.

Index